LORD BROUGHAM

MACMILLAN AND CO., Limited
LONDON · BOMBAY · CALCUTTA · MADRAS
MELBOURNE

THE MACMILLAN COMPANY
NEW YORK · BOSTON · CHICAGO
DALLAS · ATLANTA · SAN FRANCISCO

THE MACMILLAN COMPANY
OF CANADA, LIMITED
TORONTO

[*Frontispiece.*

HENRY, FIRST BARON BROUGHAM

LORD BROUGHAM

BY

G. T. GARRATT

MACMILLAN AND CO., LIMITED
ST. MARTIN'S STREET, LONDON
1935

COPYRIGHT

Walhalla's gate
Opes only for the Dead—What hand unknown
Shall carve for Brougham's vast image the grand throne?

St. Stephens.

PREFACE

THE notable revival of a general interest in history suggests that the time has come for a new and possibly a fairer estimate of Brougham's character, and of his influence upon nineteenth-century England. For some reason biographers have fought shy of the man who, as Morley wrote, " plunged with the energy of a Titan into a thousand projects," and for more than half his ninety years was a most powerful force in our politics. His own *Memoirs*, written in extreme old age, provide little more than a commentary, not too accurate, upon a mass of correspondence, some of which is valuable. Lord Campbell, his rival and coeval, included Brougham in his *Lives of the Chancellors*, that least impartial of works, which, as another Chancellor remarked, added a new terror to death. Campbell never forgave Brougham for his early success, or for having left the ordered route by which a lawyer without family should ascend the Woolsack. The " Life " is full of anecdotes and personal reminiscences, some obviously apocryphal, for Campbell was a master of *l'esprit d'escalier*, but it only gives one side of Brougham's career, and is obviously intended to " write him down " to Campbell's own stature.

Early in this century Mr. J. B. Atlay included Brougham in his *Victorian Chancellors*. This is a most valuable work, but much new material has become available since it was published, and inevitably it deals primarily with Brougham as a lawyer. Finally, there is Dr. Aspinall's *Lord Brougham and the Whig Party*, published in 1927. To this the writer, and every student of this period, must acknowledge his deep obligation. Dr. Aspinall has, however, expressly stated that his work is not a biography, and, as the name suggests, the book deals chiefly with certain aspects of Brougham's political career, about which a mass of new material was printed for the first time.

There seems, therefore, to be room for a biography written along more general lines, and intended for a less specialized public. I have avoided entering into one or two minor controversial questions connected with Brougham's career. Also, in view of the full bibliography and careful analysis of manuscript sources given in Dr. Aspinall's book, I have not thought it necessary to give a list of authorities. A few books have been published since 1927 containing material hitherto unprinted —Mr. Gore's further selection from Creevey's letters, the Centenary edition of Scott's letters, the *Huskisson Papers*, etc., and above all the new history of *The Times*, "*The Thunderer*" *in the Making*. Apart from such recent works as these, any bibliography of value to the student would be little more than a replica of that already available in *Lord Brougham and the Whig Party*. For this reason I have limited myself to a full use of footnotes to indicate the source of quotations, etc. Actually Brougham lived so long and touched life at so many points that his influence can be traced in nearly all contemporary literature.

I have to thank the Proprietors of *Punch* for permission to reproduce a cartoon, and also the little figure which appears on the title page. For the best part of a century poor Brougham's up-turned mask has been dragged, week by week, through the dirt. Perhaps there is something symbolical in the long penance which Brougham, who figured so often in the pages of *Punch*, has now to suffer upon its cover.

G. T. G.

Bishopsteignton,
South Devon.

CONTENTS

LIST OF ILLUSTRATIONS

CHAPTER I

EARLY LIFE IN SCOTLAND

Had you any conversation with Brougham ? He is an uncommon genius of a composite order, if you allow me to use the expression; he unites the greatest ardour for general information in every branch of knowledge, and, what is more remarkable, activity in the business, and interest in the pleasures of the world, with all the powers of a mathematical intellect. Did you notice his physiognomy ? I am curious to know your observation on it.
Francis Horner to the Reverend Hewlett. 1798.

HARRIET MARTINEAU was no friend of Brougham. He had been a little too offhand when he first met that earnest and very deaf young woman. Perhaps, like many others, he had been embarrassed by her ear-trumpet. Later there were disputes about suitable educational works for the poor. Worst of all, Brougham quarrelled bitterly with her eccentric hero, Lord Durham. In her Biographical Sketches she tells a story of the first daguerreotype taken at Cannes, where Brougham passed much of his old age. He should have been the centre of the group, but failed to keep perfectly still for the necessary five seconds. " There is something mournfully typical in this," writes Miss Martineau, a trifle sententiously. " In the picture of our century, as taken from the life by History, this very man should have been a central figure; but now, owing to his want of steadfastness, there will be for ever—a blur where Brougham should have been."

Our historians have been a little too ready to accept this verdict. The present generation, living as he did in an age of transition much affected by a great war, should appreciate better this versatile, unconventional man, who was always in advance of his time, who would not

B

conform to any type, and whose chief failing was a superabundance of mental and physical energy. From his great influence, from his achievements, from his queer character and unusual career, he seemed to his contemporaries the one man of his age who would certainly appeal to the biographer. They would have thought it absurd that Mr. Leigh Hunt should be remembered when the great Brougham was almost forgotten. As Disraeli pointed out, there are men—he instances some in the seventeenth century—whose importance is fully recognized by their own generation, but who have failed to find their appropriate place in history. To some extent this is true of Brougham. Posterity has not been fair to one of the great figures dominating the first half of the nineteenth century.

Perhaps this was inevitable. Brougham disobeyed the first rules for those who would become famous in politics or literature, and would be esteemed after their death. He was incurably versatile, and he neither organized a personal following nor attached himself to a group. Brougham was a politician, who became virtual leader of the Whig Party; an orator, who was " the one sole rival " of Canning; a lawyer, who rose to be Lord Chancellor; a pioneer of popular education, who helped to found London University; a reformer and controversialist, who did more than anyone to free his countrymen's minds from the lumber of eighteenth-century ideas and inhibitions. In all these capacities Brougham was a man *sui generis*, never fitting comfortably into any party or category, and as original in his methods as in his views. Historians, failing to find a suitable label, have tended to ignore him.

The strictures and sneers of his contemporaries should not be taken too seriously. Many are a tribute to his efficiency. Brougham was bound to be unpopular. During a long career he quarrelled, at one time or other, with nearly everyone in public life. He forced the English to think along new lines, a service for which they are not apt to be over-grateful. Possibly he lived too long. Some of the causes for which he had fought— the abolition of slavery, Catholic Emancipation, the sovereignty of Parliament, the State's responsibility for popular education, the easier accessibility of the law courts—these had ceased to be matters of bitter controversy, and certain general principles had been accepted some years before he died. Born in 1778, while Chatham and Dr. Johnson were still alive, he survived such younger men as Palmerston and Thackeray. For over fifty of his ninety years he impressed his vivid personality upon his countrymen, but the paradoxes of his early years had become platitudes long before he died, and the Victorians forgot the iconoclast of the Regency, who had broken the images which no longer had any significance. The wide range of his interests, his disregard for conventions, the variety of his public and private life, the political ostracism which he underwent after 1835, all these have blurred the outlines of a great career, and led to the neglect of a reformer who, directly and indirectly, did so much to fashion modern England. It is some measure of his importance that, for over a generation, a phrase like " the march of intellect "; a proposal to abolish some sinecure or some legal anomaly; the discovery of a servant reading an unexpectedly erudite work; the question who would defend some victim of political oppression; all these would instantly suggest the name of this queer, ungainly lawyer, who was continually pouring out new ideas, breaking down social barriers, attacking old abuses, or launching new schemes.

Brougham was essentially *not* a member of the governing families, though in later years he developed, as one of his less attractive eccentricities, exaggerated ideas about his ancestry, and his shadowy connection with the Vaux family. His grandfather, a busy London attorney and Steward to the Duke of Norfolk, was descended from successful farmers and cattle-dealers in Westmorland. Having interests near Penrith he bought a house and settled his family in the village of Brougham, attracted by the name, and by some vague family connection. His eldest son, Henry, was sent to Eton, a concession to social ambitions which nearly had disastrous results. Reacting from his hard-headed and hard-bitten Border ancestors, Henry developed a taste for literature, which he pursued mildly, and apparently unproductively, for the rest of his life. He settled down at Brougham Hall, with a modest income, and was to have married a lady from the neighbourhood when she died tragically on the eve of the wedding. This misfortune seems to have killed the last remnant of his ambition. After travelling abroad, he migrated to Edinburgh, where he was fortunate enough to lodge with a Mrs. Syme, sister of Dr. Robertson the historian. Within a year he married her daughter, Eleanor, and took a house near by in St. Andrews' Square.

Their eldest son, the future Chancellor, was born on September 19th, 1778, and christened Henry Peter. Four other sons, and one daughter were born during the next seventeen years. They were brought up in Edinburgh amongst those rather academic circles into which Mrs. Syme had introduced their father. None of the family showed the precocity or developed the later genius of Henry. James, the second son, and William, the youngest, followed their brother to the English Bar, and played a considerable part in his life. John, the failure of the family, tried several occupations, including an insurance agency, and a grocery shop in Edinburgh. He died at Boulogne in 1829, reputedly a bankrupt, and certainly leaving several children who were brought up by Henry. Another brother, Peter, was killed in a duel when on his way to India as a cadet in the East India Company. This was in 1800. Peter, a lad of eighteen, was shot by a senior officer at San Salvador under circumstances which certainly demanded some further explanation. No information of any kind was obtainable. This unhappy affair had a considerable effect on his eldest brother, and encouraged that independent and rather farouche attitude to the world which he was to retain, in spite of his conviviality, throughout his life.

Like so many great men, Henry Brougham owed most to his mother. He may have reverted in type to his moss-trooper forbears, but from his father he received little help. Sir Thomas Lauder, a family friend, has left some account of this harmless, ineffectual and rather portly gentleman, taking his regular walk in George Street, " confining his turns entirely to the short space between his door and the bend of Hanover Street," with " his gold-headed cane in his hand . . . the point of which he put to the ground with a mathematical exactness as regarded his steps." [1] He had little influence over his eldest son, and later there were to be difficulties about Henry's choice of a career, about his travels, and about money. He seems, however, to have been a conscientious if undistinguished father of a family, and in 1803 one of Henry's contemporaries writes irreverently to a friend, " the old Boy is become a new man, and walks about now very frequently. I sometimes meet him in the favourite walk to Leith where he looks after Johnny's shop, who you must know is about to commence grocer. I have appointed him sole agent for the sale of my West India produce, which will be a handsome sinecure." [2]

Brougham was entirely a product of Scottish education. Its course was carefully mapped out and controlled by his mother and her relations. In his old age he paid a tribute to his grandmother's " masculine intellect and clear understanding. She instilled into me from my cradle the strongest desire for information, and the first principles of that persevering energy in the pursuit of every kind of knowledge." [3] For his mother he had an

[1] Lord John Campbell : *Lives of the Chancellors*, viii. 223.
[2] R. H. M. B. Atkinson and G. A. Jackson : *Brougham and his Early Friends*, ii. 111.
[3] Lord Brougham and Vaux : *Memoirs of Life and Times*, i. 11.

equal admiration and a lifelong devotion.   All through
his busiest times he wrote to her continually, asking her
advice, and leaving important engagements to visit her
at Brougham Hall, where she was installed after the death
of his father.   He lived to repent the one important
occasion when, in accepting the Chancellorship, he disregarded her cool and admirable counsel.   When she
died, in 1840, he might well have said, like Disraeli
lamenting the death of his sister Sarah, " we've lost our
audience, we've lost our audience." [1]

Edinburgh, in those days, provided a wonderful
upbringing for a clever and ambitious youth, giving a
far wider and more intensive training than could be
obtained anywhere else in the British Isles.   Brougham
passed through the High School under the watchful eye
of Dr. Robertson, and at fourteen went to the University,
having already acquired something of a reputation as a
prodigy.   He was not quite so precocious as the young
Macaulay, some twenty years his junior, but at twelve
he was capable of refuting his Latin master on obscure
phrases in the Augustan poets, and of " studying La
Place in the original."   A clever young Scotsman was
expected to take all knowledge for his province, like
Francis Bacon or Carlyle's Professor Teufelsdröckh.   By
eighteen Brougham had attended nearly all the classes at
the University, including Church History.   He showed
his very remarkable talent for mathematics by writing a
paper on the " Inflection, Reflection, and Colour of
Light," which was published in the Transactions of the
Royal Society.   This was followed by two further
papers in succeeding years, including one " On Porisms,"
an abstruse subject to which Einstein has given a new
meaning.   The essays seemed to have caused some stir
abroad, as well as at home, in the small circles interested
in such matters.   Even in those days of less specialized
knowledge it was remarkable for a man under twenty to

[1] W. F. Moneypenny and G. E. Buckle : *Life of Disraeli*, i.
184.

attract the critical notice of Continental professors.
Brougham could probably have become one of the great
mathematicians of the century if he had chosen to keep
his active brain within the limits of academic life and
controversy. In 1803 he became a Fellow of the Royal
Society.

Cambridge might possibly have tempted him to follow
the easy road to a professorship, but the whole atmosphere of Edinburgh University at that period encouraged
any clever ambitious young man to look upon public
life as his natural career. English education had
reached its nadir at the end of the eighteenth century.
The general standard was well below that of any European
Protestant country. Five out of six children received
no education, and the proportion of Englishmen who
could read or write was about the same as that of modern
India. Higher education was confined to a very small
class, and was over-weighted with conventional classical
studies. The two Universities catered primarily for the
wealthy " landed " families, and the traditional respect in
which these were held would tend to make any student
consider that public life was a career entirely confined
to the governing families.

Edinburgh drew most of its pupils from the far better
educated Scottish middle and lower classes, though there
was also a sprinkling of English aristocrats, who were
attracted by the freer environment and wider training.
Lord Palmerston, Lord Henry Petty (afterwards Lord
Lansdowne), Lord Dudley and Ward, Lord John Russell,
all attended the great Dugald Stewart's lectures, sitting
next to hard-headed, unaristocratic North-countrymen
like Henry Cockburn, John Murray, Francis Horner,
Brougham and Jeffrey, all of whom were to achieve
celebrity in Parliament and at the Bar. From that
inspiring and unconventional teacher they acquired new
ideas about their duty as citizens, and also learnt to know
each other. It was inevitable that the old English
governing families, the Amateurs, should look to

Edinburgh for talented Professionals to strengthen their
Party sides, when the nineteenth century called for a new
type of politician, capable of understanding economic
and industrial questions.

Brougham seems to have had little doubt that he was
destined for public life. At eighteen he decided to
become an Advocate, and began to study law. The
Bar, at that time, offered more than the usual attraction
to the young politician without strong family connections.
It was a powerful trade union giving some protection
against the policy of repression which began about
1793, and continued with varying intensity until well
after the end of the Napoleonic wars. Brougham's
career was closely bound up with this long campaign
against free speech, and with the lack of any constitutional means of expressing political opinion. He saw
the system at its worst in Scotland. He was a boy of
fifteen when Muir and Palmer were tried and transported
by the notorious Lord Braxfield, who laid down the
theory, which Brougham was to combat fifteen years
later, that any public expression of a desire for reform
was necessarily seditious. Hardy, founder of the Corresponding Society, and Horne Tooke were acquitted in
England after comparatively fair trials, but in Scotland
the jury system was no protection. Braxfield's outlook
is best illustrated by his famous reply to the suggestion
that Jesus Christ had also been an " innovator "—
" Muckle he made o' that; he was hanget." Similarly
there were a few comparatively democratic constituencies in England, but all the forty-five Scottish
representatives were sent to Westminster from close
corporations, which were effectually managed by the
Lord Advocate. The Bar and the House of Commons
were almost alone in permitting some freedom of
expression to their members.

Brougham, therefore, set himself to the study of law,
together with Horner, Murray, Jeffrey and others who
were to carve out careers for themselves in England.

He was, however, from the first something of a " card," always ready to take risks with his reputation and his future, overflowing with energy, and determined to see every side of life. He had an equal facility for getting into scrapes and for getting out of them; combining a restless inquiring mind with the highest animal spirits, a difficult pair to drive through life. Typically his early companions " consisted of two sorts, viz. intellectual fellows, such as Jeffrey, Cockburn and Murray; and fellows of dissipation, fun and frolic, such as Sandie Finlay, Jack Gordon and Frank Drummond. Perhaps the two sorts of associates might have occasionally blended themselves together. But after having been found discussing literary and philosophical questions with the first set, he was sure soon after to be found rollicking in taverns, ringing bells in the streets, twisting off bell-pulls and knockers, or smashing lamps with the second." [1] At the end of the eighteenth century Auld Reekie offered every opportunity for leading this double life. In 1797 Brougham and Francis Horner were admitted as members of the famous Speculative Society, a debating club with a law against political discussion, but a law which was later rescinded " as its violation had for many years been systematic and beneficial." Here Brougham could try his prentice hand against some of the men who were later to be his political allies or opponents. As might be expected, he was a prolific writer of papers on every variety of subject from the wrongs of Scotland to one, which caused a minor scandal, on " the impossibility of the doctrine of the Trinity." [2] He had soon, in Horner's phrase, marked himself out amongst his contemporaries " as an uncommon genius of a composite order."

In June 1800 Brougham was called to the Scottish Bar. Then began a difficult period for a man of twenty-

[1] Campbell : *Lives of the Chancellors*, viii. 230.
[2] Letter from William Bryce to Loch, November '98. *Brougham and his Early Friends*, i. 52.

two, with no capital and no family influence outside the
academic world. His only prospects were those of
" heir apparent to Brougham Hall and a patrimony of a
few hundreds a year." Of Brougham's early experiences
as an Advocate there are many legends, but he was a man
round whom stories collected. He was undoubtedly
" a broth of a boy," newly introduced into a not very
strict society in which alcohol played a large part. There
is the story, circulated many years later by his enemy,
Lord Lauderdale, about a competition as to who could
find the most unconventional way of going to the races.
Brougham " got extremely intoxicated, sat up all night,
and was carried to the race-course, next morning in a
sedan chair, dressed in wig and gown." [1] Lord Campbell
repeats many stories, some probably apocryphal, about
his merciless " ragging " of that senile and ridiculous
judge, Lord Eskgrove.[2] The severity of criminal law
lent a touch of romance to anyone who could save a
guilty prisoner by raising some absurd legal objection.
It was exactly the kind of pleading which would appeal
to a clever young man with a sense of the grotesque, but
Brougham's wit and unconventionality did not bring
him many briefs. There was no short cut to success at
the Scottish Bar for a man with no legal connections.
Competition was very severe, for it was not every clever
Scotsman who could take the royal road to England.
Brougham very wisely began to write.

At that time Scottish lawyers, unlike their English
professional brethren, could take to literature without
injuring themselves professionally. Sir Walter Scott
and Lord Jeffrey are obvious examples of men who
continued the two activities simultaneously, and when
they thought fit specialized in the more attractive or

---

[1] Broughton : *Recollections*, v. 19. Dr. Aspinall, in his *Lord
Brougham and the Whig Party*, has inadvertently described this
youthful escapade as if it occurred during Brougham's tour of
Scotland when Lord Chancellor.

[2] Campbell : *Lives of the Chancellors*, viii. 230 ff.

lucrative side. A solid political or economic book might also serve as a useful passport to public office, for the supply of this kind of work did not then far exceed the demand.   Brougham, with his usual energy and self-confidence, set himself to produce a *magnum opus* on a subject of which he knew nothing, while about the same time a fortunate venture opened up another valuable field for his literary activities.   He began to plan a great work on Colonial Policy, and he joined the group of young men, led by Jeffrey and Sydney Smith, who launched the *Edinburgh Review* in 1802.

The success of both these ventures may seem surprising to a generation which has seen, in 1929, the death of the *Edinburgh Review*, and would certainly not buy a thousand-page tome on Colonial Policy, written by a young man of under twenty-five, with no first-hand knowledge of the subject.   In the early years of the nineteenth century there was a real hunger for serious political works, and a demand for a comparatively learned review amongst the growing middle class, which wished to be better informed, but badly needed a guide.   Something more solid and more reformist in tone was wanted than the Tory squibs and pamphlets, most of which fell far short of the *Anti-Jacobin* standard.   It was a natural reaction after ten years of repression.   The argumentative Scotsman longed for a little political controversy after a period so dead that when, in 1814, an anti-slavery meeting was held in Edinburgh, Cockburn remarks that " it was the first assembling of the people for a public object that had occurred for about twenty years." [1]

The *Edinburgh Review*, appearing quarterly, proved a financial success from the first.   It soon attained a circulation of about 9000, and was read by most people of any standing in the Kingdom.   " No genteel person," wrote Scott, " can pretend to be without it."   The " Blue and Buff " covered a vast number of subjects, with an appearance of great erudition.   It concealed the

[1] Lord Henry Cockburn : *Memorials*, p. 283.

superficial nature of its contributors' knowledge by a fine
slashing type of reviewing, well spiced with Sydney
Smith's humour.   Brougham entered into the game with
zest and remarkable efficiency.   All his life he wrote a
little too easily to make easy reading, but his high animal
spirits and gift of sarcasm were invaluable on a Review
which delighted, as Sydney Smith pointed out, in
" stroking the animal the contrary way to that in which
the fur lies."   " You ask what I did in No. III," wrote
Brougham to a friend.   " The short articles on Optics
and Chemistry from Phil. Trans., Guineas an Incum-
brance, Ritson on Animal Food, Stewart's Life of
Robertson, and a bit of Poggio Bracciolini." [1]   It was
a good training for two professions, Law and Politics,
in both of which a superficial omniscience is so valuable.
It must also have been great fun, for many of the reviews
were composite productions, and Brougham would sit
up half the night with Sydney Smith lambasting some
" poor little vegetarian who had put out a silly little
book."

The reviewers were bound to make mistakes in living
up to their motto, " Judex damnatur cum nocens
absolvitur."   They would occasionally get some big
fish into their net.   Brougham was responsible for delay-
ing, by an adverse review, the recognition of Professor
Young's undulatory theory of light.   In 1804 he made
himself very unpopular with many Whigs by attacking
Lord Lauderdale's book on the Origin of Public Wealth.
The general tone of the Review was Whig, though
Tories, like Sir Walter Scott, would write for it.   Jeffrey,
while he " did not dissent from Brougham's anti-
Œconomics," thought he had hardly done justice to the
prominent Whig Lord, and a Dr. Currie wrote to his
friend Thomas Creevey about this " scatter-brained
fellow, one Brougham," whom he cheerfully describes
as " a notorious prostitute " who " is setting himself up

[1] Brougham to Loch, June 1803. *Brougham and his Early
Friends*, ii. 67.

to sale. It seems Lord Lauderdale offended him by refusing to be introduced to him." [1] In this way, Brougham was first brought to the notice of Creevey, with whom he was later to be so intimately connected. There is some doubt about Brougham's connection with the attack on Byron's *Juvenilia*, which was to call forth *English Bards and Scotch Reviewers*. It was probably a composite review, and Byron himself thought Jeffrey chiefly responsible. His advice,

> " Beware lest blundering Brougham destroy the sale,
> Turn beef to bannocks, cauliflowers to kail,"

refers to the Don Cevallos article, to which reference will be made later.

The *Inquiry into the Colonial Policy of the European Powers* appeared in 1803. Like the review on Lord Lauderdale's book it suggests that Brougham, aged twenty-five, had not yet decided where to place his political allegiance. His mother's family, including the great Dr. Robertson, had inclined to be Tory, while most of Brougham's Edinburgh friends were Whig. He was certainly not a young Radical. When he was about twenty he paid a visit to London. In a letter to James Loch he wrote that " The Corresponding Society, except about six members, consists of the most despicable and brutal mobs. Men whose ignorance and savage barbarity renders them fit only for being tools—indeed they are common day labourers about town." [2] Five years later his first great work is mainly an attack on Turgot's theory of the uselessness of colonies, and there is little with which the Tories would not agree. He even suggests that the English should join the French in a joint expedition to destroy the independent negro republic of St. Domingo, though this suggestion is combined with a violent attack on the slave trade. It was

[1] *The Creevey Papers.* Edited by Sir Herbert Maxwell. Letter of Oct. 2, 1804, i. 30.
[2] Letter dated May 1798. *Brougham and his Early Friends*, i. 33.

this last argument which brought the book some celebrity, and was to affect the rest of Brougham's life, for it introduced him into the society of Wilberforce and the " Saints." Presumably there was enough Tory propaganda in existence for the confused and turgid first volume to attract little attention.

In spite of its length and prolixity the book had a fair sale, and became a minor classic for the abolitionists. Gladstone, who as a young man was a strong opponent of abolition, read the *Colonial Policy* some thirty years later. He obviously held it to be still one of the standard works on the subject. The future Prime Minister was then twenty-five, and remarks rather ponderously that " eccentricity, paradox, fast and loose reasoning and (much more) sentiment appear to have entered most deeply into the essence of this remarkable man when he wrote his *Colonial Policy*; with the rarest power of *expressing* his thoughts, has he any fixed law to guide them ? " [1] Gladstone, like Brougham, was to forswear most of his earlier views, and grow more radical with age and experience.

All through his life Brougham had a remarkable aptitude for political publicity, an art of which very little was then known. He promptly followed up his minor success with a much more effective pamphlet on the Abolition of the Slave Trade. Copies were sent to many leading members of Parliament shortly before the Slave Trade Debate in 1804. The upshot of this was fantastic, somewhat in the manner of the early chapters of a Disraeli novel. Pitt, according to good authority, made his speech with the pamphlet in his hand, and George Rose, a strong opponent of abolition, moved that the debate should be delayed because " a pamphlet had just been published, and had been very widely circulated, that he knew had produced a strong impression upon the minds of the members of that House." [2] At twenty-

[1] Morley : *Life of Gladstone*, i. 117.
[2] *Parliamentary Debates*, June 7, 1804.

six Brougham was started on his political career. He was determined to proceed by way of the English Bar, and had already, in 1803, entered his name at Lincoln's Inn, but before he moved his camp southwards he characteristically set out on his travels.

Brougham's most remarkable journey was in 1804, but he had early developed a taste for " jaunting." For a young man with little money he had a marked facility for getting about the world. At twenty-one he set out for " Sweden, Russia and Lapland " with his friend Stuart, who was afterwards the Ambassador, Baron Stuart de Rothesay. The two of them wandered through Scandinavia and Denmark, and were duly shocked at the moral turpitude of Stockholm after Gustavus III's introduction of French Court habits. Brougham also tried to get to Iceland, but only reached the Western Isles. At that period he seems to have had a severe attack of *Wanderlust*. " Ever since Brougham was at Orkney," writes his friend Clephane, " he seems perfectly mad about ships, and would hang on for hours looking at a nasty Kinghorn boat, or having his organs of smell regaled with the unloading of a herring boat." [1] In 1804, after helping to found a corps of Volunteers at the time of the invasion scare, an effort totally ignored by the Secretary of War, Brougham borrowed some money and set off for Holland. He had two immediate objects in view—to meet some of the Dutch abolitionists and to see Napoleon. The second was a sufficiently hazardous undertaking. The Peace of Amiens had come to an end in 1803, and, although war was far more casual and impersonal than now, Brougham was taking a considerable risk. He passed himself off as an American, and travelled up the Rhine in a passenger boat. This was moored off Cologne at the time of Napoleon's visit, and Brougham, in a letter to James Loch, describes how he was forced to hide in a discreet but unsavoury part

[1] Clephane to James Loch, February 1803. *Brougham and his Early Friends*, ii. 40.

of the boat while gendarmes searched for suspected characters.[1]　He caught a distant glimpse of Napoleon and then made his way to Italy.

The journey is interesting for the light which it throws on Brougham's personal courage, a matter of some dispute later.　Like all contemporary supporters of unpopular causes, Brougham was to be much pestered by challenges to duel from obscure political opponents, who thus hoped to gain some notoriety, or the gratitude of the influential.　Daniel O'Connell, who was constantly troubled in this way, killed one man and then refused to fight again.　Brougham's management of this difficult problem exposed him to the sneers of many political and personal enemies, but, whenever he was set upon any definite object, he showed great moral and ample physical courage.

Brougham returned in January 1805, and settled permanently in London.　It was a risky step.　He had no regular income, apart from his contributions to the *Edinburgh Review*.　He owed some £600, and seems to have failed to get an advance from his cautious indecisive father, whom he describes as " the damdest lazy man to deal with in the way of business." [2]

[1] Brougham to James Loch, Sept. 22, 1804.　*Id.*, ii. 203–5.
[2] *Id.*, ii. 10.

CHAPTER II

THE YOUNG WHIG

Lapland is remarkable for prodigious noble wild prospects. But, Sir, let me tell you, the noblest prospect which a Scotsman ever sees, is the highroad that leads him to England.

DR. JOHNSON.

BROUGHAM, in 1805, was a Scottish lawyer, waiting to qualify for the English Bar, but he had other aspirations besides a judgeship. He set out deliberately to make a place for himself in English politics. In those days an ambitious young man, with no family connections, could hardly avoid being either a toady or an adventurer. Parliament could not be taken by storm. Many seats were " closed," returning the nominees of the borough-owner; the others required great wealth and strong local connections. The few " democratic " constituencies, such as Preston and Westminster, were the object of intense competition. Brougham must have felt like Vivian Grey when on the verge of his Great Discovery. " My destiny should not be on a chance. Were I the son of a millionaire, or a noble, I might have all. Curse on my lot! that the want of a few rascal counters and the possession of a little rascal blood should mar my fortunes." The young Brougham and the young Disraeli had more in common than either would have ever cared to admit. Both were Professionals without the least innate respect for the Amateurs.

These two words may be used to distinguish between two main types in early nineteenth-century politics. The Amateurs were the patricians, who entered on

public life as their birthright. The Professionals had
to fight their way into politics by their ability and their
cunning, or sometimes by their wealth. Brougham
was fully cognizant of the distinction. Writing thirty
years later, he remarks that Dr. Allen, of Holland House,
never went into politics in spite of " his great talents,
long experience, many rare accomplishments, and connection with great statesmen." Brougham can account
for this " in no other way than that there is a line drawn
in this country between the ruling caste and the rest
of the community." [1] When Brougham wrote this the
line was beginning to break, and he himself had done
much to bring about this change, but had been broken
himself in the process.

It was not a question of making money out of politics.
No one could beat the old " tax-eating " patrician
families at that. Many of the Professionals were
successful lawyers and tradesmen who sacrificed their
income to go into public life. The difference was
bound up with a respect for landed property, and was
fully recognized by people throughout England. The
Amateurs expected the captain to be chosen from
their ranks, and that they should be the object of respect
and admiration for playing at all. The English, as a
whole, accepted this curious convention.

Though Brougham and Disraeli were both Professionals, they had a very different background to their
lives, and played the game with different rules. While
Vivian Grey, like the young Disraeli, was not hampered
by political principles, Brougham had already labelled
himself " reformer," and chosen the unpopular side.
If circumstances forced him to be something of a
political adventurer, he always maintained his independence and certain fundamental ideas. The English,
not taking too kindly to the political invasion from
the North, recognized two familiar types on the
stage. Brougham was qualifying to be Sir Archie

[1] Brougham : *Historical Sketches of Statesmen.* Third Series.

MacSarcasm, but he would never have done for Sir Pertinax MacSycophant.

It is impossible to understand the political world which Brougham was entering without appreciating the implications contained in the phrase, the "tax-eating families." The system had developed since the "Glorious Revolution." Up till then, Royal servants and favourites had generally received grants of land, but the aristocratic rulers of the eighteenth century had preferred to reward themselves and their followers by sinecures and pensions. Certain families had come to look upon themselves as entitled to a share in the national revenues, and the system, so convenient and pleasant to those engaged in public life, had developed until it came to be accepted, first by the Whigs and then by the Tories, as part of our constitution. When one party had been too long in power, the other was apt to be critical—the Tories towards the end of Whig rule during the first half of the eighteenth century, and the Whigs at the beginning of the nineteenth. There were, however, very few people in public life who were not benefiting or hoping to be benefited by sinecures which were recognized as legitimate perquisites, and it was only their "misuse" which was reprobated. Corruption and jobbery had two very strong buttresses in the Church and the legal profession, both of which took large sums from the public for nominal services. When Brougham was a young man, most of the wealthy families in England drew their money either from landed property—the early marks of Royal favour—or from the accumulations of public money, acquired more or less honestly. Towards the end of the eighteenth century other types of wealthy men were making their appearance; the "nabob" from India, the West Indian "planter," the stockjobber and the manufacturer. None of their fortunes had the respectability of one made, like that of Charles Fox's father, from the abuse of a public position.

Although the voice of radical criticism was beginning to be heard, the system was still flourishing during
the Napoleonic period. Dundas was a magnificent
" job-master," and so was Addington. The Hammonds,
in *The Village Labourer*, give the perfect example of
how the Church and the governing classes combined.
The clerkship of the Pells, worth £3000 a year, was
about to become vacant. Dr. Goodenough, who had
just been made Dean of Rochester, wrote to Addington,
" ' I understand that Colonel Barré is in a very precarious state. I hope you will have the fortitude to
nominate Harry to be his successor.' Harry, Addington's son, was a boy at Winchester. The father's fortitude rose to the emergency; the dean blossomed a
little later into a bishop." [1] The idea had eaten deeply
into everyone's mind. Birth—belonging to certain
families—or taking part in public life as a " Professional " were sufficient justification for some share in
the spoils. It will be seen how, in 1830, the Whigs,
when back in office at last, fell into their old ways, and
men like Creevey, who had specialized in exposing
sinecures, were to first accept them. Most of the
stately homes of England, which sprawled over eigh-
teenth- and nineteenth-century England, were built and
buttressed by public money. The King's placemen
were an important factor in Parliament up till the
Reform Act. The views of nearly every diarist, letter-
writer, historian and publicist of Brougham's period
were affected by the fact that they drew public money
under a system which was threatened by the spread of
new ideas, and the development of new classes who
were outside the magic circle.

Into this little world, thus dominated by jobbery,
Brougham entered. He was not entirely unheralded,
for the *Edinburgh Review* gave him a considerable reputation. Neither his travels nor his removal to London
interrupted the flow of his contributions. In the

---

[1] J. L. Hammond : *The Village Labourer*, p. 195.

middle of January 1805, Jeffrey is relieved by the arrival
of Brougham's "packet." "It would be a new thing,"
writes Francis Horner to the editor, "if anything connected with Brougham were to fail in despatch. He
is the surest and most voluminous among the sons of
men."[1] The *Review* provided him with an income,
and a passport into various kinds of "reformist"
society, but it did not entail any definite party attachment. Politics were in a state of hopeless confusion.
The war, the influence of the Court, the Catholic question, and reform all cut across the old party divisions.
Pitt, then in the last year of his life, attracted by his
conduct of the war many who disliked his domestic
policy. The Prince of Wales, following the Hano-
verian tradition, quarrelled with his father and became
the focus of the Opposition. The Whigs still suffered
from their ill-advised tactics of secession, while the
Grenvillite Whigs, who had joined Fox and Grey in
1804, helped to prevent the Party being connected
with any definite political principles. The Grenvillites
were little more than a clan, wholly interested in getting
a share of the "loaves and fishes," and generally averse
to all reform except Catholic Emancipation. Any
coalition of groups or individuals was possible, and
Pitt's death was followed by the short-lived "Ministry
of All the Talents."

Each of the old Parties had a reformist wing. Wilberforce and the "Saints" were Tory, their liberalism
being of the kind which might be marked "for export
only." Whitbread, Tierney, Romilly and some of the
younger Whig aristocrats formed a small radical group,
not very effective in Parliament, but in touch with
outside movements. Later these became the nucleus
of the "Mountain," with which Brougham was identified, but when he first came to London they were little
more than a collection of disgruntled Whigs, who
disliked the Grenvillites for their opposition to all

[1] Francis Horner: *Memoirs and Correspondence*, i. 278.

reform, and the older Whig leaders for their inefficiency and for the exaggerated importance they attached to landed interest. Tierney, who had been in business, Samuel Whitbread, the brewer, Mackintosh and Romilly, the lawyers, were the forerunners of the middle-class Liberal revolt against the Whig aristocracy. It is true that Whitbread was brother-in-law to Grey, but his trade connection, and his advocacy of a minimum wage and free compulsory education, marked him out as a nineteenth-century Liberal, while Grey's spasmodic radicalism never freed him from the family and landed tradition of the eighteenth-century Whigs. On their "left" was Sir Francis Burdett, representing a large but unorganized body of ultra-radical opinion in the country. Sheridan, once a fighter for liberty, was now "sinking intemperately to the West"—the old Professional, not too well treated by his employers, a baneful influence on the Party and on the Prince of Wales. The Whigs were not a party which the reformer would automatically join. Brougham's first political friends were the "Saints," to whom he was already known as the author of the Colonial Policy, and as the man who "went to Holland with the view of procuring information about the Maroons of Guiana, and the grounds upon which the Dutch still clung to their Slave Trade." [1]

Brougham's connection with Wilberforce and his circle was to last for many years, but it was never more than a friendly alliance without much political significance. At twenty-six Brougham was a very mild reformer, retaining many of his great-uncle's Conservative ideas. His opposition to the Slave Trade was keen and probably sincere, but in 1904 he was ? reprobating "any idea of *emancipating* the slaves that are already in our plantations. Such a scheme, indeed, is sufficiently answered by the story of the galley slaves

[1] Viscountess Knutsford: *Life and Letters of Zachary Macaulay*, p. 261.

in *Don Quixote*."[1] Age broadened his mind and
strengthened his passionate hatred of cruelty. He had
the "faculty of easy anger," so valuable for a reformer,
and like Voltaire, whom he greatly admired, he was
easily aroused by any kind of bullying. It was, however, only gradually that he became aware of the stupidity
and brutality of the world in which he lived. Bagehot,
writing during the lifetime of the Lord Chancellor,
rightly pointed out that with Brougham "the stimulus
is from without. He saw the technicalities of the law-
courts; observed a charitable trustee misusing the
charity moneys; perceived that George IV oppressed
Queen Caroline; went to Old Sarum. He is not
absorbed in a creed; he is pricked by facts."[2] His
natural inclination was to accept social and economic
differences as part of the natural order. His radicalism
was not theoretical, but forced upon him by specific
cases of hardship. He had to acquire a further knowledge of West Indian conditions before he became a
keen "emancipator."

For a time he threw himself, with his usual energy,
into the polyglot interests of the "Saints." A letter
written to Wilberforce, in October 1905, reads almost
like a parody of their vague, universal and self-righteous
humanitarianism, but it also explains Brougham's value
as an organizer. He had had a letter from a Dutch
friend.

"It contains an assurance that the abolition
interest remains zealous and powerful, and that
Shimmelpennick is actuated by the most liberal
views, but jealous of being thought biassed by
any English partialities. . . . From my friend Mr.
Stuart (Secretary of Embassy at St. Petersburg) I
have received a most satisfactory account of the
Russian peasantry, which I shall communicate at

[1] *Edinburgh Review*, July 1804, p. 477.
[2] Bagehot, W.: *Biographical Sketches*, p. 60.

meeting; together with a statement regarding the peasants in Polish Russia, from the celebrated historian Muller, at Berlin. . . . I have delayed writing this in consequence of a meeting I had lately with a very intelligent gentleman, who has been employed for many years on the Statistics of Ireland, and is now very anxious upon the subject of the education of the lower orders in that country. . . ." [1]

This was not a cage likely to hold Brougham for very long. His anti-Slave Trade activities, as well as his old Edinburgh friends, brought him into contact with the Whigs. He discussed abolition with Fox, and became a frequent visitor at Holland House. Wilberforce did his best for the remarkable young man. He suggests his name to Mr. Pitt for "any diplomatic business" in a letter which shows the manner in which Brougham already impressed his seniors. "You could not in the whole kingdom find anyone in all respects so qualified as Mr. Brougham, whom I formerly mentioned to you. He speaks French as well as English, and several other languages. But the great thing is, that he is a man of uncommon talents and address, and for his age, twenty-six, knowledge also, and I told you of his being so long the advocate of your government in Edinburgh. My mentioning him to you is entirely of my own head; of course he knows nothing of it." [2] This letter, so ingenuous and so inaccurate, produced no result. Pitt had then only another three months to live.

During the next fifteen months English politics were so confused that Brougham can be forgiven for not knowing whether he was a Whig or a Tory. In February 1806, the two Whig groups under Fox and Grenville

[1] William Wilberforce : *Correspondence.* Letter from Brougham to Wilberforce, Oct. 4, 1805, ii. 44.
[2] *Id.,* Wilberforce to Pitt, Oct. 25, 1805, ii. 51.

joined with Addington's Tories to form the short-lived Ministry of All the Talents. It was a very patrician Cabinet, from which Whitbread and the " Mountain " felt themselves unfairly excluded, but the only alternative was likely to be a Tory Government. Brougham, on the advice of Lord Holland, wrote an effective pamphlet in support of the Ministry—*An Inquiry into the State of the Nation at the Commencement of the Present Administration*—and like a good journalist took care to see it was adequately noticed in the *Edinburgh Review*. Wilberforce in May suggested that Lord Lonsdale should send Brougham into Parliament for one of his nine boroughs in the north of England. The seat had already been accepted by Lord Muncaster, but Lord Lonsdale would never have allowed a man of strong reformist tendencies as one of his famous " Ninepins," and the position would have become impossible in the following year when Lord Lonsdale supported the purely Tory Ministry of the Duke of Portland. However, the manner of the refusal, and a dispute with Sir Michael Le Fleming seem to have originated a kind of feud between Brougham and the Lowther interest. This was to grow much more bitter after the former had taken over Brougham Hall on the death of his father in 1810, and had began to become a personage in Westmorland.

The Coalition Ministry could not find a seat for Brougham in Parliament, but they provided him with an interesting and curious experience. In August 1806 Fox asked him to go to Lisbon as Secretary to a special Mission, consisting of Lord Rosslyn, Lord St. Vincent and General Simcoe. Napoleon was known to be working with Godoy for the partition of Portugal, and for this purpose had collected an army at Bayonne. The object of the Mission was to prevent the Portuguese fleet and the Royal family from falling into French hands. This was to be accomplished, if possible, with the co-operation of the Portuguese Government, but

Lord St. Vincent was prepared to inveigle the Regent on board, and then 'persuade' him to move the seat of Government to Brazil, taking with him such ships, property, etc. as he could transport.[1] It was a queer plan to have been sanctioned by Fox, and afterwards by Grey. Fortunately events in Prussia and Spain turned Napoleon's attention elsewhere, for the scheme, disgraceful in itself, would almost certainly have miscarried. Brougham asked to be allowed to try his diplomatic skill in Madrid, but this was refused, and the Mission returned home before the end of the year. The unfortunate Secretary was left to pay several minor accounts for which he was never reimbursed. His three months' adventure left him lighter in pocket, but with the lasting friendship of Lord Rosslyn.

The Coalition was now tottering before its fall. It had accomplished little except the abolition of the Slave Trade, and some of its measures, such as the first Order in Council, were to be the objects of Whig attacks during the long period of opposition which now lay ahead of them. Brougham was in close touch with Holland House and decided to throw in his lot with the Whigs. He was barely twenty-nine. At that age Gladstone was a Conservative, busy defending the apprenticeship system in Jamaica against Brougham's criticism. Disraeli at twenty-nine had hardly made up his mind whether he was a Tory Radical or a Radical Tory. Faced with the almost certain prospect of a clear Tory Government, Brougham saw that his place was with the Opposition. His experiences with the " Saints " must have convinced him that the negrophile of that time was not an effective fighter against repression at home. Brougham remained on friendly terms with Wilberforce and with Zachary Macaulay. During the next twenty-five years he became a leader of the abolitionists in Parliament and outside; but politically he joined the radical wing of the Whig Party.

[1] Brougham : *Memoirs*, i. 335 ff.

In the 1807 election Brougham threw his whole energies into a losing cause. Though not offered a seat he showed the astonished Lord Holland how a propagandist campaign should be run. He had already acquired some of the technique in his work for the Slave Trade agitation. At the General Election " in the course of ten days he filled every bookseller's shop with pamphlets, most London newspapers, and all country ones without exception, with paragraphs, and supplied a large proportion of the boroughs throughout the kingdom with handbills adapted to the local interests of the candidates, and all tending to enforce the principles, vindicate the conduct, elucidate the measures, or expose the adversaries of the Whigs." [1]   All this activity must have seemed a little absurd to the pre-Reform states-man, to whom Parliamentary representation suggested pocket boroughs, Court and landed interests, " nabobs " and borough-mongers. As so often in his life, Brougham was ahead of his time, foreseeing the inevitable trend of the modern democratic state, and experimenting a generation too early. He was the first politician who learnt to " manage the press," especially the provincial papers which are so often gravelled for lack of matter. He was already half a journalist, and from 1807 he began to build up a connection with men like Perry of the *Morning Chronicle*. Later he managed to obtain a place for his brother William on *The Times*. For the next thirty years Brougham was popularly supposed to have a hand in every press campaign, and to have inspired every inconvenient disclosure. It was an immensely powerful weapon, for politicians were begin-ning to grow more sensitive to public opinion, and the newspapers to carry more weight. It tended, how-ever, to make him unpopular, and largely accounts for the distrust with which the patricians always regarded him. His reputation was only partly deserved, for others, including some of the patricians themselves,

[1] Lord Holland : *Memoirs of the Whig Party*, ii. 227–8.

soon learned to imitate him, but it clung to him even after he had become Lord Chancellor, and after he had quarrelled with *The Times*. In 1834 this reputation was to play him a very scurvy trick.

Once the General Election was over, Brougham found that his Party had little further use for him. He was well known to the Whig leaders, but the Party was at sixes and sevens, and no one would, or perhaps could, persuade a Whig borough-owner to offer him a seat. He was not a good courtier, and at that time—though the clubs were important—the drawing-room was the real ante-room to the House of Commons. By October he seems to have quarrelled with Lady Holland, or perhaps merely thought he had, for there is no evidence of this in her journal. The great " Madagascar " expected a large measure of homage from her young Whigs. The genie at his birth may have promised Brougham wealth and power, but not the gift which includes the other two, that of being loved by old women. Brougham was probably too independent—not like the more adaptable Horner, his former friend and coeval, who had been taken up by the Grenvillites and already been given a pocket borough. " Think of Mr. Brougham," writes Lady Bessborough towards the end of 1807, " the protégé of Lord Holland, and apparent toad-eater and adorer of Lady Holland, abusing her violently to Corisande, and saying he detested her; there never was any woman so courted, so flatter'd, so followed, so *obey'd*, and so dislik'd, as Lady Holland." [1]

Lady Bessborough's attitude was typical of her class. A young man of no wealth or family was expected to be " toad-eater " to someone. It was Brougham's peculiarity that he settled his own terms. If he had once accepted the usual position the way would have been made very easy for him. The *Creevey Papers*, the letters of John Whishaw, the life of Horner, the careers

[1] Granville, Earl : *Private Correspondence, 1781–1821.* Lady Bessborough to Granville, Oct. 27, 1807, ii. 300.

of various members of the Holland House group all suggest that the Whigs did not expect too much from their Professionals. A good diner-out, ready to make a speech in the Commons, fulfilled most of their requirements. He could expect minor office, but, as Burke and Sheridan learnt, not Cabinet rank. Brougham never acknowledged these distinctions. Lord Campbell, who was his rival and subsequently his very hostile biographer, nevertheless admits this quality. Brougham " seemed, from his first introduction to men of the highest birth and the most distinguished position, to feel himself on an entire equality with them and, without any approach to vulgarity or impertinence, he treated them with the utmost familiarity." [1] This appeared to Campbell, himself an indefatigable careerist, to be a characteristic so remarkable as to be worth emphasizing.

Brougham now returned to his legal work. He had still some months to wait before he could be called to the English Bar, and his efforts to obtain an earlier " call " were blocked, possibly by political influence.[2] In the meantime he became a pupil of Tindal, afterwards Chief Justice of the Common Pleas, and received occasional briefs, as a Scottish Advocate, to appear before the Privy Council. Fortune and his political reputation now came to his help. He was retained as counsel for certain Liverpool merchants, who were petitioning Parliament against the Orders in Council.

Since the first Order in Council of the Coalition Ministry, in 1807, others had been issued as a reply to

[1] Lord John Campbell : *Lives of the Chancellors*, viii. 251.
[2] In a letter to Lord Grey, Brougham complains that the Government Law officers, " leaguing with Saint Alan Park (one of the greatest knaves in the profession)," used their influence to prevent his being called earlier. He adds, prophetically enough, that this is " a foretaste of what I have to expect in future when I shall stand in need of a silk gown." Park was the James Alan Park against whom he was, constitutionally and professionally, in constant opposition.

Napoleon's Berlin and Milan Decrees. Their object was to strangle French trade. " Their principle," to use Brougham's own words, " was abundantly simple. Napoleon had said that no vessel should touch a British port and then enter a French one, or one under French control. The Orders in Council said that no vessel whatever should enter any such port without having first touched at some port of Great Britain." [1] Whatever merits the Orders may have had as a war measure, they had the double defect of embroiling us with the United States, and drying up completely the feeble trickle of foreign trade which still remained. Here was a cause which suited Brougham perfectly. A group of people, with no Parliamentary status but with great influence and much popular support, was trying to force its point of view upon the Government. As a Whig and a political reformer, Brougham took full advantage of his position. For six weeks he could examine witnesses before both Houses of Parliament, and interpose a number of speeches. There was enough popular interest to ensure full attendances in the House of Commons, and Brougham was able to display his aptitude for handling commercial statistics, which very few politicians cared to touch. For the moment the petitioners were defeated, and Brougham had to wait four years until, as a Member of Parliament, he managed to get the Orders rescinded, but this first campaign had made his name.

His political reputation did not help him much on his first experience of the Northern Circuit, and Brougham passed through a disheartening period which seems to have confirmed his radicalism. He was keeping up a regular and intimate correspondence with Lord Grey,[2] who seldom came up to London, and was probably glad to get the latest political gossip, but the Whig

[1] Brougham : *Speeches*, i. 408.
[2] Brougham : *Memoirs*, i. 506 ff.

opposition was extremely feeble, and Brougham was growing more and more dissatisfied with the Party. The amateurs, the very men whose claims to seats had been preferred to Brougham's, were lazy and totally inefficient. In December 1808, Brougham was writing to Creevey, the elder and more cynical Professional, with whom he was already on familiar terms : " Lord Grey and Ld. Lauderdale *won't* come to town at all, they say, and they give as a reason Tierney's account of the state of the Party. Dissensions, etc., etc.—No good to be done—Game up and so forth. If Tierney really wrote this, he is a very bad counsellor—I could say more—but the people who can listen to it are not very wise—I conceive that this d—d faulty half-secession will not only finish the ruin of the Party, but deservedly exclude them from all public confidence." [1]

The ineffectiveness of the Whig landed gentry as reformers was obvious. They were neither able nor anxious to check the repression of all public opinion which was being enforced by Lord Sidmouth. Brougham began to turn towards the new business classes of the North as the future leaders of the country. His feelings were reflected in the *Edinburgh Review*, which under his influence was becoming more political and reformist each year. In the autumn of 1808 an article appeared which created an extraordinary sensation. It was a review of a book by Don Pedro Cevallos on the " French Usurpation in Spain," a composite review written chiefly by Jeffrey, but with political observations added by Brougham. The latter's interpolations are not difficult to recognize, partly owing to his excessive use of parentheses, a bad habit which he gradually abandoned. His articles at this period read a little like the speeches of Mr. Jingle, who also suffered from a mind which worked too quickly. All that Brougham wished to emphasize was the popular nature of the revolt against the French.

[1] *Creevey's Life and Times* : Ed. John Gore, p. 42.

" The resistance to France has been entirely
begun and carried on by the people in Spain.
Their kings betrayed them—fled, and rushed, with
the whole of their base courtiers, into the arms of
the enemy.   Their nobles followed; and it is
painful to reflect, that some of the most distinguished
of this body, after attending Ferdinand to Bayonne,
returned in the train of Joseph, and only quitted
his service when the universal insurrection of the
common people drove him from his usurped
throne.   The people, and of the people the middle,
and above all the lower orders, have alone the
merit of raising this glorious opposition to the
common enemy of national independence.   Those
who had so little of what is commonly termed
interest in the country, those who had no stake in
the community (to speak the technical language of
the aristocracy)—the persons of no *consideration* in
the state—they who could not pledge their fortunes, having only lives and liberties to lose—the
bulk—the mass of the people—nay, the very
odious, many-headed beast, the multitude—the
mob itself—alone, uncalled, unaided by the higher
classes—in spite of those higher classes, and in
direct opposition to them, as well as to the enemy
whom they so vilely joined—raised up the standard of insurrection—bore it through massacre
and through victory, until it had chased the usurper
away, and waved over his deserted courts.   Happen
what will in the sequel, here is a grand and permanent success—a lesson to all government—a warn-
ing to all oligarchies—a cheering example to every
people." [1]

It is a little difficult for the modern Englishman to
remember that this statement of an undoubted truth
would appear to the great majority of educated people

[1] *Edinburgh Review*, October 1808.

as grossly seditious, a covert attack upon the constitution, and as subversive of law and order.   Jeffrey in
some alarm writes to Horner from Edinburgh—" The
combustion which the review of Cevallos has excited here
has spread in some degree to London. . . . The Tories
having a handle are running us down with all their
might; and the ghosts of all the miserables we have
slain are rising to join in the vengeance.   Walter Scott
and William Erskine and about twenty-five persons of
consideration have forbidden the *Review* to enter their
doors.   The Earl of Buchan, I am informed, opened
his street door and actually *kicked* it out. . . ." [1]   The
article was ascribed wholly to Brougham, and at once
marked him out as a really dangerous fellow.   His
contemporaries were not used to this kind of attack
except from poets, visionaries or demagogues.   They
recognized the young Whig lawyer as a new type,
carrying very heavy guns.   " This is miching mallecho;
it means mischief," and many years later it is as Lord
Michin Malicho that Brougham appears in the good-
natured satire of *Gryll Grange*.   It was Peacock's tribute
to the demonic force which did so much to upset the
comfortable complacency of the English upper classes
he had known as a boy.

Brougham completely ignored the turmoil he had
helped to create.   They talk, let them talk!   It was an
attitude which he maintained throughout most of his
long and controversial career.   Holland House and the
wealthier Whigs were ruffled.   The Tories blustered,
and took the opportunity of hurriedly launching their
rival Review, the *Quarterly*, but Brougham continued
his usual activities, and remained on the same intimate
terms with Lord Grey, and also with the Rosslyns.
The latter were a considerable factor in Brougham's
life at this period.   " Upon their first acquaintance,"
wrote the future Lord Dudley and Ward, " the Countess
hated the Critic, and the Critic despised the Countess.

[1] Francis Horner : *Memoirs and Correspondence*, i. 438.

D

However, it seems that they have happily arrived at a due sense of each other's merits. His ' universality,' about which we always used to joke with him, prevents me from being surprised at anything he does. Otherwise it is comical enough to see the lawyer, the politician, the negotiator, the geometer, setting up all of a sudden for a man of gallantry." [1] Brougham was stopping with the Rosslyns when he collaborated with Jeffrey over the Don Cevallos article. It is even hinted that his hostess helped to inspire him, " the lady being then a great favourite, and a mad politician." [2] Grey disapproved of the article, but then he disapproved of so much that the young Whigs were doing; [3] especially their attacks upon the Duke of York in connection with the notorious case of Mrs. Clarke, a case which loomed very large in the England of 1809, distracting attention even from the way in which Napoleon was destroying the last remnants of Austrian independence.

In the autumn of 1809 Lord Grey electrified and also annoyed Creevey by remarking after dinner that " the first man this country has seen since Burke's time is Brougham." It was certainly a curious verdict, when it is remembered that Brougham was not yet in Parliament. Creevey's acid comment was that it showed Lord Grey's " spite at my conduct last session, and his own folly " ; [4] it also probably showed the astute politician that Brougham could not be kept much longer out of the House of Commons. A month later the old Lord Lansdowne died and was succeeded by Lord Henry Petty. The Duke of Bedford offered the vacant seat to Brougham, and on February 5th, 1810, he was returned to Parliament as representative of Camelford.

---

[1] Dudley and Ward, Lord: *Letters to "Ivy."* Letter of October 1808, p. 54. ("Ivy" was Mrs. Dugald Stewart, wife of the Edinburgh lecturer.)

[2] Macvey Napier : *Correspondence*, p. 309 n.

[3] *Id.*, Brougham to Napier, Oct. 27, 1839, p. 308.

[4] *Creevey Papers*, i. 107–8.

It is not known whether he ever went down to Cornwall and visited the " twenty paid electors " who formed his first constituency.   Some borough-owners preferred their nominees to stay away lest they should introduce any outside influence.

CHAPTER III

IN PARLIAMENT

From the beginnings of the century (about the time the Review began) to the death of Lord Liverpool, was an awful period for those who ventured to maintain liberal opinions; and who were too honest to sell them for the ermine of the judge or the lawn of the prelate. A long and hopeless career in your profession, the chuckling grin of noodles, the sarcastic leer of the genuine political rogue.   SYDNEY SMITH.

BROUGHAM was thirty-one when he entered Parliament. At that epoch it would have been considered a comparatively mature age, but he was already a marked man. His long gaunt figure, his queer profile and unforgettable twitching nose—" that *organum nobile*, a happy approach to *perpetuum mobile* "—his formidable eye, which Haydon said " was like a lion watching for its prey," his uncouth but effective gestures, faintly reminiscent of the Scottish preacher, all these were familiar to the great majority of Members, who had heard him arguing for the merchants' petition against the Orders in Council. Apart from this he had built up a considerable reputation as an unconventional reformer, with a caustic pen and a vitriolic tongue. Brougham never had the least difficulty in picking himself out from the crowd. His nervous energy alone was remarkable in that hard-drinking, easy-going and gourmandizing age. But he knew far more than his contemporaries about the meretricious art of self-advertisement, holding with some justification that such knowledge was a legitimate weapon for a man hampered by lack of wealth and family connections. His natural appearance was a godsend to the caricaturist, but he accentuated his physical peculiarities by his high black

" choker," and, in later days, by the invariable plaid trousers, which appear in so many cartoons. The plaid trousers ultimately became as familiar as Gladstone's collar, Joseph Chamberlain's eye-glass and orchid, or the gap—the " one lucid interval "—between Sir Charles Wetherell's jacket and breeches.

As a reformer, Brougham started with the initial disadvantage of representing a closed borough. Like many advanced Whigs he felt this anomaly very acutely, and made repeated efforts to get an open constituency before he was at last invited to stand for Yorkshire in 1830. It would, however, be a mistake to exaggerate the servility of the Member to the borough-owner. Many owners were not keen politicians, few demanded more than a general support for their Party, though they would sometimes have a special business interest which the Member might be expected to further. This was a matter of previous arrangement, and the Member's position was not unlike that of some modern parliamentarian, connected with an industrial interest from which he draws emoluments which he would probably not receive if he were not an active politician. On the Tory side there were certain constituencies bought up by men with an eye to business, or by men with Indian or West Indian connections—as, for example, the notorious " Member for Arcot "—but the Whig landlords do not seem to have looked for more than a general sympathy with the landed interest.

The Member during his period of tenancy was free to express what views he liked, but a kind of unwritten code governed both parties. If the Member found himself, owing to some re-alignment of parties, on opposite sides to the owner, he did not give up his seat, but was expected to find another as soon as possible. This happened to Brougham towards the end of his career in the Commons, and he transferred to one of the Duke of Devonshire's constituencies. On the other hand, the owner was not expected to sell or transfer the

patronage " over the Member's head."   Financial strin-
gency due to the war led to this rule being frequently
broken during the twenty years preceding the Reform
Act, when the system was falling into degradation.
Camelford was sold in 1812, losing Brougham his seat.
Six years later Creevey was turned out of Thetford under
rather similar circumstances.   His letter of protest is
worth recalling, for it suggests the rights which the
sitting Member considered that he had as against the
owner.

Creevey was an astute and not too scrupulous politician,
but he was not the " mischievous imp and toady " of
Lytton Strachey's phrase.   His letter to the Duke of
Norfolk is delightfully frank.

> " The question I put to you, Duke, is this—Why
> have you not noticed me in your arrangements for
> the new Parliament, or why have you not given me
> your reasons for not doing so ? . . . I have learnt,
> and am taught to believe, that Mr. Phillips's claims
> upon you are founded upon a large loan of money
> that he advanced to you two or three years ago. . . .
> I am certain that mature reflection will show you
> the fatal effects that such a precedent, if generally
> followed, would produce, as well upon your own
> body—the Aristocracy—as upon the Constitution
> of your country. . . . Would they not *then*, at least,
> be subject to the reproach, hitherto so unjustly and
> maliciously urged against them, of trafficking in
> seats in Parliament ? . . ." [1]

This extract may help to explain the comparative
freedom and independence of the younger Whigs in
Parliament. Lord Campbell was a " nesty " Scot,
always ready for a dig at the Northerner who had risen
in the world, but he was willing to allow that Brougham
" never, in any degree, sacrificed his independence while

---

[1] *Creevey Papers*, i. 274.

representing a peer or peeress," either when sitting for
Camelford under the Duke of Bedford, or for Winchelsea
under Lord Darlington.[1]   Within a month of taking his
seat in 1810 he became an active member of the
" Mountain," busily engaged in a number of movements for which there was not likely to have been much
enthusiasm at Woburn.

The effective Opposition was very small; some twenty
Members of the " Mountain," and a few independents.
What Peel said of the Conservative Opposition thirty
years later was true of the Whigs in the pre-reform
House of Commons.   " After you had deducted the idle,
the shuffling, the diners-out, the country gentlemen with
country occupations, and above all the moderate and
quiet men disliking the principle of a factious Opposition,
we should find the ranks pretty well thinned." [2]   Lord
John Russell, who joined the Party two years later, has
left a picture of the well-meaning but totally inefficient
leader, George Ponsonby.[3]   He was Lady Grey's uncle,
and had held a minor post in the Ministry of All the
Talents, but he had no control over the various groups
which professed some kind of allegiance to Lord Grey
and Lord Grenville.   Lord Holland, to whom Brougham
in the following year sent a " mutinous epistle " about
the state of the Party, replied frankly and pessimistically.
" There is a want of popular feelings in many individuals
of the Party.   Others are exasperated with the unjust
and uncandid treatment they have received, and are
receiving, from the modern reformers.   Another set
are violent anti-reformers, and alarmed at every speech
or measure that has the least tendency towards reform." [4]
The position was complicated by the hope, which was
keeping many Whigs very cautious, that the Prince would
bring them into office as soon as he became Regent.

[1] Lord Campbell : *Lives of the Chancellors*, viii. 283.
[2] C. S. Parker : *Sir Robert Peel*, ii. 410.
[3] Lord John Russell : *Recollections and Suggestions*, p. 30.
[4] *Creevey Papers*, i. 144.

Most of the little handful of reformers had their special subjects. "Fermentation Sam" Whitbread argued for an early peace, for universal education, and for higher agricultural wages. Romilly and Mackintosh were legal reformers, attacking the severity of our criminal code, the antiquated procedure of the Courts, and the expense of civil law. Henry Grey Bennet busied himself over the brutality of the Game Laws, the condition of the gaols, the cruelty of the madhouse system, and the ill-treatment of chimney-sweep boys. Another group, which included Lord Folkestone, "Squire" Western, Lord Townshend, and Creevey were chiefly interested in what Cobbett called "Old Corruption"— the elaborate eighteenth-century system of ministerial jobbery and Court influence.

Brougham was from the first remarkable for his versatility. He began by taking up such questions as the enforcement of the Slave Trading law, and the evils of the Orders in Council. Education was an early interest, and in 1810 he appears with James Mill, Samuel Rogers, and a number of Quaker philanthropists and Nonconformist ministers on the committee of the Royal Lancastrian Association. His defence of Leigh and John Hunt made him look into the question of military discipline. He was one of the first to expose in Parliament the scandal of flogging, and such punishments as a " thousand lashes," which were often equivalent to a sentence of death by torture. As a lawyer he naturally followed the lead of Romilly and Mackintosh, and was an early disciple of Bentham. These reforms were, for the most part, outside the ordinary day-to-day work of the Opposition. Such questions as the misconduct of the Walcheren expedition, the subject of Brougham's first speech in the Commons, loomed larger than the troubles of the poor or the scandal of the law-courts.

Wars, which provide such magnificent opportunities for wholesale domestic reforms, are usually undertaken by reactionary ministries and made an excuse for inaction.

The Radical element, inside or outside Parliament, could accomplish little directly, but " Counsellor Brougham, in a terrible fume," rapidly became a national figure. The universal nature of his interests was in itself important. It forced the English to see that all these reforms were not just individual notions, but were bound up with each other, and with the general idea of progress. People began to connect the bleeding lacerated body of a private on the " triangle " with the general degradation of the poor, and with the whole system of corrupt military appointments. The little six-year-old sweep being prodded up the chimneys of the rich was eloquent of an England which was accused with some justice of fighting the French by sacrificing her children, failing either to protect them in the factories or provide them with schools. Starvation and high prices became related to ministerial jobbery, a vicious Court, and the need for Parliamentary reform. The disabilities of the Nonconformist and the Jew became another aspect of Catholic emancipation; the scandal of the English tithe system added to the unpopularity of the clerical magistrates, the " black dragoons " of the repression.

English historians have not been over-kind to the reformer. Too often he is considered as the harmless necessary drudge, obscurely serving the cause of progress, a drab uninteresting figure compared with the jaunty defender of indefensible abuses, or the cheerful cynic who blocks all advance. Canning is remembered for the wit of the Anti-Jacobin and the Needy Knife-Grinder, but it is forgotten that he helped to give bull-baiting a new lease of life on the grounds that " it inspired courage, and produced a nobleness of sentiment and elevation of the mind." The Duke of Wellington's long and systematic obstruction in the Lords has never seriously detracted from his victories on the Continent. Melbourne survives as a paternal figure teaching the young Queen chess and constitutional practice, not as the Whig who covertly opposed reform, and the Prime

Minister who held up popular education, because he was
" against it," and " the Pagets got on damned well
without it." Possibly our attitude is due to the belief,
almost universal before 1914, that progress is inevitable,
and perhaps it had better not be too fast. Nowadays
it is less easy to take this comfortable view, or see
compensatory advantages in each reprieve for cruelty,
corruption, or inefficiency. England is not really a
happier country to-day because her education was
allowed to lag behind that of many European countries.
Lancashire is still suffering, in the stunted bodies of her
people, from the successful opposition of Lord Eldon
and others to all factory legislation. Ireland's future
was not made brighter by deferring Catholic emancipation for another twenty years. It was no gain to Britain
that Lord Lauderdale, the Whig, continued for twenty
years to block every Bill intended to stop little children
being sent up chimneys, or that the British army remained
unique for the savagery of its punishments.

An atmosphere of frustration, almost of futility,
surrounds the early nineteenth-century reformers. The
odds against them were too heavy. This was not
because they were very much in advance of their time.
Apart from a few details, such as a preference for annual
parliaments, there was nothing in the programme of the
most doctrinaire Radical which was not accepted within
a generation or two. The abuses against which they
inveighed would not have been tolerated by any section
of the public fifty years later. In many cases they only
wished to raise England to the standard of some other
European country. When Brougham began his public
career, many reforms were overdue, but they were being
opposed by a well-entrenched caste, seriously alarmed
about the continuance of its privileges, and more than
usually impervious to any moral or religious appeal.
Perhaps " caste " is a misleading word, for the " upper
classes " contained three elements, bound together by a
common fear, but not by any great affection—the old

landed aristocracy, the Church of England, and the successful London business and professional men, upon whom Pitt had so largely relied. These groups contained most of the educated people in the country, and controlled nearly all its wealth, until the North developed a new type of successful Radical industrialist.

The privileged class had three powerful weapons —repression, bribery, and the control of nearly every channel by which ideas could be spread. For the first forty-five years of Brougham's life it was almost safer, in Sydney Smith's phrase, to be a felon than a reformer. Besides Gerald, who was executed, Muir and Palmer, who were transported, there was hardly a Radical working outside Parliament who had not suffered imprisonment. Thelwall, Hardy, Horne Tooke, Cobbett, Leigh Hunt, Bamford, Knight, Prentice, and a host of obscurer men were all prosecuted for their opinions. In 1810 a man of Radical opinions had to go very warily. There was no clear path to take, no obvious party to join. In judging the reformers it is ludicrous to apply academic standards based on the comfort and security of the half-century before the last war, and we must guard carefully against accepting the prejudices of their contemporaries. The fierce light which is supposed to beat upon a throne is a feeble glimmer compared with the searchlight brought to bear on the man who sets out to criticize his generation and to attack vested interests.

Brougham, both as a lawyer and a politician, was brought into close contact with Radicals who were carrying on the dangerous work of agitation outside Parliament. He preferred, as always, to take his own line. Mob organization, then in its infancy, was one side of the modern democratic technique for which Brougham had no fondness and no aptitude, nor was he impressed by the individuals who had survived the long period of repression. Leading a small unpopular movement requires a peculiar kind of moral courage, and places an intolerable strain on the nerves and temper.

The English Radicals of the Napoleonic period had their share of the weaknesses which are apt to afflict men struggling under such conditions. There were quarrels, mutual distrust, excessive optimism interspersed with fits of despondency, a proneness to exaggeration and self-glorification. The leaders were not likely to attract a young politician who was more interested in achievement than in theory. Major Cartwright, one of the few survivors of the trials and repression of the 'nineties, was by 1810 a garrulous ineffective old gentleman; " in political matters "—according to Francis Place— " exceedingly troublesome, and sometimes as exceedingly absurd." [1] Sir Francis Burdett, the ultra-Radical member for Westminster, was the perfect Georgian replica of the " parlour Bolshevik." He had just completed his famous struggle with the House of Commons, when troops had to be marched to London and the Tower to be placed in a condition of siege before his arrest and imprisonment. He was, however, always apt to let down his friends at moments of crisis. His egoism and his great wealth prevented him being a good democrat. Cochrane, another aristocrat, was a pleasanter type, but not too well balanced, and soon to be involved in a financial scandal. Cobbett, for all his magnificent qualities, was not a person with whom anyone found it easy to work. Although he had frequently changed his own opinions, he was incessantly attacking every other Radical group, and in later years was specially hostile to Brougham. Henry Hunt, the " orator," and Burdett were both involved in a long and bitter quarrel with Francis Place, who was the one effectual, level-headed organizer amongst the Radicals. For many years Burdett suspected Place, quite unfoundedly, of being a Government spy, and would not speak to him.

To Brougham the ultra-Radicals must have seemed as limited and ineffective as the " Saints." They were

[1] Graham Wallas : *The Life of Francis Place*, p. 62.

men with whom it was possible to co-operate, but to whom it was unwise to give one's allegiance. As soon as he entered Parliament Brougham began to develop his own individual methods. He aimed at building up public opinion, especially in the north of England. The only two places where it was possible to speak freely were the House of Commons and the law-courts. Brougham used his comparative immunity as a lawyer and as a Member of Parliament to make as many propagandist speeches as possible, and he got them plenty of publicity by the judicious " salting " of the Press. A study of Hansard reveals his extraordinary skill and energy in making every conceivable subject, from sailors' rations to the duty on leather, into an object-lesson for the evils of the existing system.

The pre-reform Parliament, with its looser party organization, gave far more scope to the individual Member. Even an opposition Member, if he could show evidence of outside support, might occasionally affect legislation. Brougham, in 1811, introduced a Bill making slave-trading a felony, and successfully piloted it through the House. The next year he secured the appointment of a committee to inquire into the state of trade. By sheer force of character he turned the committee into an inquisition upon the working of the Orders in Council. He brought business men from every manufacturing town, and within six weeks had collected a mass of evidence which no Government could overlook. There was a dramatic quality about the conclusion of the inquiry which helped to build up the legend attached to Brougham's name. Perceval was murdered within earshot of the committee, but Brougham insisted on completing the evidence, thereby offending many, but emphasizing that the public good must come before private feelings. On June 16th, Brougham made his great speech on the work of the Committee, on the 23rd the Government withdrew the Orders in Council. It was five days too late. America had already declared war.

Parliament provided Brougham with one platform. His profession gave him another. He began to specialize in the " sedition line." Sir Vicary Gibbs, the Attorney-General, was doing his best to bring the law of seditious libel into disrepute by the virulence of his prosecutions. He was not satisfied with haling journalists, printers and editors before the Courts, but would pursue old ladies who had inherited a few shares in some newspaper. Yet such was the fear of the Government and the ease with which a jury could be swayed by mention of " Jacobinical tendencies " that a conviction was always considered a foregone conclusion. Brougham fought these cases with zest. He hated bullying, and he hated stupidity. In the spring of 1811 he was called upon to defend his friends Leigh and John Hunt for an article on flogging in the army, taken from the *Stamford News* and published in the *Examiner*. It was a gruesome account of a sentence of 1000 lashes, of which some 750 were inflicted before the man was carried off senseless. Sir Vicary Gibbs filed an " ex-officio " information against the brothers. The future Lord Campbell, who was present, described Brougham's speech for the defence as " the best that had been made in the King's Bench these seven years." [1] It was studiously careful in tone, took full advantage of the prosecution's absurd plea that the article would encourage the French, but concentrated on the main question " whether an Englishman still enjoys the privilege of freely discussing public matters."

A London jury decided that the Englishman did enjoy the privilege, and Brougham won a great victory. But the system of legal repression was not to be upset so easily. At Lincoln, before a jury of fox-hunting squires, he failed to get an acquittal for the editor of the *Stamford News*, who was charged with precisely the same offence as the Hunts. The Judge's summing up is worth recalling for the light which it throws upon legal ideas of prerogative. " The House of Parliament is the

---

[1] Hardcastle : *Life of Lord Campbell*, i. 260.

proper place for the discussion of subjects of this nature.
There it should appear, and not in pamphlets or newspapers.   The right to discuss the acts of our Legislature
would be a large permission indeed.   Is the libeller to
come and make the people dissatisfied with the Government under which they live ?   This is not permitted to
any man.   It is unconstitutional and seditious. . . ."
It is a great part of Brougham's legacy to England that he
made this doctrine first absurd and then obsolete.   But
he had another defeat in 1812.   The Hunts, reckless after
their success, set him an impossible task.

A poet in the *Morning Post* had called the Regent " the
Mæcenas of the Age " and " an Adonis in Loveliness."
Several of the *Examiner's* friends, including Charles
Lamb, are supposed to have helped in the compilation
of the article called " The Prince on St. Patrick's Day."
In this the Regent was described as " a corpulent man of
fifty," " a violator of his word," and " a libertine head
over ears in debt and disgrace, a despiser of domestic
ties, the companion of gamblers and demireps."   It
was the climax of a long series of attacks, including
Lamb's " The Triumph of the Whale," and it is not
surprising that Brougham, when writing to Lord Grey,
said that he was anxious about the verdict, though " full
of confidence as to the defence and its effects all over the
country—it will be a thousand times more unpleasant
than the libel ! " [1]   It probably was, for the Regent
attempted to get the trial stopped, but the Hunts would
not be bought off, and underwent their two years'
imprisonment.   Brougham would often visit Leigh in
his cell, the wonderful cell which he had fitted up in such
a way that Lamb declared " there was no other such
room except in a fairy tale."   Hunt writes to his wife
a year later to tell how " Brougham called in, and we
had a delightful conversation till six, when he was
obliged to go.   We talked on all sorts of subjects—

[1] Brougham's *Memoirs*, ii. 72.

politics, histories, poets, orators, languages, music, painting, etc. . . ." [1]

The Lancashire and Yorkshire Luddite disturbances also provided an important group of cases in which Brougham was frequently called for the defence. Magistrates and employers were busily working together to prevent any attempt at organization amongst the millhands. The textile workers had been hard hit by war conditions, high prices being combined with low wages and poor trade. The introduction of power looms completed their misery. The mill-owners, instead of making efforts to mitigate these troubles, preferred to employ spies and *agents-provocateurs*, men like MacDonald, Bent, Playfair and other forerunners of the more notorious Oliver. On the evidence of such men, most of whom were convicted criminals who had turned police " assistants," large numbers of mill-hands and their families were prosecuted not only for active offences, like rioting and arson, but for conspiracy and administering illegal oaths. Brougham appeared in both types of case, while the prosecution was usually in the hands of his old enemy, James Alan Park, the typical sycophantic careerist from the North.[2] The latter's methods are sufficiently explained by the notes which he has left scribbled on the Brief when nine men, two boys and two girls were tried for arson. " Lowness of wages—and dearness of provisions—the ground for objection—Will of Providence—Is the (word illegible) mended by destroying property—one hundred people thrown out of employment. The Means of Charity

---

[1] Leigh Hunt : *Correspondence*. Letter to Marianne, April, 1813. Brougham lent Hunt £100. Add. MS. 38108, f. 67.

[2] See note, p. 29. Park was later known as the " Christian Judge," but his Christianity, as may be gathered, was not of a kind likely to check his career. His fellow-barristers used to chant a little rhyme telling how he

" came naked stark
From Scotland."

destroyed—never was so charitable a country. The Poor shall never cease out of the land—The poor ye shall have always with you. . . ." [1]

Brougham was frequently hampered by the legal practice which forbade any speeches on behalf of the accused in cases of felony, but he was able, with the help of other barristers like Scarlett, to expose some of the informers, and he achieved one great victory in the acquittal of thirty-eight Manchester reformers, who had met together to petition Parliament, and were accused of administering an illegal oath. There is no doubt that Brougham's truculence did much to prevent the more blatant abuses of police and magisterial authority during the years of repression which followed. The effect of his reputation is shown in a confidential letter from the Secretary of State to a magistrate at Bolton, written some five years later, in which he recommends dropping the prosecution of " Blanketeers " arrested on their way to petition the Regent. " It is an extremely difficult case to deal with, and I am very much disposed to think that after the prisoners have sustained five months' Imprisonment it will be more prudent to make a merit of letting them off, than to run the risque of a Verdict after an inflammatory speech of Mr. Brougham or some such Orator." [2]

Apart from Whig politics and defending sedition cases, there was a third side to Brougham's activities. He was at this period coming under the influence of Bentham and his school of thought. He had much in common with the highly educated Radicals, men like James Mill, with their rather " Fabian Society " outlook. One of their chief tenets was the more immediate importance of education as compared with constitutional changes and Parliamentary reform. A passage from

[1] J. L. and B. Hammond : *The Skilled Labourer, 1760–1832*, p. 295. The trials are fully described in this most valuable book.
[2] *Id.*, p. 349.

E

John Stuart Mill's account of his father might apply equally to Brougham as a young man. " So complete was my father's reliance on the influence of reason over the mind of mankind, whenever it is allowed to reach them, that he felt as if all would be gained if the whole population were taught to read, if all sorts of opinions were allowed to be addressed to them by word and in writing, and if, by means of the suffrage, they could nominate a legislation to give effect to the opinions they adopted." [1] The present generation is less optimistic about the effect of universal education, but would hardly condemn anyone for being sceptical about the working of democracy in a country where most of the inhabitants could not read or write.

Of Brougham's earliest educational activities something can be gathered from the letters of Francis Place, James Mill, and Edward Wakefield, with whom he was collaborating from about 1810 onwards.   While he was striving, not very successfully, to persuade the Whigs to make universal education the first " plank " in their policy, he was working out a scheme for a complete system of primary and secondary education in London. He was, wrote Place to Wakefield, " one of the few who see the scope and extent of what it may lead to." [2] By 1813 the West London Lancastrian Association began mapping out half London into suitable school areas, so that Brougham, when he brought the question before Parliament a few years later, was far in advance of his opponents, for he had some concrete facts to place before Parliament.

The year 1812 brought many personal triumphs to Brougham, but it also saw one of those sudden reversals of fortune which are the lot of most politicians who are both independent-minded and poor.   Although he had brought new life to the Whig Opposition, and achieved

---

[1] J. S. Mill : *Autobiography*, p. 106.
[2] Graham Wallas : *Life of Francis Place*, i. 260.

two remarkable successes in his Slave Trade Act, and in the reversal of the Orders in Council, he found at the General Election that he had no real standing in the Party. He was offered the forlorn hope of contesting one of the two Liverpool seats against Canning, but Camelford had passed into other hands, and no Whig borough-owner would offer him a safe retreat if Liverpool, as was almost certain, should fall to the richer and better organized party. Brougham learnt a lesson in political strategy which had considerable effect on the rest of his career.

There are only two possible methods for the aspiring politician without influence or wealth behind him. He must decide whether to use oil or vitriol. A statistician, with a sardonic turn of mind, could probably show an overwhelming majority of successes for the former method. The young man makes himself useful to his seniors, writes their speeches, deputizes for them at dull functions, votes as he is told, is always discreet and always dignified. Such a man was Francis Horner, then rising rapidly in the Whig Party. Lockhart has recorded a ribald saying of Sir Walter Scott about Horner and Brougham. Scott was, of course, no political friend to either. Jeffrey had been praising the *Edinburgh Review* contributors. " Come," said Scott, " you can't say too much about Sydney and Brougham, but I will not admire your Horner; he always puts me into mind of Obadiah's bull, who although, as Father Shandy observed, he never produced a calf, went through the business with such a grave demeanour, that he always maintained his credit in the parish." [1] Horner was given a closed seat at St. Ives in 1806. When that was transferred over his head, he was promptly given another, and when he lost that in 1812, the Duke of Buckingham brought him in for St. Mawes in the Grenvillite interest.

Brougham, the confirmed vitriolic, still retained the support and confidence of Grey. During the abortive

[1] Lockhart's *Life of Sir Walter Scott*, p. 156.

negotiations of 1811, when the Regent, with Lord Wellesley's help, tried to form a Coalition Government, Grey made it clear that Brougham would be given office—Secretary of the Admiralty, or President of the Board of Trade. But the other Whig leaders found Brougham much too dangerous; there was more than a suspicion of Jacobinism about this universal reformer. Few of them were willing to make any real alterations in the pocket borough system. Most of them, especially the Grenvillites, thoroughly disliked the idea of parliamentary reform, and abhorred that of popular education. They would have agreed with the President of the Royal Society that " however specious in theory the project might be, of giving education to the labouring classes of the poor, it would in effect be found to be prejudicial to their morals and happiness; it would teach them to despise their lot in life, instead of making them good servants in agriculture and other laborious employments; instead of teaching them subordination, it would render them factious and refractory." [1] Brougham represented mischief, the march of new ideas, upsetting to the Whig landed proprietors. If Brougham could win Liverpool, well and good; but if not, Lord Grey himself would not be able to get him a safe seat.

There may have been some further cause for Whig annoyance in a proposal which Brougham made to Castlereagh in August 1812. The United States had already declared war, but there was an idea of opening negotiations. Brougham offered his services as negotiator, in connection with various matters in dispute. " I am induced to think that I might be of use as a negotiator in this affair, not merely from having had the honour of being employed diplomatically by Mr. Secretary Fox, but chiefly because, for the share I have accidentally had in the American question, there seems

[1] Speech by D. Giddy. Hansard, ix. 798. Quoted in J. L. Hammond's *The Town Labourer, 1760–1832*, which is invaluable for this period.

a probability of such arrangement either facilitating an adjustment with America or, should this unhappily fail, of rendering the failure less unsatisfactory to this country." [1] With England in the last stages of the Napoleonic war there was nothing absurd in such an offer from a man who was identified with a friendly policy towards America, but, like a less fortunate suggestion made twenty-two years later, it was liable to misconstruction. Brougham had yet to learn that the vitriolic politician cannot allow any chinks in his armour, especially in the back. Some of his dearest enemies began to suggest that he wished to take a post as "Minister" under the Tories. The proposal came to nothing, the negotiations were not begun. Grey, who understood his fellow-politicians, would have dissuaded Brougham, and congratulated him on his "lucky escape." [2]

Brougham in October went to Liverpool to begin his campaign. Roscoe, the historian, was the local Whig representative, and, like so many of his kind, was too optimistic. There were two seats. By relying on Whig "plumpers" one of the two should have been safe. Probably Roscoe was deceived by the popular enthusiasm against the Orders in Council, and two Whig candidates were invited, Creevey being the second. Unfortunately the electorate was limited in size, and such portion as was not corruptible was heavily weighted by the slave-owning interests under the leadership of Sir John Gladstone, father of the Prime Minister. Brougham threw himself into the game with his usual energy. Time and experience were making him more and more an enemy of the Pitt tradition, which then hung heavily over English politics, and was an excuse for every form of reactionary measure. "I have been perfectly amazed," wrote Creevey, "at the marvellous talent of Brougham in his addresses to the people. He

[1] *Memoirs and Correspondence of Viscount Castlereagh*, i. 119.
[2] Brougham's *Memoirs*, ii. 41.

poured in a volley of declamation against the *immortal memory of Pitt* the day before yesterday, describing his immortality as proclaimed by the desolation of his own country and the subjugation of mankind, that, by God, shook the very square and all the houses in it from the applause it met with." [1]   But during the long struggle —the poll was kept open a fortnight—the voters were being carefully shepherded by their opponents, and both Whig candidates knew they had little chance unless one of them withdrew.

The obvious candidate to withdraw was Creevey, who had his seat at Thetford, but the old Professional had a deeper game.   He wanted to get Liverpool later, and for this it was necessary for Brougham to be beaten as well as himself.   " To play second fiddle to Brougham," he confided to his wife, " would not be worth a dam. If it be an object worthy of my ambition to get possession of Liverpool and to *keep it*, then I say that my game, and my game only, has been played, and that the whole *dramatis personæ*, Brougham and Canning included, might have been puppets selected by myself to serve my own ulterior purposes.   Depend upon it, Diddy (Creevey himself) never played a slyer part than in his unassuming, modest character in which he has appeared before his fellow-townsmen." [2]   This was all well within the usual jungle morality of politics, though it meant that Brougham was out of Parliament, and the Mountain, to which Creevey belonged, lost its most effective member.   Brougham bore no rancour towards his fellow-professional, but was increasingly bitter against the Whig leaders, not only the landed interest but those others, like Sam Whitbread, who seem to have accepted the weakening of the left wing without any great regret. " Pray, did it strike you," Brougham was writing to Creevey a fortnight after their defeat, " that Sam is well pleased at all of us being out ?   Among other marks I was with him about a week, and he never said a syllable

[1] *Creevey Papers*, i. 172.   [2] *Id.*, i. 171.

by way of condolence or regret at my being out, or Romilly, etc. The Holland House folks, I plainly perceive from some things, don't relish attacks on Pitt. . . ." [1]

Brougham made a last minute effort to get a seat in the Inverkeithing group of boroughs, but pre-reform Scotland was no place for a free-lance. He thus found himself, at thirty-five, shelved by one Party whilst cordially hated and feared by the other. His defeat at Liverpool was " the only agreeable circumstance " which the dissolution had brought to Frederick Robinson, the future Lord Goderich. " It would," he wrote to Peel, " compensate for a world of trouble and disappointment in other respects." [2] Such a position placed a great strain on Brougham's character. A weaker man might have given up the struggle. Brougham was merely spurred to greater efforts, but his experience tempted him into the politician's most common and most characteristic weakness, the desire for personal revenge. He never really forgave the Whig leaders, and he was more than ever determined to acquire an independent position in Parliament, possibly as a Radical. He promised himself, in a letter to Creevey, " the purest of all pleasures—at once do what I most approve of in politics and give the black ones a licking every other night." [3] In the meantime he had to get more support in the country, and above all, following Iago's advice, put money in his purse. This would take time. He wrote to Lord Grey deprecating any further efforts to find him a seat. " I have no claims with those who abhor reform—which, by the way, I was so far from overrating that I never yet have said anything about it. Your urging anything in my behalf in those quarters without the possibility of serving me would only expose yourself to odium on

[1] John Gore : *Creevey's Life and Times.* Letter from Brougham, Nov. 4, 1812, p. 65.
[2] C. S. Parker : *Sir Robert Peel,* i. 61.
[3] *Creevey Papers,* i. 174.

my account, and might injure that influence over the Party which it is of the utmost consequence that you should possess unimpaired.   If Tierney, Romilly, etc. are safe (which now seems pretty certain) I can very easily be spared." [1]

[1] Brougham : *Memoirs*, ii. 70.

CHAPTER IV

THE RADICAL LAWYER

Ambition is like choler; which is an humour that maketh men active, earnest, full of alacrity, and stirring, if it be not stopped. But if it be stopped, and cannot have its way, it becometh adust, and thereby malign and venomous.　　　FRANCIS BACON.

BROUGHAM, disillusioned but energetic as ever, rapidly started on the next phase in his career. His popular reputation was not much injured by his exclusion from Parliament. The Whig Opposition in the House of Commons was so feeble, so clearly lacking in any political principle that the natural inference was obvious. Brougham was too advanced and too forceful for them. Nor had he any difficulty in picking up his work at the Bar. Horner, writing at the end of 1812, describes his success as " prodigious, much more rapid and extensive than that of any barrister since Erskine started," but both he and Campbell suggest that his interests were too varied to give him a very high professional standing. Horner expected him to take parliamentary practice, where he would be assured of a large income. " That loose rambling sort of practice is richly paid; but no professional fame or science is to be gained in that department." [1] Brougham seriously considered the idea, chiefly because it would enable him to make money quickly, and he wanted to amass the few thousands which would enable him to buy a seat.[2] In view of later criticisms about his legal knowledge, it is important to remember that he gave up this idea. He continued his general practice and returned to the Northern Circuit.

[1] Francis Horner : *Memoirs and Correspondence*, ii. 132 and 136.
[2] *Creevey Papers*, i. 174.

57

He remained as convivial as ever; a great diner-out, a versatile talker, and a mimic so clever that Kemble longed to " get him on the boards for six months." He was still a bachelor, but by no means a misogynist. In the various *chroniques scandaleuses* of that time there are hints of intimate friendships with married ladies. These innuendoes mean little more than that he was popular in society, but, like everyone with a quick tongue and a light purse, he had his enemies and detractors. Aristocratic England—the " twice two thousand, for whom earth was made "—was full of people writing each other long and gossiping letters. London, the little London which centred round Parliament, was a sounding-board upon which no pea could drop without reverberations. First there had been talk about Lady Rosslyn, but Brougham certainly retained his friendship with Lord Rosslyn for many years later. Then Lady Cowper was furious because her sister-in-law, Mrs. George Lamb, was so intimate with the lawyer, but then there were already enough scandals in the Lamb family, and the future Lady Palmerston had more than her full share of family pride and exclusiveness.[1] Brougham's connection with the Hunts helped to keep him in touch with another side of London life, the Chelsea or Bloomsbury of those days, the world of Rogers, Moore, and Campbell. To Leigh Hunt he continued to write on every subject, from translating Catullus to the Luddite riots, from books on Italy which will tell him about Ravenna to the " astounding genius " of Voltaire, whom inferior natures despise " because they cannot conceive how a man can be both lively and profound." [2]

Towards the end of this period Brougham became involved in the unhappy affairs of Lady Byron. It is possible that she consulted him professionally. He certainly corresponded with her. In 1816, according to Hobhouse, a close friend of Byron and then a violent

[1] Lady Airlie : *Lady Palmerston and Her Times*, i. 26. See also *In Whig Society*, passim.
[2] Leigh Hunt : *Correspondence*, i. *passim.*

Radical, Brougham accused Byron of cheating the Duchess of Devonshire over the rent of a house, and " attacked Byron at Brooks's for his *deformity*. Curse him." [1] For some years there are references in Byron's correspondence to this quarrel. The exiled poet, in 1820, talks of going to Calais to meet Brougham, " a matter which has been on my mind these three years." He discusses with Kinnaird the practicability of reviving a quarrel which was getting so out of date. Next year he again talks about " this little affair," and finally, in 1823, he writes to Hobhouse from Genoa : " I shall have to come home, and if I do, it shan't be for nothing, for I will bring affairs to a crisis with Henry Brougham directly on my arrival, and one or two more of the same kind ; I have nothing on my mind so much as this." [2] There is not the faintest evidence that Byron ever sent Brougham a challenge, and he never made this duelling trip to England. Characteristically enough, nothing more occurred except a reference, published that year, in the thirteenth canto of *Don Juan*.

> " There was Parolles, too, the great legal bully,
> Who limits all his battles to the bar
> And senate ; when invited elsewhere, truly,
> He shows more appetite for words than war."

The whole incident is a little obscure, but Byron undoubtedly helped to build up the Brougham legend of the violent Radical, whose energy and versatility were superhuman, but—this for aristocratic ears only—he won't fight a duel. It is a cheap but effective sneer against anyone engaged in public life, that they are men of words, not actions ; as if every administrator, business magnate or commander-in-chief was not perforce a man of words. The young Disraeli, in 1825, caught the legend as it existed then, pinned it neatly down, and

[1] Broughton : *Recollections of a Long Life*, i. 336–7.
[2] John Murray : *Lord Byron's Correspondence, chiefly with Lady Melbourne, Mr. Hobhouse, etc.*, ii. 252.

added it to his collection of contemporary portraits. "What do you think Booby says? He says Foaming Fudge can do more than any man in Britain—that he had one day to plead in the King's Bench, spout in a tavern, speak in the House, and fight a duel, and that he found time for everything but the last." [1]

As to "spouting in a tavern," this side of Brougham's activities began to develop soon after his exclusion from Parliament in 1812. The refusal to give him a seat had been chiefly due to his heretical opinions, and it was only natural that he should get into touch with other Radicals, outside the House, especially those, like James Mill and Francis Place, with whom he was already working in connection with education. He did not break off relations with his former Whig colleagues, but a certain coldness sprang up between him and the Whig "houses." His quarrel with the Hollands, from whom he was now definitely estranged, seems to have had a rather ludicrous origin. There is no reason to doubt the account which Brougham sent to Lord Grey shortly after the occurrence. He had recently settled his mother, that very independent and rather grim old lady, at Brougham Hall. Lady Holland, who was going to Scotland, determined to call on her. Mrs. Brougham refused to let the great "Madagascar" past her gate, telling the unfortunate Henry, who was then at home, that "she herself was too old to be hurt by Lady Holland or anybody of that kind, but that she had an unmarried daughter, then living with her, and therefore that no Lady Holland should set foot in her house." [2] The Hollands, in spite of their great social and political standing, remained a little sensitive about the circumstances which had led up to their marriage. Whatever excuse Brougham may have invented, he could hardly conceal the fact that Lady Holland had been snubbed, for the most galling of reasons,

---

[1] *Vivian Grey*, Chapter XII.
[2] Brougham : *Memoirs*. Letter to Lord Grey, January 1814, ii. 102.

by an elderly Scotswoman whom she had expected to patronize. The breach between them was not closed for another four years.

Brougham's educational interests brought him to the Presidency of the British and Foreign School Society in 1813, and he continued for many years to take a leading part in the great Nonconformist rival to the " National Society for Promoting the Education of the Poor in the Principles of the Church of England." He also kept in touch with the Abolitionists, and attended their Council at Sandgate. Possibly with memories of his recent experiences he afterwards warns Zachary Macaulay against taking " the mere mouth civility " of politicians as acquiescence. " I wish I may be wrong, but my estimate of the principles of these gentry is very low. Lord Wellington, by understanding (though not by feeling, of which he has none), is with us, and pretty stoutly. My remarks do not apply to him." [1] But the Abolitionists remained incurably optimistic and vague. While he was urging them towards a more radical policy there was always Hannah More to frighten them off ideas, " almost as Jacobinical as Mr. Brougham." But this period of exclusion from Parliament was to be marked by two events, more important to his career than voluntary work for causes so hopeless to tackle from outside Parliament as education and the abolition of slavery. The first was his suggested adoption by the Westminster Radicals, and the second the development of his connection with the Princess of Wales.

The Westminster Radicals were already organized as " The Friends of Purity of Elections," a body not unlike a modern Parliamentary divisional party. In 1812 they brought in Lord Cochrane as the second Member to Sir Francis Burdett. Both were returned unopposed. Cochrane was a last-minute choice. He was popular enough as the aristocratic Radical sailor, breezy and plain-

[1] Viscountess Knutsford : *Life and Letters of Zachary Macaulay*, p. 316.

spoken, but he was certainly a fool in public life, and probably a knave. Within two years he was involved in a famous scandal, when his uncle Cochrane Johnstone, also a Member of Parliament, conspired with a disreputable Prussian refugee, and others of the same kidney, to spread a false report of Napoleon's death in order to make a " bull raid " on the Funds. They were all indicted for conspiracy before Lord Ellenborough, were found guilty, and sentenced to imprisonment, fines and the pillory. The trial was famous for the standing of the accused, the doubts about Lord Cochrane's complicity, and above all for the savagery of the sentences and the supposed bias of the Judge.[1] The Whigs seized the opportunity, and rather inadvisedly turned both sentence and trial into political issues.

Brougham was doubly interested in the case. He was briefed for the defence, though as junior counsel he played only a minor part. He was also considered as the probable successor to Cochrane. In the first capacity he bitterly resented the attacks, made by Whitbread and his old colleagues of the " Mountain," upon the conduct of the defence. Writing some thirty years later, when Cochrane was an admiral of the fleet, Brougham acquitted him of anything worse than knowledge of his uncle's proceedings and a quixotic attempt to shield him, but he also gives Lord Ellenborough credit for his general handling of the case, though objecting to the sentences, and especially to the revival of the almost obsolete pillory.[2] The Whigs rushed into the attack, and, as Brougham complained to Lord Grey, " without having seen the evidence, and ignorant of the whole subject, had the

---

[1] Cochrane was restored to his rank in the Navy by the Whigs in 1833. Readers interested in the question of his complicity may be referred to J. B. Atlay's *The Trial of Lord Cochrane before Lord Ellenborough*. They will probably agree that Cochrane was definitely inculpated. Place considered he was self-condemned as a stockjobber, illegally dealing in " options." One result of the case was the abolition of the pillory as a punishment.

[2] Brougham : *Statesmen of George III*, iii. 220–2.

incredible folly to blame the counsel for not calling the witnesses. The history of presumption offers no greater instance. We had *too* good reasons for not calling them." [1] This incident and the question of Brougham's candidature at Westminster both widened the breach between him and the Party leaders.

Before the verdict had been given, the different political groups had begun to discuss a possible successor.[2] Westminster, as one of the only democratic constituencies, was a safe seat for the " left wing," but the Whigs, like modern Liberals, were naturally loth to hand over their claims to the Radical committee. There followed the usual complicated intrigues which precede a bye-election when there is no candidate already in the field. One section of the Committee put forward the worthy but quite senile Major Cartwright. The Whigs began to canvass for Sheridan, equally decrepit, but from drink rather than age. Francis Place, who had quarrelled with the Committee, but was keen for Westminster to be represented by a " live " Member, began to work for Brougham. Subsequent proceedings, though considered rather unusual at the date, have a certain interest to-day because they foreshadow, so exactly, the kind of struggle which frequently takes place in a modern Labour constituency when a candidate has to be chosen for a hopeful seat. Cartwright was the old and trusted worker for the Cause; a candidate unlikely to appeal except to the converted, or to be effective if returned to Parliament. Francis Place considered him to be " utterly incom-

---

[1] Brougham : *Memoirs*, ii. 239.

[2] Dr. Aspinall, in *Lord Brougham and the Whig Party*, talks of the " grossly indecent haste " with which the Westminster Committee began to consider a successor. Democracy does not allow too much nicety in such matters. Certainly in these modern times, when a Member is threatened with criminal, bankruptcy or divorce proceedings, local parties seldom wait for the verdict before considering possible candidates, nor are the aspirants more reticent in putting out the usual feelers.

petent," a man " for whom the electors would not vote."[1]
This opinion was justified at an election some years later.
He preferred Brougham, the experienced and very able
lawyer-politician, but distrusted him as an opportunist
with little fondness for doctrinaire tenets.

Cartwright had the support of Alderman Wood, an
uneducated man but capable and ambitious, who played
a not unimportant part in politics. As Lord Mayor in
1817, he helped to counteract some of Lord Sidmouth's
repressive measures. Three years later he was the most
prominent supporter of the unhappy Queen Caroline.
He looked upon Brougham as a rival, and there was
probably some truth in the latter's views as expressed in
a letter to Creevey. " As for Westminster—it now appears
that Ald. Wood is only making a catspaw of old C(art-
wright), and that he counts on his dying, and leaving a
place for him—the Alderman. He has avowed that he
would rather see Sheridan, or any court tool, returned
than a Whig in disguise, viz. me." [2] Brougham had the
support of Brooks, the chairman of the Committee, and
also of many Whigs like Lord Tavistock, Bennet and
Lord Ossulston. The latter had considerable influence
at a time when party affiliations were still vague. On
the other hand, Brougham complained that many of the
more conservative Whigs " have just discovered Old
Sherry to be ' an old and valued friend and an ancient
adherent of Fox.' They therefore support him." [3]

The Cartwright group naturally insisted upon Brougham subscribing to the articles of their creed, and in this
way they had the full support of Place, who was determined that Brougham, if he went to Parliament, should
go in on the Radical " ticket." Placed in the same
undignified position as many modern politicians, Brougham agreed to Burdett's three " principles of reform "—
the enfranchisement of all who paid direct taxation,
equal electoral divisions, and annual parliaments. There

[1] Graham Wallas : *The Life of Francis Place*, p. 118.
[2] *Creevey Papers*, i. 202.   [3] *Id.*, i. 195.

was nothing very formidable in these for a convinced
Parliamentary reformer. They were hardly such a
mouthful as that modern shibboleth, " the nationalisation
of the means of production, distribution and exchange."
Brougham proclaimed his acceptance of Burdett's principles on June 23rd at the annual Parliamentary Reform
dinner, though he probably, like a good politician, added
the mental reservation that they would be a fine thing for
his grandchildren. Francis Place, one of the earliest
exponents of " Hansarding," persuaded Brougham to
write out his speech, and the manuscript was carefully
filed for future reference.

Within a fortnight there came one of those curious
popular revulsions which make politics such a hazardous
occupation. The severity of Cochrane's sentence, a
moving speech which he made in his own defence
in Parliament, the sympathy which the Englishman
feels for anyone who has got on the wrong side of the
law, the fun of sending a convicted man to the House
of Commons, all united to sweep the Committee off its
feet. No other candidate would have had a chance,
and Cochrane was returned unopposed. Old Cartwright
was delighted. He was not " to be dropped and cast off
as a worn-out garment," but for Brougham it was a
severe blow. He had now had experience of two
" open " constituencies, and learnt that they required
almost as much intrigue and servility as those in the gift
of a borough-owner. His name was suggested for
Southwark, but he refused nomination.

Brougham's relations with the Princess of Wales,
afterwards Queen Caroline, were of such great importance in his life that it is necessary to recall something
of a history which is often controversial and always
sordid. The Prince of Wales, a self-indulgent, gross,
but not unintelligent man, had secretly married a certain
Mrs. Fitzherbert when he was a young man just come of
age. This marriage, which took place on December
15, 1785, was never avowed, and was of more than

F

doubtful legality. By the Royal Marriage Act the Prince of Wales could not contract a legal union before he was twenty-five, without the King's consent. A further complication was that Mrs. Fitzherbert was a Roman Catholic, and this rendered her husband liable to forfeiture of the succession to the Crown. The marriage was a *secret de Polichinelle*, suspected by everyone and definitely known to many prominent statesmen. Both Fox and Grey probably knew of the marriage early in 1787, and almost certainly prior to the latter's denials in Parliament in 1789.[1] The Whigs were then basing their hopes of office on the King's insanity and the prospect of the Prince of Wales becoming Regent. After their leaders had put themselves into a thoroughly false position, claiming powers for the Regent which were hopelessly at variance with their own constitutional theories, the King recovered and continued to rule with the help of the Tories for another twenty years. Sheridan remained the friend and boon companion of the Prince, but Grey after his initial mistake withdrew from all contact with him, nor did he renew relations in 1807, during his term of office in the Ministry of All the Talents.

Until he became Regent in 1811, the Prince remained faithful to Mrs. Fitzherbert " after his fashion." He had a succession of mistresses, the most prominent being Lady Jersey, but Mrs. Fitzherbert was the " cabbage " to whom, like King Magnus and his Jemima, he was sure to return. This relationship, which lasted for a quarter of a century, was broken for five years when the Prince was persuaded to marry Princess Caroline of Brunswick-Wolfenbüttel in 1795. It was a Royal wedding of the most gruesome kind. The Princess was a plain, grace-less, but kind-hearted girl who would have made an admirable *Hausfrau*, apart from her unfortunate upbring-ing in a German Court. She lacked all *Feinheit*, but she had a marked sense of humour, and a strong maternal

[1] On this question see, *inter alia*, Trevelyan's *Lord Grey of the Reform Bill*, pp. 8–23.

instinct which was ultimately her undoing. Lord Malmesbury has left a description, too familiar to be quoted, of bringing her to England, of the Prince's rudeness when they first met—his " Harris, I am not well, pray get me a glass of brandy "—of the wedding with the Prince still sodden in drink.[1] The Princess always looked upon this marriage, the first night of which was spent with her Royal groom drunk on the floor, as a kind of prostitution which she had had to endure. Years afterwards she remarked, " I never did commit adultery but once, and I have repented it ever since. It was with the husband of Mrs. Fitzherbert."

Somehow from this nightmarish union was born the Princess Charlotte. Shortly afterwards the Prince finally separated from his wife, whom he had already insulted by forcing her to receive Lady Jersey into her household. Caroline, who had at that time the full sympathy of her father-in-law, retired to Montagu House, near Blackheath, but her daughter was taken away when only a few months old, and she was never allowed to see her. It would have been a difficult position for a clever and discreet woman, it was impossible for one with little natural dignity and certain queer traits. For example, it always struck her as irresistibly comic that anyone who might commit adultery with her should be liable to the death penalty for treason. She laughed at Lord Eldon when he told her, and once, after dinner, she horrified Sir Walter Scott, as he limped after her into a conservatory, by turning round and saying with mock indignation, " Ah ! false and faint-hearted troubadour ! you will not trust yourself with me for fear of your neck ! "[2] It was a time when men could be extremely coarse in their talk, but women were not even allowed to use slang.

Caroline's limited knowledge of English helped to get her a reputation for making impossible remarks. This might, however, have merely been regarded as an ec-

[1] Malmesbury : *Diaries*, iii. 218 ff.
[2] Lockhart : *Life of Sir Walter Scott*, p. 140.

centricity, if it had not been for another propensity due to her thwarted maternal instincts. She was, as Brougham discovered many years later, a " child-fancier." [1] She could not resist adopting small children. The first, William Austin, was the son of a Deptford sail-maker. Inevitably there was a scandal, with a future King always looking for evidence which would justify a divorce. Lady Douglas, a disgruntled member of the Princess's household, helped to spread an absurd story that the boy was Caroline's son, and this gained such publicity that the King was forced to institute an inquiry by a committee of the Cabinet, with Sir Samuel Romilly as Secretary. This became known as the " Delicate Investigation." It cleared the Princess of the major charge, but the Ministers themselves were also in a " delicate " position, for only a feeble life lay between the Prince and the throne. With considerable worldly wisdom they drew attention to certain matters in the Princess's conduct which " might give rise to very unfavourable inter-pretation."

The Princess did not take her censure very seriously. She saw little reason for discretion on her part when her husband was openly living with other women. Later in 1806 she began her long campaign against the Prince ; to recover her daughter, and also her position at Court. Her " little Williakin " remained with her, but as he grew up her interest in him waned. " I am so sorry he is growing big," she remarked to Lady Campbell, " but I am determined to have another little boy ; I must always have a child in the house." [2]

---

[1] *Creevey Papers*. Creevey to Miss Ord, August 1821. " Brougham thought nothing of it. His creed is that she was a *child-fancier* . . ." ii. 24.

[2] Lady Charlotte Bury : *The Diary of a Lady-in-Waiting*, i. 185. Though this diary was " doctored " before its original publication in 1838 by Lady Charlotte Campbell's none too reputable second husband, Mr. Bury, it obviously contains much that the diarist jotted down at the time, and can be used with discretion. Austin remained with the Princess until her death. He accompanied her to England in 1820.

The first shot in the Princess's campaign was a letter to the King, drafted by Spencer Perceval with the help, possibly, of Lord Eldon. This was in October 1806. Five months later, as the Prince would still not consent to her being received at Court, she threatened to publish the proceedings of the " Delicate Investigation." At this time the Tories were her chief supporters, but their ardour cooled down after the Ministry of All the Talents had come to an end. The Princess moved to Kensington Palace, and was received formally at Court, but Perceval and Eldon, now back in office, were at considerable pains to suppress the printed pamphlet which contained their defence of the Princess. No great change took place in her position until the Regency. The Whigs, still hoping for much from the Prince of Wales, held aloof from his wife. The Tories, sensing rightly that the Regency did not necessarily mean a Whig Government, were also very cautious. The Princess had a few personal friends amongst the politicians, notably Canning and Ward. After 1809 Brougham was an occasional visitor, and the Princess gradually learnt to consult him about her affairs.

The Regency, with its disappointment of Whig hopes, saw a change which would justify the most cynical view of those engaged in public life. The Tories now swung over completely to the Prince's side. The Whigs began to take a new interest in the Princess. It is true there was some division on this point. The Holland House group still kept in touch with Sheridan and the Regent. Some of the older Whig families would have nothing to do with either side. The " Mountain," and especially Whitbread, identified themselves more and more with Kensington Palace, and the lady carrying on her rather undignified Court there. The general situation and the attitude of the leading politicians may seem alien to a modern Englishman, but they are familiar enough in any decaying autocracy, and could be paralleled in many Indian States, where " senior " and " junior " Maharanis may be struggling for influence over a young ruler, or where a Rajah has quarrelled with his eldest son. One finds amongst the Indian administrators and public servants the same contempt for the personnel of Royalty combined with a queer illogical respect for the institution, and a great determination that disrespect shall not spread to the common people.

Brougham, who was essentially tough-minded and instinctively an iconoclast, never made the slightest attempt to conciliate the Regent, whom he had mortally offended in the course of his defence of the Hunts. He had always a reputation as a Republican, though he certainly held that Republicanism was not then practical politics. From the first his relations with the Princess were rather formal. He neither respected nor liked her. When she consulted him as a lawyer he did his very best for her as a client, but when she merely asked his advice he did the same as Whitbread, Canning and others to whom she would appeal, he recommended the course which fitted in best with his own political ideas. Whitbread and Brougham wanted to discredit the Tories, Canning to relieve them from an embarrassing position. The Princess never gave any politician her full confidence. During the ten years from 1811 until her death, Brougham frequently communicated with her and worked for her, but she was always changing her mind, and going her own way without consulting him. Nothing would be more absurd than to picture her as a weak ignorant woman, easily led by the scheming Whigs. There is an eye-witness's account of a meeting between Brougham and the Princess in 1813, when she was beginning the second stage of her campaign, and wanted a more central house than Kensington Palace. It is probably a fair description of their relations towards each other. " Mr. Brougham came to her at last. His manner does not please her : they look at each other in a way that is very amusing to a bystander. The one thinks, ' She *may* be useful to *me*; ' and the other, ' *He* is useful to me at present.' It does not require a conjurer to read their thoughts; but they are both too cunning for each other." [1]

By 1813 there was a new factor in the struggle between "Prinny" and "Mrs. P." The Princess Charlotte was seventeen, and begins to appear, in Creevey and Brougham's letters, as "Young P.," a lady with a decided character of her own. She had sized up both her parents, and on the whole preferred her mother, of whom she was allowed to see very little. Her natural inclination to join her mother's crusade against the Regent was heightened by the latter's determination to marry her as soon as possible to a foreign Prince. His first choice was Creevey's "Young Frog," the Prince of Orange, an unattractive soldier who was afterwards to make an expensive blunder at Waterloo. Princess Charlotte found him so ugly " that I am sometimes obliged to turn my head away in disgust when he is speaking to me." [2] He had another disadvantage from the Princess's standpoint. He intended to take her to Holland, and the Princess as Heir Apparent was very unwilling to leave England. She felt that if she went abroad, her mother would also leave England, and in the absence of both the Prince would have little trouble in getting the divorce which he wanted, and then possibly would beget a male heir.

It is probable that Brougham put this point of view to her, and Creevey ascribes her refusal to be parted from her mother to " the profound resources of old Brougham . . . one of the most brilliant movements in his campaign." [3] At any rate she followed with sympathy the controversy between the Princess and Lord Liverpool.

Brougham drafted the letters, and, when necessary, arranged for publicity in the Press. If the Regent, as was his invariable rule, refused to open a letter from

[1] Lady Charlotte Bury : *The Diary of a Lady-in-Waiting*, i. 148.
[2] *Autobiography of Miss Cornelia Knight*, i. 225. Miss Knight was "sub-governess" to Princess Charlotte, a dull but trustworthy observer. [3] *Creevey Papers*, i. 198.

his wife, he had the pleasure of reading it in the *Morning Chronicle*. The vindication of the Princess by the "Delicate Investigation" was now published, and a new Commission had to be appointed to inquire into the Regent's treatment of his daughter. All through that bitter winter of 1813–14, when a fair was held for weeks on the Thames, and Napoleon was vainly attempting to revive his lost fortunes, Brougham was worrying the Regent, and the Regent was badgering his daughter to accept the young Prince of Orange, using that unpleasant ecclesiastic, the Bishop of Salisbury, to mingle spiritual and material threats.

While the older Whigs strongly objected to this meddling in Court affairs, the "Mountain" remained solidly behind Whitbread and Brougham. Napoleon's abdication helped them in the gentle sport of baiting the Regent, for it brought a host of foreign rulers and their attendants to London. Some were related to Princess Caroline, others were old friends. Her father had been a considerable figure in Germany, and been killed fighting for the King of Prussia. It was impossible for the Regent to isolate Connaught Place, where the Princess was now living, or to ignore completely her existence. The propaganda of the "Mountain" and the newspapers was also having some effect. The Regent was hooted whenever he went out, and the London crowd, wanting a concrete grievance, fixed upon his treatment of his wife, who gradually became a popular figure.

The Princess was not the easiest person to educate up to this rôle. She was unwise in the choice of her friends, and always apt to behave like a spoilt child, refusing to fulfil boring engagements, and thereby cutting herself off from that more respectable part of English society which was disgusted with the Regent and prepared to receive her. Brougham did his best. He tried to improve her calling list, arranged that she attend the Opera, and make other public appearances. He certainly harassed the Court and the Tories. Even the old Queen

Charlotte, who at the Regent's behest had refused to receive the Princess, now shared his unpopularity, and complained bitterly to her Lords, " I be fifty years and more in this country, and well respected; but now I be shspit on." But politically it was a losing game, for it led nowhere unless both King and Regent should die and be succeeded by the young Charlotte. Meanwhile Princess Caroline was growing tired of the struggle, and was every day more disposed to listen to Castlereagh's " insidious offer "—as Whitbread called it—of a large income if she would only go abroad and stay there.

Canning, who was then out of office, was always ready to paint a rosy picture of her living with her own family at Brunswick, " or in any other society in Europe, of which she might be the grace, the life, the ornament." Even if this delightful flight of fancy did not earn him, as Brougham contended, his comfortable sinecure at Lisbon, he certainly had done the Government a great service. By the end of June Brougham saw that he was beaten, with—" Mother P. bungling the thing so compleatly—snapping eagerly at the cash, and concluding with a civil observation about unwillingness to ' impair the Regent's tranquillity ! ' etc. This was all done on the spot and in a moment, and communicated to Sam and me next day, ' that we might be clear of all blame in advising it.' "[1] Brougham went down with flying colours, and the same week forced the Government to refuse the Princess a seat in St. Paul's Cathedral for the National Thanksgiving. " So the game was alive once more," but it only had a short time to run.

Brougham's one great success, the breaking-off of the Orange engagement, led to the curious incident of July 12th. The history of the rupture is a little obscure. Possibly the Duchess of Oldenburg, on the staff of the Russian Emperor, who disliked the match, may have encouraged the young Princess, and also acted as a means of communication between her and her mother,

[1] *Creevey Papers*, i. 201.

from whom she was now kept strictly separated. This was the view of Lord Castlereagh, but it would seem that the Princess needed little incitement to rebel. The Regent, acting up to his part, stormed at his daughter and threatened to move her to Carlton House. On the evening of the 12th she slipped out of Warwick House from the tutelage of her grim attendants. Taking a hackney cab, itself a great adventure, she reached her mother's house about dinner-time. It was a ludicrous, but at the same time a dangerous situation. London was in an excitable mood, and all round Westminster large crowds were collected on account of Lord Cochrane's re-election. Feeling ran very high against the Crown. It had been Brougham's policy to keep the pot simmering, but this unexpected escapade might easily have made it boil over if there had been any further resistance to the Government. He was hastily summoned by the Princess of Wales, and arrived half-asleep, thinking it was merely another of those unreasonable demands which she was always making upon all who worked for her.

There are various accounts of what happened at Connaught Place. Allowing for the different standpoints of the observers they are not seriously inconsistent. " Young Prinny " was advised to return by her mother, and also by the Duke of Sussex, who had been called from a dinner near by. No one present urged further rebellion. In the meantime the Regent, hearing of her escape, had sent his pack, headed by Lord Eldon and the Bishop of Salisbury, to bring back his daughter. They were afterwards reinforced by the Duke of York, who was allowed to go into the drawing-room, whilst the remainder waited downstairs, rather like bum-bailiffs. The Princess achieved one great object for which she had fled from Warwick House. She signed a minute, probably drafted by Brougham, in which she declared her resolution not to marry the Prince of Orange. All that was left to do was to persuade her to return. Brougham knew that Lord Ellenborough would, if necessary, issue a writ of *Habeas Corpus*. As a lawyer he had to tell her that she was still under the Regent's control, but he may well have reinforced this statement, and at the same time made it more palatable, by the arguments which he recounts in his *Memoirs*. They are worth quoting for the light they throw on Brougham's own mentality.

> " The day now began to dawn, and I took her to the window. The election of Cochrane (after his expulsion owing to the sentence of the court, which both insured his re-election and abolished the Pillory) was to take place that day. I said, ' Look there, Madam : in a few hours all the streets and the park, now empty, will be crowded with tens of thousands. I have only to take you to that window, and show you to the multitude, and tell them your grievances, and they will all rise in your behalf.' ' And why should they not ? ' I think she said, or some such words. ' The commotion,' I answered, ' will be excessive ; Carlton House will be attacked—perhaps pulled down ; the soldiers will be ordered out ; blood will be shed and if your Royal Highness were to live a hundred years, it never would be forgotten that your running away from your father's house was the cause of the mischief : and you may depend upon it, such is the English people's horror of bloodshed, you never would get over it ? " [1]

The Princess at last consented to go downstairs, and the only question is how much further pressure was needed. We have Eldon's own account. " The coalheaver's son " had not spent a pleasant night, and also liked to pose as the strong man, capable of handling Royalty with the gloves off. " When we arrived I informed her a carriage was at the door, and we would attend her home. But home she would not go. She kicked and bounced ; but would not go. Well, to do my office as gently as I could, I told her I was sorry about it, for until she did go, she would be obliged to entertain

[1] Brougham : *Memoirs*, ii. 230.

us, as she could not leave us. At last she accompanied us." [1] The details of her departure are of no great importance. The Princess returned to what was virtual incarceration, and thus she remained for two years until she was married to Prince Leopold, younger brother of the reigning Duke of Saxe-Coburg. It is pleasant to think that, from every account, she enjoyed some months' happiness before she died in childbirth.

The escapade of the young Princess was the last straw, and within a month her mother was on board the *Jason*, leaving behind her a mass of liabilities which Brougham had to help clear up, but with a vote of £35,000 a year from the Government. She might have had £50,000, but gave up £15,000 as a last gesture, which Ward, one of her Tory advisers, thought was " an act of perfect insanity." [2] Once out of the country she soon justified the worst that anyone had ever said of her discretion, appearing at a public ball, in Geneva of all places, " dressed *en Vénus*, or rather, not dressed further than the waist." [3] She rapidly discarded her English attendants, and collected a motley band of Italians and Germans, with whom she toured round the Mediterranean. Brougham was the most resilient of mortals, but five years later when she proposed coming back to England, his natural reaction was expressed honestly enough in a letter to Canning : "I am still more clear her coming would be pregnant with every sort of mischief (not to mention the infernal personal annoyance of having such a d—l to plague me for six months)." [4] With the death of " Young Prinny " any dreams he may have had of coming to power by Court influence vanished for ever, but " Old Mrs. P." was again to be a great factor in his life, and provide him with the task of defending a Queen against a Bill of Pains and Penalties.

[1] H. Twiss : *Life of Lord Eldon*, ii. 253.
[2] Lord Dudley and Ward : *Letters to " Ivy,"* p. 248.
[3] Duke of Buckingham : *Memoirs of the Regency*, ii. 92.
[4] A. G. Stapleton : *Life and Times of George Canning*, pp. 265–6.
Letter from Brougham to Canning of August 1819.

CHAPTER V

The statesman, who, in a less happy hour
  Than this, maintain'd man's right to read and know,
And gave the keys of knowledge and of power
  With equal hand alike to high and low.
                Punch.   Verses written to Brougham in 1851.

In July 1815 Lord Darlington offered Brougham the
vacant seat of Winchelsea, a friendly little borough of
unimpeachable rottenness. The origin of this arrangement was typical of the casual coincidences upon which
depended the career of the politician who was not an
aristocrat. Lord Darlington was a man of immense
wealth, who had recently quarrelled with the Regent and
the Tories. Lord Dudley and Ward told his friend
Mrs. Dugald Stewart about the return to Parliament
of her husband's old pupil. "Darlington," he wrote,
" had expected a great household office," but " somehow
that was refused him, and he therefore purchased seven
seats, for which he means to return seven patriots to
vex his ungrateful master. He could not have made a
better choice to begin with than the aforesaid Westmorland gentleman." [1]

Lord Darlington had married, *en secondes noces*, a lady
with a more than doubtful past. Not being received in
the best society she had conceived an ambition to become
a Duchess, in which position she could, presumably,
laugh at the Puritans. This provided another motive
for buying up seats and offering them to the Whigs,
whose prospects of office now seemed a little brighter

[1] Lord Dudley and Ward : *Letters to " Ivy,"* p. 292.

77

as the Napoleonic wars were ended. Lord Campbell, in his usual feline manner, suggests that the Countess herself chose " the aspiring youths of extraordinary talents " to whom Lord Darlington offered Parliamentary seats. Brougham was hardly a " youth," and even Campbell goes on to say that " he never did anything mean to gain her favour." [1] Probably the decision lay with Lord Grey, to whom Brougham himself ascribes the offer. Samuel Whitbread had recently committed suicide, an unhappy example followed by many politicians of that period. Grey may well have thought that, without his brother-in-law, the " Mountain " and generally the left wing of the Whigs would be hopelessly weak. Darlington, a queer fellow of a cynical humour, was about the only borough-owner willing to bring in a reformist. So Brougham went back to Parliament at the age of thirty-seven as member for Winchelsea, and kept the seat for fourteen years. Even democracy hardly plays such pranks.

The Whigs, if we may return to an earlier simile, had never been in such need of a fast bowler and general utility man. The few " Professionals " seem to have lost interest. Romilly was absorbed in legal work; Creevey was living in Brussels and would not be lured home; Horner was already suffering from the constitutional weakness which killed him in 1818; Mackintosh was a delicate man, with little interest outside legal reform. Amongst the " Amateurs," the elder sons of peers, and the cadets of great houses, there were many of considerable ability; Lord Folkestone and Lord Ossulston were good speakers, Lord Althorp had certain sterling qualities which gradually made him a power in the House, and Lord John Russell, wavering between politics and literature, was fortunately inclining towards the former. But English politics were no longer an affair of foreign relations and general principles, but rather of economics and of social problems. These

[1] Lord Campbell : *Lives of the Chancellors*, viii. 283.

were hardly to be handled by men who first sorted out
from their morning's post the daily letter from their
head gamekeeper or huntsman, and whose winter
thoughts turned continually to partridges in Six Mile
Bottom, to ducks flighting at dawn back to the decoys,
or to a ten-mile " point " from Rumfiddler Green to
Wandermoor Common.

On July 21, 1815, Brougham returned to the House
of Commons, but he was in poor health, and took some
months to regain his old ascendancy, or the high animal
spirits and overflowing vitality which, apart from his
ability, marked him out from the rather lackadaisical
young aristocrats on the Opposition benches. He had
learnt much, during the past three years, of what could
and could not be done under the pre-reform constitution.
He had seen that an unaristocratic politician, without a
seat in Parliament, could be treated as a nonentity, and
the Westminster election had not left him many illusions
about Whigs or Radicals. All this had made him more
of a free-lance than he had been in 1812, but he threw
himself whole-heartedly into reorganizing the Whig
Party. They were all there was to work upon, and
Brougham saw, more clearly than Lord Grey, the great
possibilities opened up by the end of the Napoleonic
wars.

The Tories were weak and divided. Already there
were signs of the coming split between the younger and
more humane Tories, who were later to follow Canning,
and the old " shell-backs," like Lord Eldon, Lord
Sidmouth, Lord Castlereagh and the Duke of Wellington,
who were to dominate and bully England during the
next six years. As a Party they had not been much
strengthened by the confused sentimentalized reaction
which almost inevitably follows the more modern
democratic war, and on which party organizers have
learnt to rely for a " khaki " election. The Crown
remained hostile to the Whigs, and Brougham had no
intention of trying to win over the Regent, whatever

may have been his secret hopes about the young Princess. The end of war would, however, mean a great weakening of the " Old Corruption," the alliance of Crown and Tories based on jobbery.

The Whigs had an overwhelming case for the reduction of war establishments, and with these would go a great mass of the sinecures and perquisites upon which the Government relied for so much of its influence. Trade was bad, the country over-taxed, the War Debt terrifying, and new life was stirring in the north of England. It was the perfect juncture at which to launch a bold policy of Retrenchment and Reform, but the " Amateurs " hung back.

To Brougham's essentially modern mind it was clear that the Whigs needed three things—a policy, a press, and some recruits, outside as well as inside Parliament. He had the greatest difficulty in making anyone in the Party see matters in this light. They had been so long out of office that most of them looked upon a coalition with some group of Tories as the only chance of sharing the spoils, while a few Stoics, like Lord Grey, despaired of seeing any change in their lifetime.

> " Nought's constant in the human race
> Except the Whigs being out of place."

Brougham's first object was to inspire his colleagues with the idea of achieving a purely Whig Government, based on a definite and moderately Radical programme. The whole conception of going to the country with a " platform " was new. Nearly twenty years were to elapse before Peel, himself a political innovator in many fields, issued his Tamworth Manifesto. This was a sufficiently vague pronouncement, but it was considered to be truckling to the new democracy created by the Reform Act of 1832. Brougham already had the idea of a short and long term policy. The first included those points on which the Opposition was to concentrate— criticism of Castlereagh's foreign policy, of the Holy

Alliance, and the treatment of Poland; retrenchment at home, the restriction of military establishments and of ministerial jobbery, the abolition of income tax and other war-time measures. The second he had already sketched out, four years before, and now brought forward again in letters to Grey, Creevey and others. He proposed a number of " measures and inquiries unconnected with ordinary Party topics, whereby much immediate real good is done to the country and great credit gained by the Party, as well as, ultimately, a check secured to the Crown and to abuses generally. For example : prison reform—education of the poor—tithes—above all the Press." [1] It was a Radical programme in everything except its failure to mention parliamentary reform. As it was less than eighteen months since Brougham had agreed to Burdett's " three points," the omission may seem remarkable, but it is clear from many references that Brougham thought it was useless to bring the question before the Commons until there was much more support both in and out of Parliament. To do so would split the Party and delay the attainment of certain reforms, especially " the education of the poor," which seemed to Brougham more important and more urgent. It was a point which was soon to be brought against him, but the history of the Reform Bill, some fifteen years later, suggests that Brougham was right in refusing to sponsor a measure for which there was then very little active enthusiasm.

The dead-weight of the older Whig leaders killed the idea of a Party programme, and the same fate seems to have attended Brougham's efforts to start a political paper. By March 1817 he " had actually down on paper £4500 for an evening paper—for reports of debates generally—of good principles—and we have £1500 more we are quite sure of—Lambton began with £500, and the D(uke) of B(edford) has just done the same." [2]

[1] *Creevey Papers*, i. 248.
[2] *Creevey's Life and Times*, p. 104.

G

The following month he promised that the newspaper—
The Guardian and Evening Reporter—would " soon be out
in great style," but it hung fire.   Like so many reformers
Brougham was apt to over-estimate the number of
people taking an intelligent interest in unorthodox
politics.   He may have been deceived by the exceptional
circumstances which had helped the *Edinburgh Review*.
It was easiest, and probably cheapest for the Whigs to
revert to their old policy of subsidizing existing papers,
which had been so successful in the years previous to
the Ministry of All the Talents, when some £3000 was
spent on the Press campaign against Lord Melville.[1]
Sydney Smith shared Brougham's views, pointing out, a
year or two later, that there were " four or five hundred
thousand readers more than there were thirty years ago,
among the lower orders.   A market is open to the
democrat writers, by which they gain in money and
distinction." [2]   But the Whigs, even Sydney Smith and
Brougham themselves, were incapable of approaching
this new population without over-emphasizing the
educational side.   Smith got nearest with his *Plymley
Letters*, which sold well in the North, but Brougham,
while providing innumerable cheap guides to knowledge, could never cater for the political interests of the
artisans.   The field was left to such writers as Cobbett
and Hunt, who neither patronized them nor expected
them to tackle undigested parliamentary reports.

Brougham's own precarious position in Parliament
showed the impossibility of bringing in new recruits to
the House of Commons.   He could do little more than
spur on to greater activity the few wealthy men of
Radical tendencies. Chief amongst these was John
Lambton, a queer character full of inconsistencies.   At
this time he was in his early twenties, an impressionable
young man with whom Brougham had developed a close

[1] See letters of James Loch, printed in appendix to *Brougham and
his Early Friends*, iii. 281 ff.
[2] Lady Holland : *Memoirs of Sydney Smith*, p. 385.

friendship. Although a millionaire he soon became "Radical Jack" to the Durham miners from whom he derived his great wealth. A valetudinarian, and something of a domestic bully, he was capable of great generosity and occasional bouts of political activity, in which he always preferred the extremer side. Late in 1816 he married Lord Grey's eldest daughter, and thus began a rather difficult family alliance which provided, however, an invaluable link between Lord Grey and the Whigs of the left wing. Brougham retained his friendship up to the time of the Reform Act, though soon afterwards they began to quarrel with extreme bitterness. Each had a little too much of the moss-trooper in his character. They could co-operate in opposition, but not when Brougham was a Lord Chancellor and Lambton had become Lord Durham. The latter, as he grew older, began to develop into the "King Jog" of Creevey's letters, a nickname which exactly fitted the extreme Radical, who was capable of remarking that £40,000 a year was "a moderate income, such a one as a man *might jog on with*." [1]

Apart from Lambton, and the aristocrats of the "Mountain," there was no one on the Whig side who was likely to be useful to Brougham. Many of the "back-benchers" belonged to the class which he used to describe as "ear-wigs"—men entirely dependent upon some great landowner, for whom they would do various odd jobs in London, sometimes managing their business affairs, as Croker, the well-known Tory, did those of Lord Hertford. They were the Tadpoles and Tapers of the pre-reform Parliament, the "£1200 a year men" as Disraeli called them. Their ambition went no higher than those minor posts with little work attached which were still available as a reward for political services. Almost inevitably such men must be produced by any Parliamentary system which expects unpaid work from its members. From Brougham's point of view

[1] *Creevey Papers*, ii. 32.

they were a dead-weight, useless and unreliable. It was impossible to build up a Party from them, and it was only natural that he should renew his relations with the leading Radicals outside Parliament.

This proved to be a fruitless and unhappy connection, which was complicated by the possibility of a vacancy in the Westminster Division. Lord Cochrane's father, Lord Dundonald, was seriously ill, and the Party began looking about for a successor in case their second Member should go to the House of Lords. There was no obvious candidate, except the ineffective Major Cartwright. Francis Place would have liked Brougham to ally himself definitely with Sir Francis Burdett, the old Radical Member. In his own words, he " wished that Brougham might be detached from the faction and make common cause with the Reformers," [1] but if there was ever a " faction " it was the little Radical caucus, the Westminster Committee. Brougham was not prepared to take his orders from them, or to give up his connection with the Whig Party. His position was not unlike that of a member of the modern Labour Party, who might find them too moderate for his liking, but would not be willing to tie himself up with the Independent Labour Party merely because they were more extreme.

Throughout 1816 Brougham took a very decided line of his own; sometimes he was too radical for the taste of the Whigs, but he was often in opposition to Burdett. His general attitude was logical enough if it is assumed that he believed the Whigs might soon be called upon to form the Government, and that the abolition of the monarchy, or the introduction of a purely democratic form of Government, would only lead to chaos. He made a fierce speech against the Regent, but voted for the grants made to Princess Charlotte on her marriage. He criticized Castlereagh's foreign policy, but supported the forcible detention of Napoleon in St. Helena. He busied himself with a Bill to reform the law of libel,

[1] Graham Wallas : *Life of Francis Place*, p. 117.

when he might have been introducing motions in favour of annual parliaments. By the autumn Francis Place had decided he was impossible as a candidate for Westminster, and also accused him of not taking enough trouble about the constituency. " Several good opportunities were offered him to mix in a proper way with the electors," wrote Place in October; " he availed himself of none of them." [1] When it is remembered that Cochrane was still a Member of Parliament, and remained so until he accepted command of the Chilian fleet in 1818, a certain diffidence on Brougham's part is understandable. But Place was a severe taskmaster, and, as Brougham wrote to Lord Grey, Westminster " would be a seat somewhat hard to sit upon." [2] The Westminster Committee turned towards " Orator " Hunt, who was then becoming very prominent through his great public meetings.

The split between Brougham and the Radicals was widened by the increasing truculence of the latter. Bad harvests and famine prices were leading to disorder in the country areas as well as in London and the North. The Radicals outside Parliament naturally and justifiably took advantage of this distress to drive home their arguments, for if ever distress was due to politicians it was during the five years following the Napoleonic wars, but the form of their agitation made it difficult to support them in Parliament. Hunt made speeches which were definitely inflammatory, and at Spa Fields, in Bermondsey, he was responsible for a serious riot. Cobbett in his *Political Register* was pouring scorn on Whigs and Tories alike. Cartwright's " Hampden Clubs " and the " Spencean Philanthropists " were preaching strange doctrines, and causing acute apprehensions amongst the more comfortable classes. This was one of those periods when a constructive reformer, who is unwise enough to emerge from his library, is almost certain to find himself

[1] Graham Wallas : *Life of Francis Place*, p. 118.
[2] Brougham : *Memoirs*, ii. 198.

in an undignified position. Brougham never worried much about criticism. He steered a course somewhat to the left of the " Mountain," but it gave him few friends in or out of Parliament.

He began by a remarkable success in a doubtful cause. In March 1816 he led the attack upon Vansittart's Income Tax Bill, and had it thrown out by the Commons. It now seems incongruous that the party which claimed to be the more advanced should have concentrated upon abolishing a direct tax on the rich when there were so many indirect taxes on the poor. Probably much of Brougham's support was due to selfish motives, but Whig objection to the tax was based partly on its inquisitorial character. It was also so " productive "—we should now say so " elastic "—that it tended, as Brougham said in his speech, " to make Ministers profuse and extravagant." Every country has had to be educated up to making returns of income, and there was probably much sympathy with the Irishman who filled up his assessment paper as follows :—" Take notice. I have cut the throats of all my horses—I have shot all my dogs—I have burned all my carriages—I have dismissed all my servants, except my wife, and therefore conceive that I cannot be liable to any tax whatever." [1] Brougham, like nearly all his contemporaries, had very hazy ideas about the incidence of taxation, but he can have had few illusions about the nature of his victory. He undoubtedly found his success embarrassing. He knew that no Whig Party, worthy of the name, could come into office based on a casual majority of thirty-seven, obtain on such a favourable subject as the remission of an unpopular tax. Nor was anything likely to be gained by forcing a General Election at that juncture.

The Tadpoles and the Tapers of the Whig side thought otherwise, hoping at least for a coalition which would include a few Grenvillite Whigs, and would lead to the distribution of some sinecures. Brougham deliberately

[1] Smart : *Economic Annals*, p. 469.

19 March attempt to renew property tax defeated by a majority of 37.

From a sketch by Cruikshank.

killed their hopes. Within a few days he made what can only be called a calculated indiscretion. Taking advantage of a Whig motion for reducing the salaries of Secretaries to the Admiralty, he launched out upon a violent attack on the Regent. The most remarkable passage is worth reproducing as an example of his methods, and as showing how far he and the Radicals had gone along the road to republicanism. He compared unfavourably the conduct of the Regent and his advisers with that of the Stuarts.

> "Far otherwise must those be estimated who entertained no scruples of religion, who experienced no tenderness of conscience; who, in utter disregard of the feelings of an oppressed and insulted nation, proceeded from one wasteful extravagance to another; who decorated and crowded their houses with the splendid results of their extravagance; who associated with the most profligate of human beings; who, when the gaols were filled with wretches, could not suspend for a moment their thoughtless amusements, to end the sad suspense between life and death; who, alone, or surrounded by an establishment of mercenaries, and unable to trust to the attachment of the nation for their security, yet desired the House of Commons to enable them to lavish on their favourites the money extracted from the pockets of the suffering people of England." [1]

The speech made a great stir. The newspapers reproduced its more virulent passages in full. Tory politicians talked cheerfully about high treason, the lesser fry about " that gin-drinking, straddling, corduroy scoundrel," or, even worse, " that American-minded Brougham." [2] More than ever was he recognized as

[1] *Parl. Debates*, xxxiii. 497.
[2] Sir Charles Bagot to Mr. Binning. *Canning and His Friends*, ii. 14.

the most dangerous man in Parliament, the scourge of
Carlton House, the bogy of the country vicarage.   The
Whigs, jolted out of their usual ruts, were equally upset,
though only the less intelligent thought they had been
robbed of office.   Romilly considered the speech to have
been " injudicious as well as very unjust," but he " had
no doubt that whatever had been the division, the
Ministers would still have continued in office." [1]   John
Whishaw, the " Pope of Holland House " and a very
level-headed observer, was not certain whether the speech
even lost them the division, " because weak and timid
people are glad to avail themselves of *any* pretext in such
cases; but certainly Brougham's imprudence afforded
them very plausible reasons for declining to act with a
Party avowing personal hostility to the Sovereign." [2]
Only the Radicals outside Parliament gave Brougham
a little encouragement.   Francis Place wrote to congratulate him, though the speech was not held sufficient
to counterbalance his other lapses from the Westminster
standard.

Tactically the speech was a mistake.   It had been
made   without   sufficient   previous   consultations.
Brougham alienated the old Whig leaders without
rallying the more adventurous spirits in the Party.
" Mr. Ponsonby was grieved, Mr. Tierney appalled at
this fresh instance of indiscretion.   It was the more
unaccountable because Brougham had during the session
evinced more disposition to concert with the Party than
he had affected for some years." [3]   So wrote Lord
Holland, ignoring the fact that Brougham had been out
of Parliament and out of the Whig counsels for nearly
four years, and might have remained so permanently if
it had not been for Lord Grey's friendship and the
Countess of Darlington's social aspirations.   But if the
Whig leaders were selfish and unreasonable, Brougham

[1] Sir S. Romilly : *Memoirs*, iii. 236.
[2] Lady Seymour : *The " Pope " of Holland House*, p. 149.
[3] Vassall Holland : *Further Memoirs*, p. 234.

was also ill-advised. His primary object, that of preventing the Whigs from making a premature grasp at office, could have been achieved by less drastic means. The next few months proved that the Tories were as safely in power as ever. They had only to abolish a few sinecures, and make a few concessions about expenditure, such as the abandonment of the malt tax, in order to ensure their majority in the Commons. Their position was even stronger when they began their policy of repression. Country gentlemen on both sides had been disturbed by the way in which unrest was spreading from the towns into the villages. The Whigs were faced with the secession of the Grenvillite section and another difficult period in opposition. It was not a happy moment to emphasize their divisions.

Brougham recognized his mistake. With his usual resilience he ignored criticism and continued as active as ever, but for the next three or four years he was far more circumspect. He dropped his connection with the Radicals during the autumn of 1816, and was therefore not associated with the movements which led to such futile demonstrations as the Spa Fields Riot, or the " Pop-gun plot " when the Regent had his coach windows broken on the way back from opening Parliament. Brougham had found the Radicals impossible people to work with, and his relations with them grew steadily worse during the first years of the repression.

Early in 1817 the Ministers appointed Secret Committees of the House of Lords and the House of Commons. This was the beginning of three lamentable years, in which Lord Sidmouth, Lord Castlereagh and Lord Eldon used every weapon in a Government's armoury to harass and destroy the few miserable men in the industrial areas who were trying to do something for their fellow-workers. It was a repetition of the anti-Luddite campaign of 1812, but without the justification of the Napoleonic war. Brougham combined with Lord Grey, Tierney and Lambton to fight each repressive measure, and to expose each scandalous method employed by the Government. In Parliament they had only a remnant of the Whigs behind them. The secession of the Grenvillites relieved them from the dead-weight of a group with little stomach for reform, but it seriously depleted their numbers. They were, however, supported by a rapidly increasing number of educated people in their struggle against the suspension of the Habeas Corpus Act; the Seditious Meetings Act; the " Six Acts "; the suborning of spies, such as the notorious Oliver; the packing of juries; the constant use of undisciplined Yeomanry drawn from the employing class; the brutal and sometimes grotesque punishments.

Brougham's reputation as a fighting lawyer had survived from the days of the Lancashire and Yorkshire Luddites. In a previous chapter it was shown how this restrained the more flagrant misuse of legal machinery when the " Blanketeers " began the first " hunger march " to London.[1] His truculent opposition in the House of Commons was equally important because he made it impossible for well-intentioned people to remain neutral over such a matter as the " Peterloo Massacre," the most famous of several collisions between Yeomanry and demonstrators. Only a study of Parliamentary debates at this period can do justice to Brougham's watchfulness, the extent of his interests, and his ready anger, the *sæva indignatio* of the true reformer. More than anyone in England he determined that if there was to be repression, then it should not be a thing " done in a corner." In the end it was " Peterloo " which broke the old Tory Party. It shamed the younger men into a revolt against the old gang as certainly as it inspired the Masque of Anarchy. Brougham was building up a reformist middle-class movement, for he had learnt that the Whigs would never move without such pressure, yet all through this period he was exposed to constant attacks from the Radicals. Cobbett and Place outside Parlia-

[1] See above, p. 49.

ment, Cochrane and Burdett within it, pursued him with that relentless bitterness which advanced Radicals always reserve for those in partial but not complete agreement with them. The gravamen of their charge was that he refused to support, and denounced as untimely and absurd, the purely doctrinaire demands then being put forward for complete Parliamentary reform. His Westminster speech of 1814 was brought up against him, and printed. His efforts and those of the Whigs to combat repression were derided.[1] It was a dispute along lines which are sufficiently familiar to anyone interested in modern politics, but it had some influence on Brougham's career. He retained his personal friendship with some of the ultra-Radicals, like James Mill, but he made up his mind to work entirely through the Whig Party, and he set himself to educate the Party on the lines of his long-term policy.

[1] Thus Francis Place, writing to Hodgskin in May 1817 :—
" These dirty Whigs who had vigour itself against the claims of the people were perfectly imbecile against the abominable measures of the Ministers, who have all the power and all the law in their own hands to imprison whom they please, at their own will and pleasure, and without any accusation even." But Place himself is the best witness of the impossibility of working with men like Hunt, who " says that his mode of acting is to dash at good points, and to care for no one; that he will mix with no committee, or any party; he will act by himself; that he does not intend to affront anyone, but cares not who is offended." See *Life of Francis Place*, pp. 122–3 and 119–20.

CHAPTER VI

FOUNDING A LIBERAL PARTY

Nought remains
But vindictiveness here amid the strong,
And there amid the weak an impotent rage.
THOMAS HARDY : *The Dynasts.*

THE fourteen years during which Brougham sat for
Winchelsea were the most productive of his life, but,
apart from his defence of Queen Caroline in 1820, they
were not the most spectacular. From the age of thirty-
eight to fifty-two Brougham was the most active member
of the Opposition, the virtual leader of the Whig Party,
though never its nominal head. It was a period of
solid political drudgery. Brougham set himself to give
some cohesion to a group of amateur politicians, who had
never known Party discipline; to force a reformist
policy upon men who were mostly opportunists; and
to set some standards of work amongst a collection of
country gentlemen who looked upon Parliament as a
club. It was a measure of his success that at the end of
this period the Whigs could force a very drastic Reform
Bill through a hostile House of Lords, and follow up
their success with other important measures. Afterwards there was some reversion to the old Whig inefficiency and indecision, but the nucleus of nineteenth-
century Liberalism existed in the Opposition Party during
these pre-reform years, and the man most responsible
for its incubation was Brougham. Time plays some
curious tricks. Gladstone, who was to inherit the fruit
of these early labours, was then a small boy learning from
his father a special hatred for the unmannerly lawyer
who was continually bringing before Parliament scandals
connected with the slaves on his great estates in Demerara.

Although, as a Parliamentarian, Brougham had no serious rival on the Opposition benches, he had to contend with many difficulties, some personal and some political. His father had died, and left him a small private income, but he was chiefly dependent upon his earnings at the Bar. It was difficult to combine the two activities. John Campbell writes to his brother in 1816 that " my friend Brougham, you will see, is making a prodigious splash in the House of Commons, but is doing nothing at the Bar. He may almost be considered to have left the law, or the law to have left him. I really do not think I have heard his voice in the Court of the King's Bench these three terms. But he may be considered the leader of the Opposition, which is rather a more splendid situation than that of a ' rising junior.' " [1] Brougham's reputation in " the sedition line," and his quarrels with Lord Eldon cannot have helped him to get briefs in the more lucrative civil cases. A year later Campbell wrote that " he might almost be considered as having left the Bar," though he continued to go on the Northern Circuit. After 1820 his practice improved, though he was then to be hampered by Lord Eldon's refusal to make him a King's Counsel, but up to 1830 his lack of private fortune emphasized his dependence upon the good-will of Lord Darlington for his seat in Parliament. He continued his periodic attempts to win an " open " constituency, but this was an almost impossible ambition for a Whig without landed property.

It was not easy to work with Whig gentry, even after the secession of the more conservative members, who followed Lord Grenville. The rank and file disliked Brougham's keenness, distrusted his versatility, and had been frightened by his attack on the Regent. Like all parties which have been too long in opposition they were broken up into warring factions. Palmerston, from a Government bench, watched their unhappy plight with

[1] Hardcastle : *Life of Lord Campbell*, i. 334.

cheerful venom, and helped to produce that amusing pasquinade, *The New Whig Guide*, which in later years he disowned and tried to suppress. Brougham appears as the " Broom fireship," dangerous to both sides because of her " combustibles, in particular the quantity of brimstone she had taken on board." In spite of remonstrances from the Ponsonby flag-ship she " insisted upon running in to blow up Fort Regent," and was finally left " *lying* in a pitiable condition." In another skit Brougham is tried before Lord Grenville and a special jury of the Whig club for disrespect towards George Ponsonby, for making propositions or motions without consulting him, and for declaring that " the Right Honourable George Ponsonby was ' an old woman,' or words to that effect." The prisoner's attempt to prove an alibi was defeated by evidence that " he had spoken thirty-two times on the night in which he alleged he was absent from the House." [1]

There was enough truth behind this to explain why Brougham met with such difficulties in the House of Commons. He retained his close intimacy with men like Lord Grey and Lambton, who were outside the petty squabbles of the Party. He seems to have been a frequent visitor at both their houses, and to this period belongs one of the most famous stories of the Brougham legend. He was riding across a ford at Alnwick with Lord Grey, when his host, noticing the height of the water, asked him if he could swim. " I never have swum," was the reply, " but I have no doubt I could if I tried." With these two leaders, Brougham's difficulty was that they were too immersed—the one in his large family, the other in his estates—to spend enough time in London. With the smaller men his trouble turned mainly on the question of leadership, and such matters of policy as parliamentary reform and the Whig attitude towards sinecures. Brougham was too opinionated, too keen, and too little of the courtier to win over the Whig country gentlemen as

[1] *The New Whig Guide*, p. 83 ff.

Disraeli won over the Conservatives. This he fully
recognized, but, unlike the rest of the " Mountain," he
would have preferred an aristocrat, Lord Althorp or
Lord George Cavendish, as leader rather than one of
the more professional politicians. Events were to
prove him right. In 1817 George Ponsonby died, and
Tierney took his place. A letter from Bennet shows how
a prominent member of the " Mountain " viewed this
choice, and explains by inference what was the real
state of the Whig organization.

> " Have you heard of our plan for a leader ?
> Some persons last year thought of one of straw,
> such as Althorp or Ld. G. Cavendish, but that would
> not do, and we, the Mountaineers, resented the
> scheme. At present we all concur in the necessity
> of someone, and taking all circumstances into con-
> sideration, Tierney is the man selected in this choice.
> Romilly and Brougham cordially concur, and I do so
> likewise : not that Mrs. Cole has not many grievous
> faults, but there is no one else who has not more.
> Romilly cannot, from his business ; and Brougham
> cannot from his unpopularity, and want of discre-
> tion. I think the old lady can be kept in order, and
> tho' she be timid and idle, yet she is very popular
> in the House, easy and conciliatory; in no way
> perfect, in many ways better than any other person.
> The proposition takes immensely, and at present
> 60 or 70 persons have signified their adherence. . . ."[1]

Tierney proved a complete failure. His nickname of
" Mrs. Cole " he owed to a character in one of Foote's
farces, a very naughty lady too fond of making flattering
references to her own character. Tierney combined this
same unfortunate habit with an indecisive manner and a
doubtful political past—he had been an opponent of
Fox, a supporter of Addington, and an apologist for

---

[1] Letter to Creevey. *Creevey Papers*, i. 264.

the East India Company. From Brougham's point of view he was too closely identified with the Holland House group, and he lacked the force of character to give the Party the unity it needed. No man without either birth or supreme intelligence could hope to control the Whigs. Tierney had neither. He was despised as a " tradesman," and he temporized on every subject.

Two questions perpetually embarrassed the keener Whigs. The Radicals were continually organizing petitions for Reform, but there was no Whig policy on the subject. Brougham went so far as to support the enfranchisement of all who paid direct taxes, but, as a Whig, he would not tie himself to the " three points " which he had formerly accepted. The other difficulty was the continual jobbery with which some of the Whigs were connected. Tierney was an ally of that arch " jobmaster," Lord Lauderdale, an old opponent of Brougham. This robbed the Whigs of their claim to be the enemies of corruption. It was Lauderdale, for example, who arranged in 1815 that William Adam, a Scottish judge, should also be Attorney-General to the Regent. Brougham had protested against this, even though he foresaw " a rupture with Grey as by no means an unlikely result of my doing my duty, and taking my swing. We have lately had an approach to that point in consequence of my urgency against Adam's job, Lauderdale's general jobbery, and other tender points, including the *Cole* faction, and their getting round him."[1] Brougham had now to submit to working with the head of the " Cole faction " as his chief.

Under such leadership Brougham could get little support for his programme—a very modern conception —and his views as to how an Opposition should behave. He wanted the Whigs to take up every good debating point, to force divisions when possible, and to get all

[1] *Creever Papers*, i. p. 253. This letter is misdated (May 1816). It must have been written a year earlier, when Brougham was not in Parliament.

the publicity they could for some different and alternative policy. He was blocked by the older Whigs and their dependents, who only wanted to play the game of the " ins and outs." The " ear-wigs " still hoped to get into office through a split amongst the Tories, or even by Court influence, though the chances of the latter contingency were not very rosy after the death of Princess Charlotte towards the end of 1817. Brougham put his point of view very clearly in a letter to Lord Lansdowne, leader of the Whigs in the House of Lords during Lord Grey's long absences.

> " One principle they have is that an Opposition should do little or nothing, but be quiet and wait for blunders and await the event. Another is that we should seldom divide, and never but when we are strong—as if an Opposition could lose by being beaten in numbers. They really seem to confound the Opposition with the Ministry, to whom being beaten is, of course, very dangerous. To adopt feeble, milk-and-water measures and couch motions in unmeaning terms, for the sake of catching a stray vote or two, is another error. But the grand and general one is that of seeking popularity from the other side—addressing speeches as well as measures to the majority—conciliating the enemy—in short, playing his game. They make stout speeches enough, and many able ones now and then upon a set, regular party question, which no Ministry that is firmly seated cares much about. They shrink from—disapprove—shake their heads at the constant galling opposition which alone does the business; which, for example, destroyed the Orders in Council and the income tax." [1]

The last sentence contains a powerful argument.

[1] From a long letter dated July 21, 1817. It is printed in full from the Lansdowne MS. in Aspinall's *Lord Brougham and the Whig Party*, pp. 80–2.

H

Brougham had himself shown that the House of Commons, though totally unrepresentative, with half the Members chosen by some 200 Peers, and the rest selected by a few thousand voters, nevertheless was amenable to pressure from outside opinion, if only this public opinion was well organized and sufficiently aggressive. The Whigs, however, would not see this, and for the next six years they stultified Brougham's work until, by the time Canning had succeeded Castlereagh, he was willing to modify his ideas about the proper functions of an Opposition. The day-to-day questions before the House of Commons were concerned chiefly with foreign affairs, national expenditure, and the treatment of the economic unrest spreading over the north of England and the industrial parts of Scotland. On all of these Brougham gave his Party a lead. He denounced the Holy Alliance with humour as well as bitterness, laughed at the " Three Gentlemen of Verona," but could only get thirty Whigs to follow him into the lobby against Lord Castlereagh. He took up Creevey's old line of exposing the worst sinecures, but had little help from men who looked upon such posts as the proper reward for political work. There was more unity in attacking the unconstitutional methods of repression. It was a Whig tradition to stand upon the letter of the law, and uphold the Habeas Corpus Act, but they could achieve little except that they shamed the Government out of the use of *agents provocateurs*, which had become a normal part of police procedure. The Whigs were hampered by their fear of the Radicals. They were almost as afraid of a popular demonstration as the Tories, and had never really overcome the anti-Jacobin complex of twenty years before. Brougham saw the French Revolution as a rising of the uneducated, foredoomed to failure. Most of the Whigs were not so impersonal, and felt like Sir Walter Scott, that " property is aimed at, and that is a very feverish sensation for those that have it."

With little hopes of defeating the Tories by " in-fighting," Brougham concentrated much of his energies upon advocating a long-term policy for the Whigs. He foreshadowed his future legal reforms by introducing a Bill to amend the law of libel, he made a number of speeches on economics, and, most important of all, he took the place of Whitbread as the leading advocate of popular education. As an economist Brougham is interesting. Like all his contemporaries he was groping about round a subject of which very little was then known, but his powerful and unconventional mind brought him to a very modern position. He became an empirical free trader, often running foul of the orthodox economists, like Ricardo, but preferring to examine cases on their merits rather than according to some general principle.

In two great speeches, made early in 1817, Brougham surveyed the state of industrial England, where wages had sunk so low that cheap labour discouraged the introduction of new machinery and better methods.[1] (In this, as in so many other points, England in the early nineteenth century was curiously akin to present-day India.) He urged a policy of commercial treaties for reviving trade with Europe, and specially attacked the retention, after the end of the war, of trade restrictions originally imposed on political grounds. He argued that the old mercantile theory was " long exploded and repudiated by all who had received a liberal education," but was prepared to allow the prevailing restrictive policy to remain unaltered whenever there were special grounds for protection, and specifically mentioned the case of corn. The speech, wrote Sir Robert Wilson to Lord Grey, " has made a great impression in the City, and will have a powerful effect in the country."[2]

The same sturdy unconventional common-sense characterized most of Brougham's views on economics. He was opposed to any further extension of the empire until

[1] The speech is printed in Brougham's *Speeches*, vol. 1. See also *passim* Smart's *Economic Annals*. [2] Add. MSS. 30121, f. 266.

we had consolidated our trade position. Above all, and this was unusual in his time, he refused to accept the prevailing poverty and faulty distribution of goods as being inevitable. Unfortunately, he went back on this position in later life, but his remarks, made when introducing a petition from unemployed workmen in Birmingham, have a curiously modern ring.

> "They cannot but think that these calamities originate in natural causes, which it is in the power of human wisdom to discover and remove; they cannot but think that, in a country abounding with every blessing, some means may be devised by which the blessings of Providence may be distributed and enjoyed, by which the productive powers of industry may again be brought into action, and the honest labourer be able to earn an honest bread by the sweat of his brow."

Brougham's economic theories raise questions which are still in dispute. His support of the Corn Laws, his defence, in later years, of the Navigation Laws, his insistence of the evil effects of the heavy land tax, his belief that farmers were suffering from the habit of drinking tea rather than beer, his scepticism about the " balance of trade," all these views were ridiculed by the orthodox free traders, whose verdicts have been accepted far too readily by English historians. Brougham was speaking to men whose ideas about economic nationalism were almost as crude as those held by most European Governments to-day. He wanted a gradual modification of the system, made with due regard to English agriculture. He held that imports, such as tea, which displaced an English produce, such as malt, did not necessarily cause an equivalent amount of employment in the export trades. If he was an economic obscurantist, then those to whom the light is revealed to-day are a small and diminishing minority.

Brougham's educational activities are less contro-versial. Here, indubitably, he was in advance of his time. For over a quarter of a century he was continually driving successive Governments towards a system of State-aided popular education, cheap and universal. Until he began this long struggle there had been little recognition of any State responsibility for the education of its children. He had to force his views upon a generation in which the overwhelming majority of intelligent people took little interest in social questions. The bishops, and the clergy generally, were hostile. They were bitterly jealous of any interference in the parishes, and resented any light being thrown upon their neglect or upon the gross abuse of those charitable trusts which had survived from centuries with a higher regard for learning. The wealthier classes, Whigs as well as Tories, were inclined to hold that any education of the poor was dangerous. Even charity schools were likely to be accused of Jacobinism. When Hannah More, that staunch defender of the existing order, opened schools for Somerset day labourers, she was accused of " methodism " although she was careful to teach " no writing, nor any reading, but the Bible, catechism, and such little tracts as may enable them to understand the Church Service." Brougham argued repeatedly that this fear of popular education was a " modern idea," and in 1820 he quoted with great effect Pope Benedict's Bull of 1724, in which the establishment of schools was encouraged because the source of all evils was ignorance.[1] He was combating the great wave of deliberate obscurantism which swept over England during the Napoleonic period, and which was the meaner and more deadly because it was based, not on some religious misconception, but on the selfish prejudices of the wealthier classes. Francis Place once had an illuminating conversation with Lord Grosvenor, whom he had asked to subscribe towards the London Mechanics'

[1] *Hansard*, N. S. ii. 57.

Institute.   " He said he had a strong desire to assist the
institution, but he had also some apprehension that the
education the people were getting would make them discontented with the Government.   I said that the whole
mass of the people were discontented with the Government, and that although teaching them would not remove
their discontent, it would make them less disposed to be
turbulent. . . . He said, ' True, but *we* must take care of
ourselves.' " [1]   Few of Brougham's opponents were so
honest.   They preferred to organize covertly the powerful vested interests which any large educational scheme
was bound to disturb.

England, at the beginning of the nineteenth century,
was almost the worst educated country in Western
Europe, with only a small percentage of her population
able to read or write.   Two early attempts to improve
matters had been unsuccessful.   The Factory Act of
1802 had made it obligatory upon masters to see that
their apprentices were taught the elements of knowledge
and the principles of Christianity.   It might have been
better if the Government had begun by teaching the
masters.   The first year produced a crop of indignant
petitions against this " harsh " and " impractical " law
which cut down the hours for child labour to twelve
daily, and insisted that they should not be made to sleep
more than two in a bed.   The Act could only have been
enforced by local magistrates.   Most of these were
employers or their friends, and without any system of
Government inspection the Act soon became a dead
letter.   A few years later Whitbread brought in his Poor
Law Reform Bill of 1807.   This included a scheme,
afterwards made the subject of a separate Bill, under
which all children between seven and fourteen should
be entitled to two years' schooling.   Land and houses
should be rated for this purpose, and the local magistrates would be responsible for the provision of schools
and teachers.   The Bill passed the Commons in a

[1] *Life of Francis Place*, p. 112.

modified form, but was killed in the Lords by the Archbishop of Canterbury, Dr. Manners Sutton, and the Chancellor, Lord Eldon, a permanent and effective combination against any weak-kneed attempts at social reform.

After Whitbread's death Brougham began tackling the problem by his usual method. He moved for the appointment of a Committee of Inquiry. The Government had not learnt the modern trick of making such committees ineffective, either by over-weighting them with cranks and obstructionists, or using them as a kind of *oubliette* for shelving some awkward question. For Brougham they were an invaluable means of collecting evidence, and working up a widespread agitation outside as well as inside Parliament. He had already used a Committee of Inquiry to kill the Orders in Council. In 1816 the Commons agreed to appoint a Select Committee on the Education of the Lower Orders.

Brougham was the chairman. The Committee began their investigations in the London area, where Brougham had already privately mapped out the ground.[1] He was able to mobilize all those interested in the subject, including a number of Nonconformist ministers, and a few devoted clergymen who had undertaken this work undeterred by the apathy of their superiors. Within a few weeks the Committee could prove that there were 120,000 children in the metropolis without any means of education. It was the London of Dickens, of dark unpoliced slums, of "Tom-all-Alone's" from which half-starved children would creep in order to pick up a living. "The poor," according to the Report, "were in general anxious for education, yet in some cases they objected to send their children to school," preferring to "let them out to common beggars. From 2000 to 4000 children were in this situation, and out of this number came most of the juvenile depredators who swelled the calendar of Newgate."[2]

[1] See above, p. 50.   [2] *Hansard*, xxxiv. 633.

From London the Committee extended their work over the rest of England. They found conditions rather better in the provincial towns, but bad in the villages and in the new industrial areas. " The efforts of individuals combined in societies are almost wholly confined to populous places." From the first the Committee was brought up against the religious question, which for the next three generations was to be the curse of English education. The solution of the Committee, which was incorporated in Brougham's Education Bill of 1820, was " to place the choice of the schoolmaster in the parish vestry, subject to the approbation of the parson and the visitation of the diocesan; but to provide that the children of sectarians shall not be compelled to learn any catechism or attend any church, other than those of their parents." [1] The Report foreshadowed the dual system, as it is known to-day, recommending grants for schools where there was some organization, but in parishes where there was none, setting up rate-supported free parochial schools. The Select Committee dissolved in 1818; two years later Brougham brought forward its natural sequel, the Bill for the Education of the Poor.

This was one of the finest pieces of constructive work in Brougham's career, which, if it had been carried, would have entirely altered nineteenth-century history. Brougham introduced it in a speech of great moderation and breadth of vision.[2] Its first object was to plant schools wherever needed, the power of allocation being left to the Quarter Sessions. Considerable authority was left with the parson of the parish, who would decide on the course of education, but no form of worship would be allowed in the school except the Lord's Prayer and passages from Scripture. Schoolmasters were to

[1] *Third Report of Select Committee on Education of Lower Orders.*
[2] The speech is printed in full as an Appendix to J. E. G. De Montmorency's *State Intervention in English Education.* This work contains a valuable account of educational developments up to 1833.

be members of the Established Church. Brougham
reckoned that the cost of erecting schools would be about
half a million, and that some £150,000 a year would be
needed for maintenance.   The Bill was conceived on the
same broad and generous lines as Forster's Act, half
a century later.   The religious solution was very akin
to the "Cowper-Temple clause," which ultimately
brought something approaching a permanent settlement.   But in 1820 there was no real urge behind the
demand for educating the children of men who were
voteless and politically inarticulate.   The Bill passed
its second reading, but was killed in the Committee
stage, apparently owing to the opposition of Catholics
and Dissenters, but on this point there seems to be some
doubt.   It might only have been spared to be massacred
by the Lords.

Before the Select Committee dissolved in 1818 they
had started another political hare, the pursuit of which
was to cause far more excitement amongst the comfortable classes than any scheme for building schools for the
lower orders.   During their investigations the Committee had come across several cases of old educational
charities being grossly misapplied.   The subject was
really outside their scope, but Brougham was the last
man to miss an opportunity of exposing the " Old
Corruption " in one of its least defensible forms.   During
the times of the Tudors and Stuarts large grants of money
and land had been made by founders and benefactors to
various schools and colleges.   This property had often
been misappropriated during the eighteenth century.
The Committee discovered the most flagrant irregularities.
In several cases, as at Huntingon and St. Bees, the land
had been leased to the trustees at ridiculously low rents,
while the income was used for political purposes.
Pocklington School, which was nominally under the
supervision of St. John's College, Cambridge, still
boasted a headmaster, but the building was used for
storing lumber, and the one pupil was discovered working

in a saw-pit. The Provost of Eton and the Fellows of Winchester were made to produce their accounts. The arcana of College Bursaries at Oxford and Cambridge were dragged out into the open. The Master of St. John's College was so upset by his cross-examination about the disposal of Fellowships that he burst into tears. The general public were delighted, the Tories seriously alarmed, for they knew that there was hardly an institution in the country, political or educational, which could bear this kind of inquisition.

Brougham brought in a Bill to appoint Commissioners to inquire into scholastic endowments. The Government very shrewdly substituted their own Bill, in itself a recognition of Brougham's case, but carefully designed to prevent the elucidation of the grosser scandals. The Lords modified it still further. Lord Eldon, as usual, did his best to burke any inquiry. "No man," he declared, "would take upon himself the responsibility of a charitable trust if he were to be exposed to suspicious and vexatious inquiries." The Universities and the larger Public Schools were put outside the purview of the Commissioners, the new personnel was carefully chosen by Lord Sidmouth so as to avoid any excessive keenness in ferreting out new scandals. Brougham put up as good a fight as he could. His open *Letter to Samuel Romilly, M.P., on the Abuse of Charities* ran into several editions, and he engaged in a fierce wrangle with Sir Robert Peel, the new Member for Oxford, but, as with most men in advance of their time, the chief effect of his work was indirect. The Commissioners wandered round the country. Baulked of their larger prey they probably wasted much time on small misappropriations, like the " one pound an annum," the charitable donation which Farmer Seedling " lumped in with his tithes," but a generation later Dr. Folliott would have thought the last place for such an inconsiderable trifle was his own pocket.[1]

[1] Peacock's *Crotchet Castle*, Chapter VIII.

Brougham fought his educational battle single-handed. It was the way he liked to work, and the way he worked best. If his restless spirit ever suffered reincarnation, surely it must have been in the hound, which, following its own line after the pack had been whipped off at nightfall, arrived tired but " full of fox " at the kennels next morning. Such hounds are admired but not too popular. The older Whigs were as afraid as the Tories about where all these radical inquiries would end. " Lord Grenville," wrote Charles Wynn, " seems to be too much engrossed by Brougham's report and apprehension of an unhallowed Committee of the House of Commons, within the sacred precincts of Alma Mater, to think of anything else." [1]   The " Mountain " and the " Saints " gave some cautious support, but it was a lonely fight and tended to make Brougham more independent than ever. He looked upon himself as the representative of educated Radical opinion in the North. As the Whigs would not join him, he felt free to take his own line when they fought upon some constitutional point with which he did not agree. He refused to support an attack on the Septennial Act, and voted against his Party when the Government suggested an allowance of £6000 to the Duke of Kent. Probably he felt that if England was to have a monarchy, this was a small sum to pay the Duke for putting away Madame St. Laurent, with whom he had lived in amity for twenty-seven years, in order to provide the country with a legitimate heir. It certainly proved a cheap price to pay for a little Victoria in place of the unspeakable Duke of Cumberland. But all this gave Brougham a reputation amongst the Whigs for being perverse, and his position was in some ways anomalous. He had every qualification for being the strong man from the North except an independent constituency. This was his vulnerable spot, he

[1] C. W. W. Wynn to Marquis of Buckingham. Nov. 18, 1818. Duke of Buckingham : *Memoirs of the Regency*, ii. 289.

was dependent upon Lord Darlington for a seat in Parliament.

If Westminster would have been a " hard " seat, Winchelsea was an uneasy one. Lord Darlington's early fury against the Regent had abated. He still patronized the Whigs, but was very little of a " reformer," and ten years later he was to support the Duke of Wellington's frankly reactionary Government. The difficulty was recognized by both. At each General Election Brougham, with Lord Darlington's encouragement, attempted to fight an open constituency. In 1818 Lord Darlington himself, in a very courteous letter, suggested that Brougham might try again at Liverpool. " I entreat you," he wrote in January, " to believe that nothing could induce me to name the following subject to you but from the great regard that I entertain for yourself, the considerable anxiety that I feel to serve our esteemed and mutual friends, and for the support of that cause and those political principles which I am endeavouring to aid, at immense expense and trouble, and on a more extended scale than you can possibly be aware of." [1]   Brougham probably had little desire to be returned as second string to Canning, which was the most he could hope from a constituency with such a very restricted franchise. He decided to fight Westmorland, where he had his little family property. It was a bold move, for up till then the seat had always been considered a close preserve of the Lowther family.

The Whigs were fighting on two fronts. In the few urban constituencies with wide franchises they opposed Radicals—Romilly stood successfully at Westminster and Sir Robert Wilson at Southwark. They hoped to win a few county seats from the Tories. Brougham was undoubtedly happier tackling a Tory stronghold. He had been ill in 1817, and not, as his contemporaries would say, " in full force," but for the General Election he started a canvass of the county with all his old zest

---

[1] The letter is printed in full in Brougham's *Memoirs*, ii. 336.

and combativeness. Westmorland soon became the centre of interest for the whole country, and the election was probably the first outside London which was reported upon, day by day, in the Press. Special correspondents from *The Times, Morning Post,* and *Morning Chronicle* toured round the constituency, collecting news and views from the surprised villages of the fells, whose 2500 "forty-shilling freeholders" were a deciding factor in the contest. The election soon began to resemble military manœuvres carried on without much discipline and with considerable animosity. The Lowthers used their influence to bring as many troops as possible into the district and imported gangs of "toughs"—miners from Cumberland, sailors from Liverpool. Both sides had to organize their voters to march into the only polling station at Appleby, just as to-day an Indian *zemindar* will collect his tenants and send them, shepherded by his agent, to walk some miles to camp by the poll. Brougham in a letter to Lambton has left a lively picture of his activities ten days before the poll opened.

> "I addressed the people last night in myriads, and a troop of horse under arms. . . . Troops are drawn round us everywhere. They are stationed in every direction leading to Appleby, etc. I mean to protest against them on every occasion. The *men* are all with us and speak very freely. Our people live with them, and are assured they would not touch them. Indeed they generally wear my ribbons. The enemy are downcast to a degree. I *have* the original of a letter from a captain in the navy offering £150 for four votes. It was received by his uncle on Monday, and I had possession of it on Thursday in a remote part of the county, so good is our intelligence. . . .
> "I have succeeded everywhere in organizing my forces and marshalling them under leaders, to

march in bodies with music and colours, the lame following in carts, etc., and those who have horses to ride. We have beds for them all in houses and barns, etc. The multitude, which is enormous, are to be camped. We have got the best arrangements for polling booths, on *sure and convenient ground*, and shall have the entire command of them. The enemy are hiring a mob of miners, chiefly from Aldstone Moor, but we shall defeat them signally if they give battle." [1]

Lord Lonsdale carried the heavier guns, and Brougham had to withdraw on the fifth day of the poll. The Lowther contingent were almost as active as the Whigs. Apart from bribery and physical violence they organized a propagandist campaign, in which De Quincey, as editor of the *Westmorland Gazette*, played an unaccustomed rôle.[2] Wilberforce's letter of 1806 was also unearthed, and used for what it was worth. But it was the old landed tradition and interest which pulled them through. This proved overwhelming in 1818, and was sufficient on two later occasions when Brougham fought the constituency again, in 1820 and 1826. The important point about these contests was that Brougham did not rely on the local Whig interest. The Party in London had promised him some financial help, but even that was not forthcoming. Brougham made a direct and personal canvass. This was a real innovation, and its comparative success marked the first breach in the bastard feudalism which had obtained such a hold over the English countryside during the eighteenth century.

The Whigs had increased their strength by about thirty, but Brougham returned as member for Winchelsea, did not find them any more effective as a reformist

---

[1] This letter from the Lambton MSS. is printed in full in Aspinall's *Lord Brougham and the Whig Party*, p. 90.

[2] See Pollitt: *De Quincey's Editorship of the Westmorland Gazette*.

party.   In the *Edinburgh Review* he had, perforce, to take
the line that the country, desiring reform, had turned
to the Whigs as their natural leaders.   Sir Robert
Wilson, hopeful as ever, told Lord Grey that if he would
only take up electoral reform the " Whigs would be in
power before Xmas." [1]   Brougham must have known
that there were no grounds for such optimism.   The
Party, in spite of a few close votes on such subjects as
Criminal Law Reform and Catholic Emancipation, soon
showed itself incapable of replacing Lord Liverpool's
Government.   The handful of Whigs who were serious
reformers were weakened and disheartened by the
growing bitterness of their quarrel with the Radicals.
The position is sufficiently familiar in modern democracy.
A small group on the extreme " left " alienates the moderate reformers by the virulence of their attacks, tending to
make them both conservative and ineffective.

The suicide of Romilly was a further disaster.   Death
had not been kind to the reforming Whigs.   First
Whitbread had committed suicide, then the young
Princess had been taken and the Regent spared, and
now Romilly, a true knight too decent and too scrupulous
for those times, had died under his own hand.   To
Brougham it was a deep personal loss.   For ten years he
had fought with Romilly against the Philistines.   Together they had attacked the slave trade, flogging in the
army, the savage penal code, the scandals of the law-
courts, conditions in factories, the use of children as
chimney-sweeps, the neglect of education, the long line
of abuses which the Tories had inherited from the
eighteenth century.   There were so few who saw the
world as they did, and now Romilly, the noblest of them
all, was dead.   Brougham wrote to Lord Grey that " he
never thought we should live to sustain a loss which
might make even Whitbread's seem inconsiderable." [2]
It seemed to have knocked the heart out of Brougham.
Lady Granville met him " looking like something dug up.

[1] Add. MSS. 30122, f. 230.   [2] Brougham : *Memoirs*, ii. 339.

He says he has never recovered Sir Samuel's death, and the shock of attending the funeral." [1]

During the following sessions Brougham and Lord Grey carried on their opposition to the Six Acts and other repressive measures, but their quarrel with the Radicals made it difficult for them to defend with any fervour the men who were consistently abusing them. Another contest at Westminster, caused by Romilly's death, added to the bitterness of this dispute. The Radicals put up Hobhouse, the young aristocrat and friend of Byron. The Whigs, after failing to persuade Brougham or Bennet to stand, fell back upon a very moderate Whig in George Lamb. So bitter were the attacks on Lord Grey, that Lambton went down to defend his father-in-law and support Lamb, though his political views were probably far closer to those of Hobhouse. This election marked the nadir of the " reformists." It left them in such a state that Grey could write as follows to Sir Robert Wilson about the impossibility of having any dealings with the Radicals :

> " Look at the men, at their characters, at their conduct. What is there more base, more detestable, more at variance with all taste and decency, as well as all morality, truth and honour ? A cause so supported cannot be a good cause. They may use Burdett for their instrument for a time, and you also if you place yourself in their trammels, but depend upon it, if a convulsion follows, I shall not precede you many months on the scaffold, which you will have assisted in preparing for us both." [2]

Tierney continued to lead the Whigs, a sad disgruntled band, throughout 1819. Both he and Brougham had serious illnesses, and the Party remained equally ineffective inside and outside Parliament. Even the little

---

[1] Lady Granville : *Letters*, 1810–45, i. 138.
[2] The letter is printed in G. M. Trevelyan's *Lord Grey of the Reform Bill*, p. 188.

triumph of placing Brougham on the Civil List Committee was dashed by the suspicion that Castlereagh
wished to be outvoted to save himself from giving the
Crown as much as it had demanded.   In county after
county public meetings were being organized by Hunt
and the Radicals, demanding Parliamentary Reform and
attacking the repressive Acts.   The Whigs could never
make up their minds whether to support these or discourage them.   This all played into the hands of the
Tories.   Under Lord Liverpool's weak leadership the
alarmists had matters their own way.   They dismissed
Lord FitzWilliam, Lord Lieutenant of Yorkshire, for
attending a county meeting, and they began secretly to
build up a new army.   Everything seemed staged for a
virtual dictatorship by Wellington and Castlereagh,
against which the Whigs could have done nothing but
protest feebly.

   Suddenly the whole position was reversed.   The Tories
were put upon the defensive, and the Whigs became
temporarily a united Party with popular opinion behind
them.   The cause of this was the death of the " old, mad,
blind, despised, and dying King," the accession of the
Regent and the affair of Queen Caroline.

I

CHAPTER VII

BROUGHAM AT FORTY

Such at the age of forty was the worldly result of labour, which the world had chosen to regard as successful. The world also thought that Mr. Arabin was, in his own estimation, sufficiently paid. Alas, alas, the world was mistaken . . .

ANTHONY TROLLOPE : *Barchester Towers.*

BEFORE discussing the most spectacular incident in Brougham's life—his defence of Queen Caroline—it may be well to have a glance at the man himself, some fifteen years after he had migrated to London. He had still the same long lean figure, the same tireless energy.

> " A meagre form, a face so wondrous thin,
> That it resembles Milton's Death and Sin,
> Long arms that saw the air like windmill sails,
> And tongue whose force and fury never fails."

It was this remarkable physical energy which first struck nearly everyone who met him, either in his prime or in his old age. About this middle period he had occasional bouts of illness, possibly due to the mixture of hard work and the gross eating and drinking of the times, but these had no permanent effect on the wonderful constitution which served him so well for ninety years. He never spared himself, could sleep when he wanted, and took a pride in the mental agility which enabled him to switch from one subject to another. Le Marchant, who was his private Secretary, describes the early days of his Chancellorship, ten years later. " He had known him work incessantly from nine in the morning till one at night, and at the end be as fresh apparently as when he began. He could turn from one subject to another with

A CHRISTMAS FIRESIDE

Intended as a Present to the Rising Generation

" *And I can never cease to be*
Affectionate and kind to Thee."

From a sketch by H. B. Doyle.

Jan. 8, 1833.

MASSACRE AT ST. PETER'S, OR "BRITONS STRIKE *HOME*"!!!

The charge of the Yeomanry at Peterloo.

surprising facility and promptitude, in the same day travelling through details of a Chancery cause, writing a philosophical or mathematical treatise, correcting articles for the ' Library of Useful Knowledge,' and preparing a great speech for the Lords." [1]

Like Mr. Asquith he despised the " pampered athletes " who need exercise and games.   When stopping with friends he would ride, but showed little skill with horse or gun.   He deplored the addiction to field sports of the amateur politicians, and their pose of treating politics as a dull and disagreeable duty.   His busy contentious life provided all the sport he needed.

> " Go, stalk the red deer o'er the heather,
>   Ride, follow the fox if you can !
> But, for pleasure and profit together,
>   Allow me the hunting of Man."

Travel was his one relaxation.   Though he did not repeat the adventurous journeys of his youth, he went nearly every year to France, and sometimes to Switzerland and Italy.   Like most of his contemporaries he was not interested in scenery, but went abroad to meet interesting people, or to see works of art.   He found Geneva uninhabitable.   " It is a country to be in for two hours, or two and a half, if the weather is fine, and no longer.   Ennui comes on the third hour, and suicide attacks you before night.   There is *no* resource whatever for passing the time, except looking at lakes and hills, which is over immediately." [2]

Brougham in 1819 was a notable but not a very successful member of the Junior Bar.   His political standing made him unpopular with the leaders, but he was well liked by his fellows, and took his full share in the boisterous fun of the Northern Circuit in those pre-Victorian days.   His comparative lack of success was partly due

---

[1] Greville : *Journal of the Reigns of George IV, etc.*, iv. 33.
[2] Letter to Creevey, Aug. 25, 1816.   *Creevey Papers*, i. 258.

to his rule of giving political work the first claim on his time and energies. This involved much visiting at country houses, frequent attendance at Brooks's Club, and calls upon those Whig hostesses who played such an important part in the political game. He was popular in society. His wit was ready if a little ponderous. His originality and independence of thought compensated for any lack of finesse due to his harder upbringing. He never quite accepted, or was accepted by, the London Society in which he had to spend his life. Lady Granville complains that he goes to dinner, in 1820, with " his hair and beard grown, looking like an orangoutang." [1]

All through his life he was a notable talker, with a fund of quotations remarkable even in that age. He had the defects common to most great talkers. Like Dr. Middleton, he tended to be pontifical, and " would ride down a duke when the wine is in him." The famous remark of Samuel Rogers, after seeing him off one morning, suggests that the poet found him rather overwhelming. " This morning, Solon, Lycurgus, Demosthenes, Archimedes, Sir Isaac Newton, Lord Chesterfield, and a great many more went away in one post-chaise." But Greville, who repeats the story, was chiefly struck by Brougham's " almost childish gaiety and animal spirits." [2]

The pose of omniscience, which probably began as a form of humour, became rather annoying in later life. There was always a touch of the pedagogue about Brougham. " Lady Sefton told me that he went with them to the British Museum, where all the officers of the Museum were in attendance to receive them. He would not let anyone explain anything, but did all the honours himself. At last they came to a collection of minerals. . . . Their conductor began to describe them, when Brougham took the words out of his mouth, and

---

[1] Lady Granville : *Letters, 1810–45*, i. 200.
[2] Greville : *Journal*, i. 120.

dashed off with as much ease and familiarity as if he had been a Buckland or Cuvier." [1] But in spite of this Brougham's hostesses seldom found him heavy in hand. He was witty in an age when wit was appreciated and a high standard demanded.

It is necessary to mention the question of his eccentricity, for it has been seized upon by many later writers as if it was his chief characteristic and bordered at times on mental derangement. This would seem to be the least justifiable part of the legend which has grown round his name. It must, first, be remembered that, over a long period, certainly between 1810 and 1835, he incurred, more than any of his contemporaries, the hatred of the educated classes, and this at a time when personalities, especially in private letters and the Press, were exceptionally unscrupulous and virulent. His exposition of Radical ideas got under their skin far more effectually than the rant of more popular demagogues like " Orator " Hunt, or the diatribes of writers like Cobbett. More especially Brougham was hated for his ideas on education, his attacks on the older seats of learning, and his efforts to spread what was believed to be a dangerous knowledge of science and economics. This roused against him, not only the regular politicians, whose attacks we automatically discount, but a host of writers, including Peacock, Mackworth Praed, Barham of the *Ingoldsby Legends*, the young Disraeli, and others, most of whom had no personal knowledge of Brougham, but were ready to put the worst construction on anything they heard about this dangerous iconoclast. The legend of his eccentricity seems to be based partly on his early escapades, which, as has been seen, were sometimes ascribed to a later date; partly on his unconventionality—just as Mr. Arnold Bennett's " card " drove a mule and found it a useful animal, so Brougham invented the very convenient " box on wheels " which is always associated with his name; but chiefly the legend rests on his

[1] Greville; *Journal*, ii. 152.

uncanny versatility and energy, and what " Squire "
Western, the M.P., called his " flow of jaw."

The words " mad " and " frantic " were frequently
used in correspondence about anyone with whom the
writer had had a temporary disagreement.   Thus Creevey
writes to his stepdaughter about a letter which he had
from Brougham.   " I had charity enough for him not
to show it to anyone but Sefton, and he quite agrees with
me that he is *mad*.   His lunacy, you may plainly see, is
to be in power."   The letter, fortunately preserved,
turns out to be both sane and sensible.   It deprecates
any idea of the Whigs joining with Joseph Hume in an
attack on the Church of England.   Brougham suggests
that " there is a vast mass of religion in the country."
" Some Church establishment this feeling must have;
and I am quite clear that a much-reformed Church of
England is the safest form in which such an establishment can exist.   It is a quiet and somewhat lazy Church :
certainly not a persecuting one." [1]   But Creevey and
Sefton were having one of their periodic attacks of
extreme radicalism, so that Brougham is dubbed as
" mad."   Similarly, Lord Dudley and Ward wrote to
Mrs. Stewart about meeting Brougham some years later,
when he was supposed to be in a fever of excitement in
the days preceding the formation of the first Whig
Ministry.   " Brougham was here a few hours to see his
wife who is come for her health.   I met him in the
street, and he came up to this room for a quarter of an
hour.   People talk of his being *frantic*.   I never saw
anybody more composed, more easy, more agreeable. . . ." [2]   At various periods in Brougham's life
there are covert hints at mental derangement.   They
are much on a par with accusations of cowardice about
fighting duels.   Both came from the same source—
from men who were trying to drive Brougham out of
public life.   In each case there were some grounds.

[1] *Creevey Papers*, ii. 65–7.
[2] Lord Dudley and Ward : *Letters to " Ivy*," p. 340.

Brougham, like many of his contemporaries, had to deal with wanton challenges from men of straw. Similarly he had to face severe attacks of depression, such as assail many men of active brain who have had to fight their way against adversity.

Few English politicians have experienced greater vicissitudes, but Brougham took these bouts of depression very seriously, and set himself to conquer them systematically. There is a curious passage in his life of Dr. Johnson in which, as he showed later, he explained his own symptoms and cure.[1]

> " To these miseries, the general lot of the literary man's life, was added in Johnson's the far worse suffering from his constitutional complaint, a suffering bad enough in itself if the companion of ease and of affluence, but altogether intolerable when it weighs down the spirits and the faculties of him whose mental labour must contribute to the supply of his bodily needs. The exertion, no doubt, when once made, is the best medicine for the disease; but it is the peculiar operation of the disease to render all such exertion painful in the extreme, to make the mind recoil from it, and render the intellectual powers both torpid and sluggish, when a painful effort has put them in motion. I speak with some confidence on a subject which accident has enabled me to study in the case of one with whom I was well acquainted for many years."

Brougham goes on to describe in great detail the course of the disease, and the hygiene of mind and body which are necessary to cure it. Many years afterwards,

[1] Mr. J. B. Atlay draws attention to this allusion in his biography of Brougham in the *Victorian Chancellors*, p. 346. The writer has already acknowledged his indebtedness to this work, especially in regard to Brougham's legal career. The *Life of Dr. Johnson* is included in Brougham's *Men of Letters and Science*. Published 1846.

writing to his lawyer friend Forsyth, he says of this passage, " I am the person alluded to. Your case is a shade worse than mine." [1] There seems no evidence of any mental derangement, only the periodic reactions of a highly-strung person who never spared himself. The best proof of the absence of any disease, and of Brougham's ultimate self-control, was that he lived to be an eminently sane and healthy octogenarian.

Brougham's enemies were not only political. At the beginning of the nineteenth century the countryside was still dominated by a few " landed " families, and Society generally by a powerful if irrational caste system. Brougham belonged to the rapidly growing educated professional class. Like the smaller " rentiers," these were " quality " compared with traders or working men, but they were not admitted to equality with that exclusive sub-caste, the Governing class. The division was never really based on heredity or race, but not much logic need be expected in a people who could maintain up to modern times a rigid distinction between wholesale and retail traders amongst their compatriots in India. In eighteenth-century England a generation or two of great wealth or of landed property was sufficient quali- fication for the governing class. Chatham belonged to it, though his grandfather had been an East Indian " interloper," at one time little better than a pirate. Burke and Sheridan did not belong, though, if they had been given peerages, and drawn sufficient money from the public funds, their sons would have been accepted. Dundas was a doubtful case until a peerage completed the process of adoption. In Brougham's time the caste system was decaying. The younger Pitt, by his indis- criminate distribution of peerages, had hastened its end. The Tories were always less exclusive. Peel, for example, was accepted into the governing class, though his father had built up an enormous fortune from nothing, and Peel himself had a strong provincial accent. But caste

---

[1] *Letters of Lord Brougham to William Forsyth, Q.C.*, pp. 45–9, 82.

ideas were still powerful and deeply embedded in the common mind. Of the three characteristics of the caste system—" endogamy, commensality and mutual control by members "—the feeling against " mixed marriages " remained strong, but the governing class were already finding it convenient to muzzle the rising " plebeian " by inviting him to dinner, and the enforcement of caste rules on such subjects as duelling was becoming increasingly difficult.

The women of that time tended to cling to these caste distinctions longer than their men-folk. There is an illuminating passage in the *Creevey Papers* suggesting how far the process had gone by the 'thirties. Joseph Parkes, the famous Birmingham attorney, became a very important person at the time of the Reform Bill. He was " mixed up with all classes—Church, Chapels, and State; and as well or better calculated for utility as any man I know. . . . He has great influence in the Trade Unions; he is a prime leader of the Dissenters." He was, in fact, the typical " key " man of modern politics. Lord Grey saw that such men were essential for his Party in the new " reformed " House of Commons. " He had formed a great opinion of him, with a strong desire to see him; and then he got on to say that he *would* know him; upon which our dear Lady Grey, in a tone and manner quite her own, said : ' I hope there is no *Mrs.* Parks ! ' " [1] In this changing society Brougham was recognized as a disruptive force. He had, it is true, that strong sense of " property " which was then almost universal, but he was certainly not more obsessed by its importance than such advanced Radicals as Sir Francis Burdett, J. C. Hobhouse, or Lord Cochrane. For " family " he had little regard, and he wandered, amused and unimpressed, round the Whig " Houses " —Croxteth, Arundel, Middleton, Howick, and the rest.

[1] *Creevey Papers*, ii. 270. There *was*, of course, a Mrs. Parkes, a lady of considerable distinction, daughter of the famous Dr. Priestley.

He flits through the memoirs and correspondence of that period, recognized as something of a portent, but making the ladies laugh, and a great favourite with the children. He initiates Lady Bessborough into the mystery of Highland beds, " which are generally in a hole in the wall," and when she suggested pulling the mattress out, " he said I had better leave them where they were—

> Nor further seek their merits to disclose,
> Or draw them farther from their dread abode." [1]

But Lady Bessborough came to consider that he was harbouring a deep resentment against the Whig leaders, and " whether friend or foe, he will never be a favourite of mine." His friendships with Lady Rosslyn and later with Mrs. George Lamb have already been mentioned. It is possible that he preferred the rather naughtier ladies of the Whig circle, and of these there was a sufficiently plentiful and varied selection. He certainly got on better with Lady Jersey and Lady Darlington than with Lady Grey, who ultimately became his bitter enemy. There is already some hint of this preference when, in 1819, he offers to take Creevey down to Middleton. " Rely upon me—I am the last and shyest man in the world to do these things at such places as Holland House, Chatsworth, Croxteth, etc., but I am on a footing of friendship with the Jerseys as intimate as if I were a brother, and I know them thoroughly and you may trust me." [2] In later years this failing developed, and he became a little contemptuous of women, preferring to lump them in a not too flattering category. It was a tendency which was undoubtedly encouraged by his marriage.

Brougham married, at the age of forty, into the fringes of the Governing caste. His wife was " a Mrs. Spalding, a rather dashing widow with three children, a good

[1] Earl Granville: *Private Correspondence, 1781–1821*, p. 324.
[2] *Creevey Papers*, i. 294.

jointure, and a house in Hill Street." [1]   She had been a
Miss Mary Eden, granddaughter of the first Lord Auck-
land, and therefore niece of the future Viceroy and of
his sister Miss Emily Eden, who nearly married Lord
Melbourne, and wrote that entertaining account of her
brother's Indian experiences in *Up the Country*.   There
was some mystery about Brougham's marriage, which
took place, perhaps a little ominously, on April 1, 1819.[2]
It was not a wedding to which any friends were invited,
and for some reason it was kept secret for a month or
two.   This gave the malicious an opportunity for talking
scandal, and Mrs. Brougham did not improve matters
by presenting her husband with a seven-months child, a
fact duly noted by Brougham's many enemies.   A year
afterwards, " Mrs. Brougham's seven-months child "
was commented upon in *John Bull*, the scandalous
periodical which the Tories brought out under Theodore
Hook's editorship.[3]

This first child died in infancy.   The second, also a
daughter, was Eleanor Louise, who lived to be eighteen,
but was a constant invalid.   It was an inauspicious
opening to a marriage.   There may even have been
some truth in the accusations of a "forced marriage"
which were periodically brought against Brougham.
Seven years later, at the time of his quarrel with " Dandy
Raikes," Creevey opined that Raikes " had been worked
up to this step by such chaps as Lowther, Glengall and
Belfast, and that he was made to believe that Brougham
was a shy cock; for Lady Glengall has always been
harping upon that tack of late, as that he was made to
marry Mrs. Brougham, by one of her brothers upon a
certain event being known, and such stuff as this." [4]   It
is unlikely that anyone made Brougham take an im-

---

[1] Letter from John Whishaw, July 17, 1819.   *The " Pope " of
Holland House*, p. 205.
[2] The *Dictionary of National Biography*, by a curious slip, gives the
date as 1821.   [3] Lady Granville : *Letters*, i. 201.
[4] *Creevey Papers*, ii. 106–7.

portant step against his will, but he may have believed
that he had compromised Mrs. Spalding.

The marriage was not a great success. Mrs. Spalding
seems to have been a stupid woman and a failure socially.
Creevey frankly disliked her, so it is necessary to discount
his descriptions of her " sitting like an overgrown doll
at the top of the table in a bandeau of roses, her face a
perpetual simper, without utterance "; [1] or his account
of a lamentable dinner, in 1825, with the Darlingtons,
when " she came in more languishing than ever," and,
as Creevey foretold, accomplished " her favourite trick
of fainting before she left the house. She was going
her lengths the whole of dinner, so that I made Ly
Arabella nearly die with laughing at her. At last,
however, the colour really did desert her face, and she
actually bolted." [2] Brougham himself cannot have been
the easiest of husbands, but this queerly assorted couple
remained together in comparative amity until her death
in 1865. She was his rather inefficient hostess when he
was Lord Chancellor, and in later years accompanied
him each winter to Cannes, until her own health gave
way.

If Brougham's marriage was not altogether happy, it
brought him some consolations. He loved children,
and was admirable with them. In the very thick of
the Queen's trial, " how do you think he was occupied
the greater part of Sunday morning? Playing at leap-
frog with Duncannon's children." [3] He loved his
invalid daughter—his little Tullia, as he called her—
with a passionate intensity. Her death, in 1839, clouded
the rest of his life. While she was growing up he filled
the house with children. He seems to have got on
admirably with his step-children, and when he became
Lord Chancellor the elder Miss Spalding went everywhere with him. His brother John, the unsuccessful

---

[1] Creevey Papers, ii. 89.
[2] J. Gore : *Creevey's Life and Times*, p. 178.
[3] Lady Granville : *Letters*, i. 168.

wine merchant and grocer, died in Boulogne in 1829, and Brougham at once adopted his large family. " Be Brougham's political errors what they may," wrote Greville the following year, " his gaiety, temper and admirable social qualities make him delightful, to say nothing of his more solid merits, of liberality, generosity and charity; for charity it is to have taken the whole family of one of his brothers who is dead—nine children —and maintained and educated them." [1]

Wordsworth, like the other Lake Poets, had no reason to love the prominent Edinburgh Reviewer. During one of the Westmorland elections he wrote a violent pamphlet against Brougham, but, in 1831, he went out of his way to say how much he admired him personally. " He was very generous and affectionate in his disposition, full of duty and attention to his mother, and had adopted and provided for a whole family of his brother's children, and treats his wife's children as if they were his own. He insisted on taking them both with him to the Drawing Room when he went in State as Chancellor." [2]

Brougham moved into his wife's house at No. 5, Hill Street, but most of the children were brought up in Westmorland, where he gradually built up a little estate round Brougham Hall. Two of his brothers were beginning to play some part in his life. James, the second son, was at the English Bar, and seems to have " devilled " for his brother in more ways than one. Brougham found him a seat in Parliament in 1829, but he died four years later. The youngest brother, William, was also a barrister, but combined that work with writing leading articles for *The Times*, and Henry undoubtedly used him to keep up his connection with the Press. He also went into Parliament and had a legal career of some distinction, finally, in 1868, succeeding to his brother's title. Brougham's strong family feeling found its outlet

[1] Greville : *Journal of the Reigns of George IV, etc.* Under date Nov. 22, 1830.   [2] Greville : *Journal*, ii. 123.

in looking after his mother, his two brothers, and this
army of children, some thirteen in all, for whom he was
responsible. Miss Berry, who stopped at Brougham
Hall in 1824, clearly liked the family and appreciated
the matriarchal rule which prevailed while old Mrs.
Brougham was still alive. "We found there the
mother of the family, her daughter, her three sons, and
the wife of the renowned eldest. The mother is a charm-
ing person, the best specimen of an old Scotch lady, well-
informed and liberal-minded, without the least *cant*. Their
house is delightful; an old manor-house, well situated
and very conveniently disposed, and arranged with
good taste within." [1]

It was Brougham's custom to spend every Christmas
with his mother. It would seem that such filial piety
was not too common. At any rate John Doyle (" H.
B."), who was not always very friendly, made it the
subject of a cartoon in the year which followed
Brougham's elevation to the Chancellorship.

[1] Miss Berry : *Journals and Correspondence*, iii. 357.

CHAPTER VIII

ATTORNEY-GENERAL TO THE QUEEN

An old, mad, blind, despised, and dying king—
Princes, the dregs of their dull race, who flow
Through public scorn, mud from a muddy spring—
Rulers who neither see nor feel nor know,
But leech-like to their fainting country cling,
Till they drop, blind in blood, without a blow—
A people starved and stabbed in the untilled field—
An army which liberticide and prey
Make as a two-edged sword to all who wield,—
Golden and sanguine laws which tempt and slay,—
Religion Christless, Godless, a book sealed,—
A Senate—time's worst statute unrepealed,—
Are graves from which a glorious Phantom may
Burst to illumine our tempestuous day.
                              SHELLEY : *England in 1819.*

Two events, one in 1819 and the other in 1820, helped
to destroy the decaying structure of " Old Corruption,"
under which the Crown had, for over half a century,
retained its influence by wholesale bribery, a venal job-
hunting aristocracy, an antiquated electoral system, and
the suppression of all independent opinion or working-
class movements. There had been much steady under-
mining during the previous ten years. The efforts of
the Whig " Mountain " and of the Radicals had taught
the country to connect this system of corruption with
their economic distress, and two men of genius, Cobbett
and Cruikshank, had with pen and pencil made people
visualize the pillars on which the system rested. They
saw the Regent as a selfish voluptuary, the Yeomanry
as a class weapon lacking even the restraining discipline
of the Regular Army. In 1819 the Yeomanry came
into action at " Peterloo." In 1820 the Regent, who

had just succeeded to the throne, was involved in the
scandal of the Queen's trial. Neither event was in
itself of great importance. The so-called " massacre of
Peterloo " was a comparatively small affair according to
modern standards of political and industrial repression.
The Queen's affair, if it had not from the first aroused
great popular excitement, would have certainly been
" settled out of court." Both caused an immense stir
because millions of people, who had not yet learnt to
think politically, saw in them the typical working of a
system which they abhorred, though they had little idea
as to what would replace it.

Peterloo was also important because it shamed the
educated classes and the younger Tories, and roused the
old English dislike of anything approaching military rule.
The trial shook the whole foundations of English society.
The King, the Court, the Lords and the Ministers were
all dragged through the dirt, and Brougham, in Professor
Trevelyan's phrase, was " showman of the spectacle."
Neither Toryism nor the old Whiggism was ever quite
the same after 1820. Just as the extraordinary mani-
festations at the end of Lord Ripon's period of office
showed a surprised officialdom that there was an Indian
public opinion, so the popular turmoil at the Queen's
return to England proved that there was a new force in
England which could not be permanently ignored.
Sir Walter Scott took a narrow one-sided view when
he ascribed the Queen's popularity solely to hatred of
the new King. " What they seek was expressed in the
comment of the Irish gallery to Lady C.—huzza for
Lady C., and long may she live to cuckold the Chancellor." [1] The crowd may not have worried much about
the Queen's innocence, but her prosecution seemed to
them typical of the way in which England was being
run by Lord Eldon, Lord Liverpool and Lord Castlereagh, when even a Queen could be bullied if she hap-

[1] *Letters of Sir Walter Scott, 1819–21.* Centenary Edition,
p. 237.

pened to offend the King, or the little group which
governed the country.

Brougham, perhaps the chief actor in this queer
drama, was naturally exposed to every kind of criticism.
He was accused of using the Queen for party purposes,
of endangering her interests for his private advantage,
and injuring his country by not preventing the scandal
of what was virtually the trial of a queen for adultery.[1]
Such accusations were to be expected from Tory apolo-
gists endeavouring to defend a difficult case by imputing
personal motives, but they have influenced many
subsequent writers. The first two points will be
considered later. They present difficulties because little
is known of what passed verbally between the Queen
and her legal advisers, Brougham and Denman. As to
whether Brougham should have prevented the case, it is
enough to say that the conduct of the preliminary
negotiations was the Ministry's responsibility, that
Brougham was never their agent, and that on a long
view it was probably best that the affair should be
thrashed out in public. The attitude of the French in
such matters is sound. It is better for a scandal, such as
the Stavisky case, to be investigated, even if it reflects
upon the administration, than that the Government and
society should be corrupted by rumours and veiled
accusations. Queen Victoria was born in 1819. During
the eighteen years before she came to the throne most of
the corrupt influence of the Crown had disappeared, and
the Court was purged from the taint of immorality.
The rapidity of this change was largely due to the
publicity of the trial, and the conduct of the Queen's
defence.

In 1819 Brougham can have had little idea of what
would happen when George III died. As a politician
he had given up much interest in the Royal family since

---

[1] It was not, as will be seen later, a legal " trial." A Bill of
Pains and Penalties was introduced in the House of Lords, and
counsel and witnesses were heard.

K

Princess Charlotte's death. The birth of the little Victoria in May did not relieve the Whigs from the prospect of a long series of Royal brothers, as Kings or Regents, none of whom would be more sympathetic than the Regent, and who would be much less trouble-some to the Tory Ministers. Brougham was theoret-ically a legal adviser to the Princess of Wales. She had promised to make him her Attorney-General when she became Queen, but he had had little communication with her while she was touring about in Italy and the Near East. He knew that the Regent was pressing for a divorce, and that some incriminating evidence had been collected by the " Milan Commission," which had been sent out, under the instigation of Sir John Leach, to inquire into reports of the Queen's misbehaviour. In July 1819, Mr. Cooke and his two colleagues placed such evidence as they had collected before the Cabinet, which accepted their view that there was sufficient proof of adultery, but doubted whether it could be established by reputable witnesses. Brougham was not shown the evidence, but knew about these accusations, and, according to his own account, " was acquainted with circumstances, unknown to them, of great indiscretions on her part, though entirely unconnected with the charges against her." [1] She had undoubtedly been appallingly indiscreet, and for the next year Brougham almost certainly believed that she had actually com-mitted adultery with her steward Pergami.[2] It was only after the case had started that he changed his mind, and decided that the Queen was a " child fancier," more interested in Pergami's daughter Victorine than in the stalwart handsome father. Plumer Ward reports a conversation in 1820 when Brougham remarked that " at first he did not think it possible that she was inno-

[1] Brougham : *Memoirs*, ii. 382.
[2] Bartolomeo Pergami was mistakenly called Bergami at the beginning of the trial. See Nightingale, *Report of the Trial*, iii. 689.

cent. But the more the case had opened, the more had her innocence appeared; and now in his conscience he believed her guiltless." [1]

The Ministry were in the unhappy position of being pressed by the Regent to procure a divorce which they knew could only be obtained on evidence of adultery given by foreigners, " many of whom appear to be in a low station of life." Two valuable groups of Tory supporters—the Bishops and the " Saints "—would be affronted by any proposal to grant a divorce to a man who had deserted his wife and was openly living with other women, while any trial might bring up the dangerous question of the Fitzherbert marriage. On the other hand, Brougham was not too happy as the legal adviser of a woman who was indiscreet, unreliable and unbusinesslike, and whom he gravely suspected of having committed the offence, possibly treasonable, of adultery. The Princess was in an irritable mood, annoyed at her treatment by the French and Italian Governments, and angry about the delay in paying her some money under her brother's will.

Negotiations were begun between the Government and Brougham on behalf of the Regent and the Princess, but along lines which would not then have been acceptable to either of the principals. In June Brougham wrote to Lord Hutchinson that he was " disposed to advise the Princess to accede to an arrangement grounded on some such basis as the following :—That she shall agree to a formal separation, to be ratified by Act of Parliament, if such a proceeding can be accomplished; that she shall renounce the right to be crowned in the event of a demise of the Crown, and shall from thenceforth take some other style and title, as that of Duchess of Cornwall; that she shall renounce the jointure to which she is entitled in the event of her surviving the Prince Regent, and that her present annuity shall be

[1] *Memoirs of the Political and Literary Life of R. Plumer Ward*, ii. 60. Ed. E. Phipps.

granted for her life. . . ." [1]   Probably the Government
would have accepted such terms, but they did not feel
able to force them on to the Regent, who might have
tried to form an alternate Government.   Lord Liverpool made the obvious " face-saving " gesture of asking
that the request should be made in writing.   This, of
course, would have put the Princess hopelessly in the
wrong.   In such negotiations agreement has to be
reached privately between the agents, and then between
them and their respective principals before either side
can make an overt move.

In August the Princess talked of making a visit to
England, and wrote in this sense to Lord Liverpool
as Premier.   Brougham eventually dissuaded her.   He
wanted to keep the *threat* of her coming as a bargaining
counter, but certainly did not want her to come.   There
is no reason to doubt the sincerity of his letter to Canning,
quoted in a previous chapter, in which he talked of the
" personal annoyance of having such a devil to plague
me for six months."   Canning was one of the few
genuine supporters of the Princess on the Tory side, and
later resigned his office because of Lord Liverpool's
policy towards her.   Brougham went on to express his
real objections to the Princess landing in England.

" I think it exposes things to the risk of clamour
and violence, which no one can hope to estimate,
far less to direct, or in case of necessity to disarm.
In short, the question, both before being brought
on and after, would not be considered with even

[1] Letter of June 14, 1819.   This is given in full in C. D. Yonge's
Life and Administration of Earl of Liverpool, iii. 15.   This volume
contains a very full and documented account of the negotiations
before the introduction of the Bill of Pains and Penalties.   It is
important to note that this author expressly acquits Brougham of
" having stimulated her in the rejection of all terms of compromise.
The imputation was wholly undeserved.   It is now clear that in
all the advice which he pressed on the lady, whom we may already
term his client, his motives were as disinterested as his advice was
judicious for all parties."

tolerable coolness and fairness were she here. I therefore am disposed to stop her coming by every means in my power. I have written instantly, but shall set out suddenly myself to stop her if I find that nothing else will do; even if she had begun her journey, I had rather meet her on the road and make her turn—in short, anything better than her coming here. You had better communicate this. I rely on the honour of the party concerned to have justice done to my motives in the event of the other setting the mob against me, which she is quite capable of doing." [1]

The letter suggests Brougham's difficulties. The Queen was already in communication with Alderman Wood and others who were promising her every kind of popular support. The "Mountain" wished to make the dispute into a straight political issue. Brougham objected to his client being identified either with the Radicals or the "Mountain." He knew too much about the weakness of either group when it came to a trial of strength in Parliament or outside. Very wisely he consulted Lord Grey, who thought that the Princess might have "beaten the Prince and his foolish adviser Leach" if she had come over, but made it clear that "whatever course this business may take, we, as a party, have nothing to do but to observe the most perfect neutrality, and to decide upon the evidence as we should do in any other case." [2]

There is some mystery about an arrangement to meet the Princess at Lyons. Creevey, writing after her death, accuses Brougham of bringing the Princess from Italy to France, and then refusing to go to Lyons "because he was too busy." [3] We have not the full correspondence

[1] Brougham to Canning, August 5, 1819. Letter printed in full in Stapleton's *George Canning and his Times*, pp. 265–6.
[2] Lord Grey to Brougham, August 25, 1819. Printed in Brougham's *Memoirs*, ii. 342.
[3] *Creevey Papers*, ii. 23.

between her and Brougham, but Creevey is not a safe
guide. He was very keen to make the case a political
issue, and furious with Grey and Tierney for their
" insanity " in refusing to do so.[1] Brougham took
Creevey to visit Lady Jersey in the autumn of 1819, and
promised him a seat in his carriage when he went to see
the Princess, which he then expected to do in the
following spring. He was not likely to confide fully
in the cheerful but not too responsible gossip, who was
also pressing for a policy with which he privately disagreed. He probably fobbed Creevey off with some
casual remark about his reasons for not going to the
south of France. We only know that Brougham did
not go, and that the Princess gave up her idea of coming
to England. In December she wrote to him from
Marseilles, not suggesting that he had upset her plans,
but still harping on the question of her recognition by
foreign Courts, and clearly uncertain about the Radical
promises of popular support if she came to England.

> " By the newspapers I have been informed that
> our dear King is very ill; of course, if it should be
> his lot to follow his ancestors, I think I could not
> remain in France, having yet not received any mark
> of attention from that Court. I would probably
> return to Italy; the whole aspect for me would
> then change. If the *country* would protect me I
> certainly would fly to England." [2]

At the end of January the old King died. George IV
nearly followed him within a week, but recovered from
his pleurisy and returned to the attack. His keenness
for a divorce had become an obsession. The Cabinet
pressed for a separation. The King would not hear of
it. He entirely disapproved of settling an annuity upon
the " Princess," as he still called her, though it should

---

[1] *Creevey Papers*, i. 313.
[2] *Life and Administration of Earl of Liverpool*, iii. 22–3.

be payable only on her remaining abroad. He refused to allow her name to be mentioned in the Liturgy, a point of urgent importance, and an insult which ultimately caused the break-down of negotiations. The Cabinet were firm on the subject of divorce, and their Minute makes an obvious reference to the Royal manner of life. " If your Majesty and the Princess were in the situation of private individuals, it may be assumed as certain that a divorce could not possibly be obtained." It was a home thrust which made the King bluster and threaten to change his Ministers, but the Cabinet were on strong ground. Not even the " ear-wigs " amongst the Opposition would have accepted office on condition of being more compliant.

While these discussions were proceeding the Queen was growing angrier and more difficult to control. Brougham had sent a special messenger suggesting that she should come to France, intending that she should issue her ultimatum from there, but by April she had, as it were, taken the bit between her teeth. One annoyance had succeeded another. Her official income ceased with the death of George III. The Roman Foreign Minister described her as " Princess," the French Minister refused to give her a passport at all. She was furious about the Liturgy, and received reports describing the newspaper agitation in her favour which was rapidly developing in England. She wrote queer unbalanced letters to Alderman Wood, the draper, in which she enumerated her grievances, while she gave him various business commissions. He was to find a suitable house for her in London, and arrange about her silks—" them which are in gold should be made into all sorts of collers." With both principals spoiling for a fight the position of Lord Liverpool and Brougham became increasingly difficult. Their common troubles brought them together. Brougham looked upon Wood as a dishonest nuisance, though he modified this opinion later. He wrote to Lord Hutchinson, the Government intermediary, suggesting that the Tories should use their Press to keep him quiet. It is a good example of Brougham's lively but extremely indiscreet correspondence, for Hutchinson was a political opponent.

> " Wood, the ass and alderman whom they call *Thistle*-wood, talks of going to see his son at Paris. But I suspect he means to see the Queen also, for he tried to get my approbation, which I withheld. He has his job to do in making her take Castlehill; and I am clear that Carlton House ought in Monday's newspapers to put in all manner of hints and squibs against him on the score of his having a job to do. This may keep her from listening to so great a blockhead if well done and quickly." [1]

Clearly at this period Brougham was working for a settlement on the basis of the Queen remaining abroad, except possibly for a short visit to settle her private affairs. But Alderman Wood's influence was at least as strong on the other side, and fitted in better with her inclinations. By the end of May she had reached St. Omer with the avowed intention of crossing over to England. She summoned her Attorney-General to meet her there.

A digression is necessary on the subject of the " silk gown." This question of Brougham being made a King's Counsel was to crop up repeatedly during the next seven years, and has injured his reputation historically. The professional and political allegiances of Law officers form a delicate subject. The present generation has seen a succession of political lawyers drift in and out of office, and change their political parties with a careless grace which would have certainly surprised Brougham and his contemporaries. Even if

---

[1] *Life and Administration of Earl of Liverpool*, iii. 51. The allusion in the first line is, of course, to the Cato Street conspiracy with Thistlewood as ringleader. " Having a job to do " apparently then meant making a commission for oneself.

we adopt the more rigorous standards of the later Victorian era, Brougham's conduct, when carefully examined, can be fully justified. Too much attention has been paid to a series of carefully organized attacks made upon him at the time of the Queen's " trial," when a discredited Government used its Press and propagandists to impugn the good faith of the Counsel for the defence. With the object of poisoning the relations between the Queen and her law officers, they strove to create the impression that Brougham was considering his personal interests as against those of his client. It is a painful thought that a hundred years hence the lives of our Lord Chancellors may be illustrated chiefly by extracts from the *Workers' Weekly*. It is to be hoped that they will make as good a showing in the matter of political and professional consistency as does Brougham.

At the end of 1819 neither Denman nor Brougham had been " called within the Bar," though their standing as barristers and Members of Parliament might normally have entitled them to this privilege. Both applied early in the following year, independently of their position as officers of the Queen, but the application was not admitted. They were unpopular with the Crown and with Lord Eldon. As lawyers they had defended sedition cases, as politicians they were " reformers."

Brougham considered the Attorney-Generalship to the Queen as a professional rather than a political appointment. It brought him some distinction, an almost incontestable claim to be called temporarily within the Bar, but very little else. It involved him in much unremunerative work, and ensured the perpetual odium of the King. There was always a chance of some political game developing, but up to May 1820 there was little reason to anticipate a *cause célèbre* in which the Queen would be a principal. Brougham might well have resigned his position at any time before the introduction of the penal Bill. It is known that he seriously

considered doing so. He was merely the adviser of a
client with whom he did not get on too well, and whom
he believed to have committed grave indiscretions. She
found him insufficiently subservient; he was annoyed
by her capriciousness and pretensions to regal
infallibility.

On the first day of the Easter Term Denman and
Brougham were " called within the Bar " by Abbott,
the Lord Chief Justice.[1] Their precedence was given
to them as office-holders, not as barristers, so that they
would revert to the junior Bar, to " the tie-wig and stuff
gown," if the Queen died or they gave up their posts.
Now it is certain that Lord Liverpool, during the preliminary negotiations already described, would have
been glad to see the Queen's affairs in the hands of an
ordinary lawyer rather than those of his doughty political
opponent. He knew that Brougham's relations with his
client were unsatisfactory, and he felt that he might
encourage a tendency to resign by having Brougham
made a King's Counsel, and thus cancel one of the chief
professional attractions of the Attorney-Generalship.
He approached Eldon with this object, but it is probable
that the Chancellor did not consent. There was certainly no evidence of a " bargain " in which Brougham
was in any way involved; nor is being called within
the Bar a political appointment which would have made
an iota of difference to Brougham's political allegiance,
or his freedom, as a politician, to espouse the Queen's
cause. Finally, it is clear that if any offer was made to

---

[1] Lord Campbell, in his entertaining but very unreliable life of
Brougham, liked to introduce his own personal reminiscences.
They are as often as inaccurate as the rest of his work. Thus
he describes " Lord Chief-Justice Ellenborough, who had conducted the ' Delicate Investigation ' in 1806, and who had a great
dislike to Caroline," calling Denman and Brougham within the
Bar, and adds, " I well remember the sarcastic smile with which
this speech was accompanied." It must have been a smile as ghostly
as that of the Cheshire Cat. Lord Ellenborough had been dead for
over a year. *Lives of the Chancellors*, viii. 297.

Brougham it certainly was not accepted. Brougham was not made a King's Counsel for another seven years, shortly after Lord Liverpool's death. The only reason why the matter of the " silk gown " became important was that the Tories, hard pressed at the time of the Bill of Pains and Penalties, wished to stir up trouble between the Queen and her advisers, and to impute personal or political motives to the Counsel for the defence. They mobilized for this purpose the whole of Grub Street from Theodore Hook downwards, or perhaps it would be fairer to say from Theodore Hook upwards, as it would be difficult to imagine anything meaner or more scurrilous than *John Bull* under his editorship. At any rate an army of scribblers, having little else to work upon, concentrated their attack on Brougham as the man

> " who offered to bilk
> For a gown of silk
> The Queen—and the whole Opposition."

Returning to the events of the end of May 1820, the Queen was then at St. Omer, surrounded by a collection of Italian attendants, and with a few unofficial advisers, chief of whom were Alderman Wood and Lady Ann Hamilton. Brougham and Lord Hutchinson set off to meet her. The terms which the Cabinet were prepared to offer made few concessions to the Queen's self-respect. She was to receive an annuity of £50,000, but on condition that she should never come into any part of the British dominions, should take some title other than Queen of England, and should exercise none of the rights and privileges of Queen except the appointment of Law officers. Brougham made it clear, by a series of written answers obtained from Lord Liverpool, that he was in no way a negotiator for the Government, and left himself free to advise the Queen to reject these terms.[1] The only confusion related to the standing of Lord Hutchinson, but if there was any question of

[1] *Life and Administration of Earl of Liverpool*, iii. 59, 60.

modifying terms he was obviously the one person who could speak for the Government.

Some small misadventures, due partly to the Queen's precipitancy, led to further complications. A storm delayed both men, and caused their crossing by the same boat and arriving together. Brougham found the Queen determined to leave for England, and much upset by her disputes with foreign officials. She was inclined to distrust Brougham, who saw at once that in such a mood she would never look at the terms which were the Cabinet's first offer. After an interview with her, on June 3rd, he wrote to Lord Liverpool that he had not " even ventured to hint at the renunciation proposed by your Lordship; indeed I never deemed that at all within the possibility of the case, and I am now certain that the bare mention of the thing would have been followed within five minutes by an order of post-horses to go to Calais." [1] He had, however, to protect himself, and the next day he got Lord Hutchinson to state the terms. The latter seems to have added a further prohibition that any title the Queen might take must not be one belonging to the Royal family. The Queen set out for Calais, as Brougham wrote to Liverpool, " five minutes after she rejected Lord Hutchinson's proposition, which she did the moment it was made." Lord Hutchinson sent a long letter to the Premier with the unwelcome news of her approach. He is inclined to blame Brougham, not for the failure of their mission, but for over-estimating his influence with the Queen. There is no suggestion that Brougham did not do his best to avoid a crisis.

> " I am now to observe to you that in the whole of this negotiation, Mr. Brougham, as far as my judgment enables me to go, does not appear to have possessed the smallest degree of power, weight or

[1] *Life and Administration of Earl of Liverpool, Id.*, Letter from Brougham to Liverpool, June 3, 1820.

authority over the mind of the Queen; he exaggerated to himself, and consequently to others, the
influence which he thought he possessed over her.
To speak to you in confidence, I think that her
violence and determination subdued him, and that
he failed in making the slightest impression upon
her. He may be, and I dare say has been, most
sincere; but as for influence, if it ever did exist,
there certainly was no appearance of it on the present
occasion. I do not know who her counsellors
were. I cannot attribute much to Alderman Wood,
Lady Anne Hamilton, or the Italians who surround
her. I believe she took counsel from her own
rashness, presumption and obstinacy. She appears
to be a woman of most decided and determined
character." [1]

Lord Hutchinson was right. The Queen was " determined." She was a woman of fifty-two, and for twenty-
four years her life had been anomalous and unnatural, a
wife without a husband, a mother separated from her child,
a princess not accepted at Court. She was heartily sick
of trapesing round Europe with her raggle-taggle Court.
It was her last chance of regaining her rights, and then
came this final spur to action—the insulting demand
that she should renounce her position, and the scarcely
veiled accusation that she was cohabiting with her steward.
It is not surprising that she swept lawyers and politicians aside and started for England as if on a crusade.
 Denman, as her Solicitor-General, met her when she
arrived in London, after driving up with her queer caval-
cade from Dover. He has left an account of her reception by the crowd, a remarkable phenomenon, which
was partly a tribute to the work of Cobbett and the
Radicals, but more to the Englishman's sense of fair play.

[1] *Life and Administration of Earl of Liverpool, Id.*, Hutchinson to
Liverpool, June 5, 1820, iii. 72–4.

" Her progress was slow through the countless populace, her travelling equipage mean and miserable; her attendants appeared ill calculated to conciliate good-will in this country. Hardly a well-dressed person was to be seen in the crowd. Two or three men on horseback assumed a rather more respectable appearance; but one of these was my bankrupt cousin John Holloway; another a sheriff's broker well known in courts of justice. I need not relate that the Alderman was seated in the carriage by Her Majesty's side, and Lady Ann Hamilton sat opposite. It was an open barouche of shabby appearance. Six or seven carriages followed; on the box of one was a man with a turban, in another Hieronymo and Carlo Forti, with immense mustachios. The press of people, the cheers, the acclamations, beggared all description." [1]

Brougham, who had slipped discreetly back to London, met his colleague with the remark, " So now we are in for it, Mr. Denman." He was in a very difficult position, having misjudged and to some extent alienated his client. He had been misled, partly by the lawyer's tendency to suspect fornication on all occasions, possible and impossible, but more justifiably by reports he had privately received of the Queen's indiscretions, which included an accusation of connivance at the forging of the Duke of Brunswick's signature on a bill. He would have liked to resign, but he knew that if a Bill of Pains and Penalties was to be introduced, such a step would fatally compromise the Queen. It was the old problem of defending a client believed to be guilty, but it was complicated by political and other considerations. Either that night, or possibly the next day when Lord Castlereagh moved for the appointment of a committee to inquire into the evidence contained in the famous " Green Bag," Brougham made

[1] Arnould: *Life of Denman*, i. 145.

up his mind not to resign. He was to have further difficulties with his client, but there is no reason to doubt the tribute which Denman paid to his devotion to her case from the time of her arrival in England.

"Let me here state, once for all, that from this moment I am sure that Brougham thought of nothing but serving and saving his client. I, who saw him more nearly than any man, can bear witness that from the period in question his whole powers were devoted to her safety and welfare. He felt that the battle must be fought, and resolved to fight it, manfully, and 'to the utterance.'

"Nothing remarkable passed on our return to Her Majesty, except that she suffered Brougham to leave the room first, and detained me some moments with an observation on him. She said, 'He is afraid.' She was certainly right, but his fears were on her account, not on his own." [1]

[1] Arnould: *Life of Denman*, i. 147.

CHAPTER IX

THE QUEEN'S "TRIAL"

At the former village were on one end of a decent white house, these words, "*Queen Caroline; for her Britons mourn,*" and a crown over a I in black. I need not have looked to see: I might have been sure that the owner of the house was a shoemaker, a trade which numbers more men of sense and of public spirit than any other in the Kingdom.   *Rural Rides.*

THE House of Lords obediently passed the motion for appointing a committee to inquire into the accusations against the Queen. The Commons were not so compliant. Brougham at once intervened with a powerful and very dexterous speech, which must have given the Ministers some idea of the resistance they would have to overcome. He demanded a preliminary inquiry into the credentials of the witnesses, accused the Government of prejudging the case by their treatment of the Queen since George III's death, but suggested the possibility of further negotiations. He was supported not only by many Whigs—some of whom like Sir Robert Wilson still hoped to turn out the Government—but also by a number of Tories. Canning came out boldly in the Queen's defence, and the "Saints" showed their disapproval of the whole business. Some of the country gentlemen rose "to implore Lord Castlereagh not to press the matter further; not from any feeling for the unhappy Queen, not from any sense of attachment to the despicable King, but because they thought their property might be compromised by the proceeding."[1] Finally, Wilberforce moved the adjournment, and it was carried by acclamation.

[1] Arnould: *Life of Denman,* i. 148.

The Queen made the next move by a letter to the Premier in which she " commands Mr. Brougham to announce her own readiness to consider any arrangement that can be suggested consistent with her dignity and honour." Lord Liverpool replied, somewhat unfairly, by a reference to the Memorandum of April 15th, which he knew, from Brougham's letter of June 3rd, had never been put before the Queen, though she had heard the general terms from Lord Hutchinson. It was a clever and possibly a justifiable move on the part of the much-harassed Premier. The Queen merely helped him to reopen negotiations when she replied that " the memorandum of April 15th, 1820, which the proposition made through Lord Hutchinson appeared to supersede, has now been submitted to her for the first time." Unfortunately the public had been taught to believe that Brougham acted partly as a negotiator for the Government, and were impressed by propaganda aimed at increasing the breach between him and the Queen. His position was very difficult. On the assumption that he was doing his best for a client whom he believed to have hopelessly compromised herself, Brougham's conduct is unassailable, but Lord Liverpool's action forced him to justify his behaviour at St. Omer before the House of Commons. A full explanation would have seriously weakened his client's case. He was driven to make a rather feeble statement about " strange unaccountable accidents of which no one who was not on the spot could form any idea." As a politician he was exposed on both flanks. The Tories wanted some scapegoat for the intolerable scandal of the Queen's return, while the " Mountain " were prepared to make the Queen's innocence into a party question. Between the two sides the unfortunate Brougham came under the undeserved suspicion of playing a double game, and keeping his client in the dark.

The best justification of Brougham's strategy was that negotiations were again begun, and on much the same

L

basis as at St. Omer, but he was still hampered by his belief in the Queen's guilt.   His relations with his client were further complicated by the refusal of the Whig ladies to call at " the Queen's miserable residence in Portman Street."   Mrs. Brougham herself did not go to pay her respects, the general attitude being explained in a remarkable passage from Denman's narrative.

> " My wife was extremely anxious to call, but I begged her to wait till Mrs. Brougham should do so, *dreading that such scenes of vice and debauchery would be proved as would overwhelm with shame any woman who had formed acquaintance with the criminal.*" [1]

On June 14th, Brougham and Denman, " two meagre lawyers," were " received by Lord Castlereagh in his parlour, after he had entertained a party of foreign ambassadors.   He was covered with diamonds, stars and ribands; the Duke of Wellington was equally splendid." [2] The basis of the negotiations was that " the Queen must not be understood to admit, or the King to retract, anything."   Brougham won a number of concessions— the settled income for her life, her " unimpeachable and unsuspected title," the use of the Royal yacht, etc.—but after five days they could reach no settlement about the Liturgy.   This might seem a minor point, but the Queen, a thwarted, lonely, middle-aged woman, was tasting for the first time the heady mixture of popularity and notoriety.   Every day the excitement was growing more intense, the crowds larger and more clamorous, until even the army was believed to be affected—" the extinguisher was taking fire."

The Queen knew that she would lose this popular support the moment that she agreed to go abroad, or gave way on the question of the Church service, which would be considered as tantamount to a confession of

[1] *Life of Denman*, i. 149.   The italics are Denman's.
[2] *Id.*, i. 153.

guilt. She certainly hesitated on June 19th. Brougham, talking to Greville some years later, said she would have probably accepted the Ministers' terms if she had got her two advisers to recommend this course; " her intention was, if they had, to act on their advice, but to save her popularity by throwing the odium upon them, and devoting them to popular execration." [1] Her Radical friends were undoubtedly afraid of this, and Alderman Wood went so far as to say in a public speech that, if the Queen went abroad he would not vote a shilling for her allowance. The final decision was reached in the drawing-room at Lady Ann Hamilton's house in Portman Street, with a large crowd waiting in the street outside. The two lawyers were sufficiently canny not to give any advice on the main question, and after an angry scene the Queen made up her mind. Amongst the crowd outside the house was Lord Sefton, perhaps the most attractive member of the " Mountain," and to him Brougham signalled the Queen's decision by strolling to the window and stroking his chin. It was the beginning of a great political and forensic struggle. Lord Liverpool promptly decided to introduce a Bill into the House of Lords which, when it passed both Houses, would have degraded and divorced the Queen.

The appearance of the House of Lords when discussing the Bill of Pains and Penalties was familiar to many Victorians from prints of Hayter's famous picture. The attendance of counsel, the examination of witnesses, and the presence of the Queen herself, all helped to give the illusion that the Queen received a legal trial. This is unfair to her and to her counsel. It was only by " courtesy "—or from fear of exasperating public opinion—that some of the ordinary safeguards of a criminal or a divorce case were permitted. The Queen would not normally have been present. This was permitted at her request. Counsel attended for and against the Bill, but the position of the Law officers was

[1] Greville, C. *Journal*, iii. 37.

anomalous. It was not clear why they should have appeared on behalf of what was technically a private Bill. Their duty was confined to proving the truth of statements in the preamble of the Bill about the Queen's general behaviour and her relations with Pergami. Witnesses were called, but the ordinary rules of evidence did not apply, and it was only the legal instincts and intervention of the Lord Chancellor which kept the examination within any bounds. The Queen's counsel were hampered from the start by receiving no list of witnesses, and no specification of the times and places where offences were supposed to have been committed.

Finally, there was neither judge nor jury. Peers could vote on the Bill whether they had heard the evidence or not, and a bare majority would decide the verdict. As it was a Bill of Divorce, as well as Degradation, other considerations would sway their votes besides the facts stated in the preamble. Nor could they claim, even theoretically, to be impartial. The movers of the Bill would vote although they had shown that they had already made up their minds from the evidence in the " Green Bag," accepting the statement of witnesses not on oath, and not subject to cross-examination. Party loyalty would obviously influence votes, for the Bill was moved by the Premier, was supported by the Law officers, and its failure must endanger the Government. In the Lords the party demarcation was not so definite as it might have been if the Bill had reached the House of Commons. The Whig leaders, notably Grey and Holland, were far from friendly to the Queen, and insisted from the first that they would give their votes according to the merits of the case as put before them.[1] But the

---

[1] Cf. Creevey's account of a dinner with Grey on August 25th, who, " in consequence of the day's evidence being unfavourable to the Queen, was a rigid lover of justice : he did not care a damn about the cause : he was come to do his duty, and should act accordingly. Wilson, on the other hand, was perfectly certain the Bill would never pass the House of Lords, and that, if it did, it must take at least two years in the Commons. . . . So much for the chiefs in

THE TRIAL OF QUEEN CAROLINE

Copley.   Majocchi.   Lushington.   The Queen   Earl Grey
                             Denman.   Brougham.   (speaking).
                                       (with paper).

promoters of the Bill and the place-men formed a solid block, which was far more than sufficient to account for the narrow majority which passed the third reading of the Bill before it was withdrawn.

These considerations explain and justify the extra-ordinary truculence of Brougham's methods. He was not arguing a case before an impartial tribunal, he was not humbly pleading a cause, he was fighting the Lords, and the whole corrupt and oligarchical system which they represented. He might hope to win over some peers by discrediting the witnesses, by argument or eloquence, but chiefly he was marshalling public opinion against the Bill and against the King, with a view to fighting the case in the House of Commons, which was more amenable to outside opinion.

There was also a powerful weapon which the defence kept in reserve, as being too dangerous to use except in extremity. Lord Liverpool had been forced by the King to include a clause in the Bill annulling the marriage. Brougham had sufficient evidence of the first marriage with Mrs. Fitzherbert to have forced Parliament to take it into consideration, with all the consequences which might have followed in the excited state of the country. His weak point was his quite legitimate fear of the ministerial evidence, and his doubts as to the Queen's innocence. Everything tended to make attack the best defence, and it was also the policy which suited his own temperament. His attitude was made plain in the preliminary discussion, when the Queen protested against the "mode and manner of the proceedings." He argued that his client would be in a far stronger position if she was "the lowest subject in the realm," and proceeded to elaborate the point in a speech which is worth quoting. It set the tone of the defence, and, in 1820, was a very original way in which to address the Lords.

---

the Whig camp. Thanet and I agreed afterwards as to their insanity." *Creevey Papers*, i. 313.

" God grant that she had never risen to a higher
rank than the humblest individual who owed
allegiance to his Majesty. She would then have
been fenced round by the triple fence whereby the
law of England guards the life and honour of the
poorest female. Before such a Bill could have been
introduced against any other individual, there must
have been a sentence of divorce in the Consistory
Court, there must have been a verdict of a jury
who might have sympathised with her feelings. . . .
There would then have been among her judges none
who were servants of her husband, for her counsel
would have had the right of challenging all such—
none who were hired by him during his pleasure—
none who were placed in a situation to feel gratitude
for the past or expectation for the future favours
which he has it in his power to bestow. She would
have been tried by twelve honest, impartial and
disinterested Englishmen—at whose doors the
influence which may act upon her present judges
might agitate for years without making the slightest
impression either upon the hopes or the fears which
it was calculated to excite."

It is not usually wise to attack the competence or
credentials of a body before whom a case is being laid,
but Brougham was probably right not to flatter the Lords
by treating them as if they were a serious judicial body.
He had an extremely powerful team behind him. Denman, with his obvious probity and weight, was only
hampered by a deficient sense of humour which betrayed
him in his final speech. Dr. Lushington was an advocate
of great experience, Vizard was an attorney full of guile.
Wilde, who as Lord Truro became Chancellor thirty
years later, was specially engaged by the Queen, much to
the annoyance of Brougham and Denman, but in the
end they full recognized his worth, and he probably
eased the difficult relations which continued between the

Queen and her Law officers. Nicholas Tindal and John Williams proved effective at cross-examination, and between them all they were too much for the Government's Law officers; "their sixth man would walk round the counsel for the Bill."

Brougham set himself out to make the Government ridiculous, and to strengthen the general feeling voiced by Lord Grey : "The Ministers ought to be hanged for the situation into which they have brought this unfortunate business, and I am by no means sure that this will not happen before its conclusion." Public disgust grew steadily as the witnesses appeared, drawn from all parts of Europe to give evidence of crumpled beds, soiled linen, or the suggestive gestures of Turkish dancers. As these prurient and often irrelevant details were slowly elicited, translated and often denied under cross-examination, the absurdity of the whole proceeding became overwhelming. Grey, the patrician, was gradually converted in spite of his hatred of the Queen's vulgarity. Towards the end of August he wrote to his wife : "Brougham, I think, is not a good cross-examiner, and indeed it is difficult through an interpreter, but he has damaged the witness Majocchi a good deal. Majocchi answers, nine cases out of ten, 'non mi ricordo,' and often in cases in which, if he had told the truth in the first instance, not to recollect is impossible. It will be a singular event if with such strong presumption of her guilt as can leave little doubt of it, the nature of the evidence should allow the Queen to escape."[1] Brougham continued his attack, fighting on points of procedure with Lord Eldon, who was caught between his professional pride and the intransigeance of the promoters of the Bill. Several of the peers, wearying of these interminable proceedings, insisted on taking part in examining the witnesses, and added to the confusion. "Non mi ricordo" became a catchword throughout the country, and the general

[1] Letter of August 22nd, quoted in Professor Trevelyan's *Lord Grey and the Reform Bill*, p. 195.

impression of the evidence for the Bill is conveyed by
Leigh Hunt's cheerful verses :

> " You swear—you swear—' Oh Signor, si,'
> That through a double door, eh,
> You've seen her *think* adulterously ?
> ' Ver' true, Sir—Si, Signore ! ' "

The Government's Law officers, Sir Robert Gifford
and Sir John Copley, completed their case on September
9th. Brougham had achieved part of his object. He
had dragged the " Old Corruption," the whole eighteenth-
century system of Government, through the mud. He
had made it unlikely that the Commons would submit
to a repetition of the performance in the Lower House.
The Queen's Counsel had shaken the witnesses sufficiently
to ensure that she did not lose her popularity with the
crowd. But Brougham, when he obtained an adjournment for four weeks, knew that he had not won over a
majority of the peers, and that his witnesses could con-
tribute very little, even if they did not—as actually
happened—weaken his case. The Government witnesses might not have proved the Queen's lack of chastity,
but the cumulative effect of their evidence showed her
completely lacking in all sense of decorum, and, in the
opinion of most peers, totally unfitted to be upon the
throne. She had obviously lived on terms of considerable intimacy with Pergami, even if they had not committed adultery. The Lords would undoubtedly have
voted for the Queen's degradation, but many, especially
the Bishops, fought shy about the divorce, either on
general grounds or because they felt it was unjust to
push through a divorce without bringing in the husband
as a party to the case.

Brougham, therefore, left most of the further dissec-
tion of the Government evidence to Lushington and
Williams. His opening speech for the defence, on
October 3rd, was a great oratorical effort in the style of
the period. It was clearly aimed at an audience far

wider than the House of Lords.   It stressed the scurvy
treatment which Caroline had received since she first
landed in the country, and emphasized the political
dangers which threatened the constitution if the Bill was
passed.   Brougham's object was to frighten the waverers
into getting the Bill withdrawn on account of the
obnoxious divorce clause, and in the end he was successful.   He did not actually play his trump card of the
Fitzherbert marriage, but he let his opponents know that
he still had it in reserve.

> " He must also observe, that it was no light
> addition to the anxiety of this feeling to foresee
> that, before these proceedings closed, it might be
> his unexampled lot to act in a way which might
> appear inconsistent with the duty of a good subject
> —to state what might make some call in question
> his loyalty, though that was not what he antici-
> pated from their lordships. . . . The evidence
> against her Majesty, he felt, did not now call upon
> him to utter one whisper against the conduct of her
> illustrious consort, and he solemnly assured their
> lordships that but for that conviction his lips would
> not at that time be closed.   In this discretionary
> exercise of his duty, in postponing the case which he
> possessed, their lordships must know that he was
> waving a right which belonged to him, and abstain-
> ing from the use of materials which were unquestion-
> ably his own. . . . He had before stated to their
> lordships that an advocate, in the discharge of his
> duty, knows but one person in all the world, and
> that person is his client. . . . Separating the duty of
> a patriot from that of an advocate, he must go on
> reckless of consequences, though it should be his
> unhappy fate to involve his country in confusion." [1]

Brougham was much abused for the doctrine contained
in these latter sentences, but most people would now

[1] Nightingale : *Report of the Trial*, ii. 7.

agree that an advocate is entitled, after due notice, to bring forward any relevant facts, and it is for the Court to decide whether these facts are to be heard in public or not. The threat may have been obscure to some of the peers, but not to the King, nor to the Ministers, nor to Lord Grey. A letter from Brougham to John Croker, written a generation later, shows that this was no empty bluff, and explains the general strategy of the Queen's counsel.

" I lose no time in setting you right about a very important point of history, namely, the Fitzherbert marriage. I see you more than half lean to a belief in it, but you may at once change that into an entire belief. I could have proved it in 1820. I had as my witness, H. Errington, Mrs. F.'s uncle, who no doubt would have sheltered himself under the privilege of not committing himself, for he incurred a *præmunire* by being present. Mrs. F. in like manner; and I had a communication from her in great alarm, and I rather think I quieted her with a promise not to call her. . . . It was this and not recrimination to which I alluded mysteriously, and in a way that has been much censured, when I spoke of throwing the country into confusion. Recrimination of adultery was supposed to be the thing threatened. Nothing was more absurd. We had abundant proof of that, but it was of no value; for who ever doubted the adultery? But the other meant a forfeiture of the Crown, or at least a disputed succession, and I am quite confident, from something Hutchinson told me, that George IV was aware of what the real trump was I had in my hand." [1]

The famous peroration, which is said to have made Erskine burst into tears, and which Denman described as " sublime," is equally menacing. Brougham was appeal-

[1] J. W. Croker : *Correspondence and Diaries*, iii. 335.

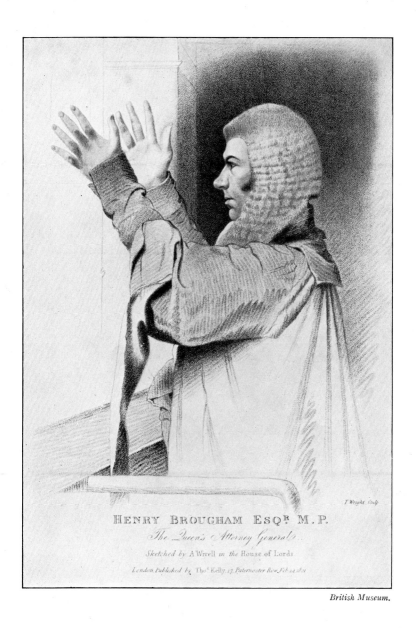

HENRY BROUGHAM ESQ.^R M.P.

The Queen's Attorney General

Sketched by A.Wivell in the House of Lords

London Published by Thos Kelly, 17, Paternoster Row, Feb.24.1821.

T Wright Sculp.

ing, not for the suffrages of his audience, but to the fears of the Ministers and of the King.   It was his instinct to fly high.   He was always a falcon rather than a " mousing owl," and there is a magnificent impertinence about this ending, even though, in the fashion of the times, it tore a passion to tatters.   Behind its balanced periods was the voice of a new and impatient democracy.

" Such, my lords, is the case now before you, and such is the evidence by which it is attempted to be upheld.   It is evidence—inadequate, to prove any proposition;   impotent,   to   deprive   the   lowest subject of any civil right;   ridiculous, to establish the least offence;   scandalous, to support a charge of the highest nature;   monstrous, to ruin the honour of the Queen of England.   What shall I say of it, then, as evidence to support a judicial act of legis-lature, an *ex-post facto* law ?   My lords, I call upon you to pause.   You stand on the brink of a preci-pice.   If your judgment shall go out against your Queen, it will be the only act that ever went out without effecting your purpose; and it will return to you upon your heads.   Save the country—save yourselves.   Rescue the country;   save the people, of whom you are the ornaments;   but severed from whom, you can no more live than the blossom that is severed from the root and tree on which it grows. Save the country, therefore, that you may continue to adorn it—save the Crown which is threatened with irreparable injury—save the aristocracy, which is surrounded with danger—save the altar, which is no longer safe when its kindred throne is shaken. You see that when the Church and the throne would allow of no Church solemnity on behalf of the Queen, the heart-felt prayers of the people rose to Heaven for her protection.   I pray Heaven for her; and I here pour forth my fervent supplications at the throne of mercy, that mercies may descend on

the people of this country richer than their rulers
have deserved, and that your hearts may be turned
to justice." [1]

As the case for the defence proceeded, the atmosphere
grew more like an election and less like a trial.   Witnesses
were cajoled, threatened, or hidden away.   The most
serious accusation of adultery concerned events on the
Syrian journey, when the Queen was supposed to have
spent a night with Pergami in a tent on board a *polacca*.
Apart from two officers, whose evidence on the whole
was compromising, there was only one British seaman on
board.   This man, named Adams, turned up in a man-
of-war, docked at Bristol, shortly after the *Courier* had
delicately suggested that the Queen had had him assassin-
ated.   He immediately offered to give evidence favourable to the Queen, and was promptly spirited away, first
to Portsmouth—whither he was pursued by Alderman
Wood—and then to sea.   Powell, the official organizer
of the prosecution, was less efficient in his management
of Restelli, whom he had treated as a kind of foreman
for the Italian witnesses.   These unfortunates were
growing restive.   They were never allowed out for fear
of the mob, and their families were getting anxious about
them.   Powell allowed Restelli to go back to Italy,
though Counsel for the Bill had given an undertaking
that witnesses would remain in the country.   Brougham
seized his opportunity.   He called Restelli, and elicited
the admission that he had been sent to Milan.

The Whig Lords insisted that the matter should be
investigated, and they finally pinned the responsibility
down to Powell, who was called as a witness.   Brougham
bided his time until he was asked if he wished to examine
this witness.   His first question, if answered, would
have upset the whole convention under which the Bill
was supposed to be a private Bill, and the Law officers
of the Crown to be appearing for an unnamed client.

[1] *Trial*, ii. 80.

" *Who is your client or employer in this case ?* "

Shouts of " Order " prevented any danger of Powell replying, but Brougham was able to get in his protest. It was by far the most truculent of all his interventions, and memorable for a quotation which was much too apt to be politic.   The general line was clear enough.   " My lords, if I knew who the party is against whom I appeared, *non constat* that I may not bring forward a mass of evidence furnished by himself—namely, speeches, declarations, and acts of that opposite party."   But at some period Spencer Perceval, the brilliant erratic son of the murdered Premier, had suggested to Brougham a reference to Satan's arrival at the gates of Hell.   A smaller man would not have dared to use it, a wiser man might have refrained, but Brougham had the fox-terrier's instinct too strongly marked.   Was it a rat or a King behind the arras ?   Nothing would stop him.   " Prove to me who the party is," he went on, " and I will not disturb the professional confidence of his agent.   And who is the party ?   I know nothing about this shrouded, this mysterious being—this retiring phantom—this uncertain shape——

> ' If shape it might be call'd, that shape had none
> Distinguishable in member, joint, or limb—
> Or substance might be call'd—

(and such your lordships will admit)

>   that shadow seem'd,
> For each seem'd either . . . what seemed his head
> The likeness of a Kingly Crown had on.'

Yet under this shape, this ' airy nothing '—and I know not whether it be one, or either, or neither . . ." [1]   The Lord Chancellor soon interposed.   But Brougham had got well under the King's guard.   In those days it was comparatively safe to attack Royalty's morals, but not

---

[1] *Trial*, ii. 463.   The quotation is from *Paradise Lost*, Bk. 11, line 666.   Greville (*Journal*, i. 36–40) was sitting near Brougham, and is the authority for Spencer Perceval's intervention.

their figures. George IV's growing corpulency was almost an obsession with him.[1] He still had another ten years to live, but he never forgave Brougham this thrust, nor Denman a later and far less felicitous reference to Nero.

The Bill dragged on its slow course, passing through the committee stage. Proceedings had become little more than a *Schauspiel* played for the edification of the public, while, behind the scenes, the Ministers were trying to cajole the King and find some way out of a difficult and undignified situation. Long speeches were delivered by peers as well as by counsel, all embellished by quotations from the classics, from Shakespeare, and from Mr. Foote's latest farce. Lord Grey made an oration which did much to establish him as the political leader of the popular party. It was the beginning of that alliance between the aristocratic Whigs and the crowd which was to become so important at the time of the Reform Bill. Grey remarks to his wife that his white beaver hat—the symbol of radicalism—was cheered by a mob which apparently did not recognize him.

Liverpool, who saw his majority weakening and could have small hopes of getting the Bill through the Commons, decided that he must jettison the divorce clause. He managed to get the King's consent, itself evidence of the effectiveness of Brougham's attack, but the affair was mismanaged. Party discipline was not strong, and many peers must have seen the absurdity of passing the " Degradation " without the " Divorce " clause. This would have converted the Bill of Pains and Penalties into what Creevey cheerfully described as a " Bill to declare the Queen a w——, and to settle her upon the King for life, because from his own conduct he

---

[1] " He was more vain of his person and slim figure than of almost anything else; and he said to Lord Donoughmore . . . that he thought everybody allowed, whatever faults he might have, that his legs were not as I described them."—Brougham, *Memoirs*, ii. 412.

is not entitled to a divorce." [1]   The second reading was passed with the Divorce clause still retained, but before the third reading the Bishops attended in greater force, and some of the Lords had begun to lose their nerve. The majority dropped to nine (108 against 99).   Lord Liverpool, in spite of Lord Eldon's objections, took the only possible course in withdrawing the Bill.

It was a great victory for the public, and was celebrated as such.   London and other cities were illuminated, Church bells were rung, and the crowd, as at the time of the Reform Bill, went round the mansions of the great, breaking any windows which did not " show a candle." For Brougham it was a personal triumph.   With Denman and Lushington he was given the freedom of the City of London.   All over the country, the " Brougham's Head " swung over the doors of inns and beer-shops as a challenge to the old order of society.   Yet the position was full of danger.   Brougham received the credit, but also bore the responsibility, of having led a successful attack upon the King and the whole system of Government.   The visible result of his efforts was the Queen attending a great Thanksgiving Service at St. Paul's, escorted by an immense crowd with banners bearing such titles as " The Queen's Guards are her People."   But no one knew better than Brougham the weakness of the human material upon which he had to depend.

Caroline never had much sense, and after this success she was less amenable to advice than ever.   There was truth in Lord Holland's description of her.   " She was at best a very sorry and uninteresting heroine.   She had, they say, some talent, some pleasantry, some good-humour, and great spirit and courage.   But she was utterly destitute of all female delicacy, and exhibited, in the whole course of the transactions relating to herself, very little feeling for anybody, and very little regard for honour or truth, or even for the interests of those who were devoted to her, whether the people in the aggregate

[1] *Creevey Papers*, i. 315.

or the individuals who enthusiastically espoused her
cause." [1]   Like so many of the great, she could never
understand that she was only the symbol of a cause about
which she knew little, and that the cheering crowds
were a testimony to the work of her lieutenants rather
than to her personal merits.   There was bound to be some
reaction, but the Queen made it impossible for Brougham
or her other supporters to prevent the last few months of
her life being a miserable tragedy.

No woman ever needed to walk with greater circum-
spection.   Her position was almost without precedent,
and she had against her the King and his principal
Ministers, who soon showed that they were not squeamish
in the weapons they chose.   This was sufficiently evident
when, within a month of the end of the trial, a new
publication appeared, called *John Bull*.   The Tories
already had a subsidized paper, the *Courier*.   This had
poured out a commentary on the trial which was remarkable for its venom and lack of scruples, but *John Bull*
exceeded anything known at the time.   Its aim was to
prevent anyone in society from calling on the Queen.
Denman described it as the " climax and consummation
of all villainy."   Creevey wrote that " its personal
scurrility exceeds by miles anything ever written before.
In accounting for the motives which have influenced the
different ladies who have called upon the Queen, it states
yesterday, without equivocation, reserve, or any in-
nuendo, but plainly, that Lady T—— and Lady M——
B—— were induced to go by threats respecting the
criminal intercourse that took place between Lady
C—— W—— and a menial servant." [2]   Poor Mrs.
Brougham, as already mentioned, was drawn into the
business, being attacked for her " seven-months child "
in company with the far more vulnerable Lady Jersey
and Lady Ossulston, " a foreigner married to a weak
little lord." [3]

[1] Lord Holland : *Memoirs of the Whig Party*, ii. 120.
[2] *Creevey Papers*, ii. 2.   [3] Lady Granville : *Letters*, i. 202.

Brougham did his best to provide the Queen with an ultra-respectable household. He negotiated with the Duke of Roxburgh to act as Grand Chamberlain, " a young nobleman of eighty-six, so that the breath of scandal can never touch him." Money was a serious problem, for the Queen was completely feckless. Characteristically, when the Bill was withdrawn, she had offered her Counsel a large sum of money, which of course they refused, but she then forgot to pay them their fees and expenses, which were ultimately settled by the Treasury. Brougham saw that the Queen would weaken her case by asking the Government for an allowance. He attempted to raise a fund inside the Whig Party, but those who had been keenest supporters of the Queen were not the type likely to put up large sums of money. A meeting was held at Brooks's in February, " very thinly attended, and things looked damned ill and black." [1] But the Queen settled matters by writing to Lord Liverpool asking for an income. The Government gave her the full £50,000 a year, and the Queen began living in her old undignified manner, filling her house with a casual and often ostentatious company, attending theatres where she received a mixed reception, and generally behaving in a way best fitted to spoil her popularity.

During the last five months of her life, Brougham continued to act for the Queen on all legal matters. He defended before the Privy Council her claim to be crowned, " with the King, on the same day, and at the same place," but he had a weak case, for many Queens were never crowned. No more successful was his attempt to get her name in the Prayer Book. Brougham also fulfilled an old promise by testifying, from his place in the House of Commons, to his personal belief in her innocence, though it might be argued that his speech, when carefully examined, only shows that he believed the case " not proven." Apart from these professional activities he seems to have had little personal influence

[1] *Creevey Papers*, ii. 15.

M

over the headstrong lady at Brandenburgh House.   He
certainly cannot be blamed for the lamentable fiasco
when the Queen tried to force her way into the Abbey
at the time of the King's coronation.   The most that
can be said is that he did not join Dr. Parr and others in
urging her not to go, possibly because he suspected that
opposition would only confirm her determination.

The affair was completely mismanaged, and the crowd
hostile.   The Queen made herself ridiculous.   As
Brougham wrote to Creevey, she " lost incalculably by
getting out of her carriage and tramping about ; going,
and being refused, and damaging the Coronation was all
very well, but the way of doing it was bad." [1]   He had
some idea of encouraging her to make a tour in Scotland,
passing through the industrial areas and Birmingham—
" where the King refused to go "—but it is doubtful if
the Queen would have consented, or whether it would
have been a success.   She settled matters by falling ill,
and after undergoing medical treatment of the most
appalling nature the poor creature died.   She faced
death with the courage which was her redeeming virtue.
Viscount Hood, who had been appointed Chamberlain
in place of the octogenarian Duke, wrote to Brougham
that " she died in peace with all her enemies. *Je ne
mourrai sans douleur, mais je mourrai sans regret*—was
frequently expressed by her Majesty." [2]

Her death revived some of her old popularity.   There
were wild scenes as the coffin was taken down to Harwich
to be shipped to Brunswick.   The funeral procession
was not allowed through the City.   Brougham, travelling
down to Harwich with Sir Robert Wilson, could hear
the Life Guards firing on the crowd, some of the bullets
hitting his coach.   The circumstances of her death and
burial were a fitting climax to her life.   While the coffin,
bearing the inscription " Caroline of Brunswick, the
injured Queen of England," was being lowered into a

---

[1] Brougham to Creevey, July 26, 1821.   *Id.*, ii. 20.
[2] Viscount Hood to Brougham, Aug. 8, 1821.   *Id.*, ii. 21.

German grave, the King was arriving in Ireland, and declaring it was the happiest day of his life. No one was in mourning, and the King, in a state of tipsy benevolence, seems to have won the hearts of the Irish, who "clawed and pawed him all over, and called him his Ethereal Majesty."

> " Ere the daughter of Brunswick is cold in her grave,
> And her ashes still float to their home o'er the tide,
> Lo ! George the triumphant speeds over the wave,
> To the long-cherish'd isle which he loved like his—bride."

So ended the most squalid chapter in English history. Two legal cases arose out of these events. From these Brougham may have derived some minor satisfaction. Both arose from the virulent Toryism of the established Church. The Reverend Richard Blacow, a clergyman of no great standing, thought fit to deliver himself of a sermon on the Queen's Thanksgiving Service. *Inter alia et enormia* was the following sentence, which seems worth rescuing from obscurity.

> " After compassing sea and land with her guilty paramour to gratify to the full her impure desires, and even polluting the Holy Sepulchre itself with her presence—to which she was carried in mock majesty astride upon an ass—she returned to this hallowed soil so hardened in sin, so bronzed in infamy, so callous to every feeling of decency or shame, as to go on Sunday last, clothed in the mantle of adultery, to kneel down at the altar of that God who is ' of purer eyes than to behold iniquity ' when she ought rather to have stood barefooted in the aisle, covered with a shirt as white as unsunned snow, doing penance for her sins."

The case came up for hearing after the Queen's death, but Brougham, who had now reverted to a stuff gown, conducted the prosecution, and Blacow was sentenced to three months' imprisonment. Compared with the savage penalties meted out to those who attacked the

King or the Government, this was a sentence so mild as to suggest considerable judicial partiality, but it served as a valuable precedent in future cases of criminal libel. It thus helped to discourage those political prosecutions which Sir Vicary Gibbs had made iniquitous.

The other case was more important. The *Durham Chronicle* had criticized the clergy of that city because " no single bell had announced the departure of the magnanimous spirit of the most injured of Queens," and suggested that " such conduct renders the very name of our established clergy odious till it stinks in the nostrils." Amongst the clergy in that city was the future Bishop Phillpotts of Exeter, who was to become famous, ten years later, as the most violent of Tories, and a leading opponent of Catholic Emancipation and the Reform Bill. He instituted the prosecution of Williams, the proprietor of the newspaper, for libelling the clergy of Durham. At the same time, as if to show that the Church was itself above the law, he issued a pamphlet in which he described Williams as " a miserable mercenary, who eats the bread of prostitution and panders to the low appetites of those who cannot, or who dare not, cater for their own malignity." It was a case after Brougham's own heart. He loved to do battle with the Church Tory and Militant. Campbell tells a story of a colleague who met him pacing up and down by the river bank. " Brougham suddenly turned round, held up both hands, and exclaimed in a hollow voice, ' Avaunt ! Depart ! I am distilling venom for the Durham clergy ! ' " [1]

He certainly distilled a very potent brew. Only a man of the most extraordinarily wide and varied erudition could have unearthed the Elizabethan Bishop, who had said of the Durham clergy that " they do stink in the nose of God and His people." There was no nonsense about defence, no pleading for mercy. Freed from the comparative restraint of two months before the House of Lords, Brougham set himself to castigate the whole

[1] Campbell : *Lives of the Chancellors*, viii. 332.

hierarchy of the Church. The result was a magnificent example of sustained invective, worthy of comparison with a sermon by John Knox or the satire of Swift. He affected to lament the unhappy state of Scotland, across the border, " sitting in outer darkness," but managing to survive and educate its children, though " without a mitre or a minor canon," and although " they support no cathedrals, maintain no pluralists, suffer no non-residence; nay, the poor benighted creatures are ignorant even of tithes." Having finished with these episcopal shepherds, " whose operations are so constant that the flock actually live under the knife," he turned to the lesser fry, " the watchful and eager animals that attend them (some of them too with a cross of the fox, or even the wolf, in their breed)." Finally, Brougham cast his eye upon Dr. Phillpotts, who had unwisely ensconced himself upon the Bench, near the Judge. He began by a few remarks about the insect which, " brought into life by corruption, and nestled in filth, though its flight be lowly and its sting puny, can swarm and buzz, and irritate the skin, and offend the nostril." He then proceeded to deal with " these reverend slanderers—these pious backbiters "; " the much venerated personages whose harmless and unprotected state is now deplored, have been the wholesale dealers in calumny," and continued with an obvious reference to the Phillpotts pamphlet.[1]

It was only the strongest pressure from the Bench which prevented this Philippic gaining a verdict of not guilty, but Brougham gained the ultimate victory. A rule was granted to show cause why judgment should not be arrested, and finally the prosecution was dropped.

[1] The speech is printed in Brougham's *Speeches*, i. 333.

CHAPTER X

We may therefore visit on the laches of this ministry (that of Lord Liverpool after the introduction of Canning) the introduction of that new principle and power into our constitution which ultimately may absorb all, AGITATION. The cabinet, then, with so much brilliancy on its surface, is the real parent of the Roman Catholic Association, the Political Union, the Anti-Corn Law League. DISRAELI : *Coningsby*.

THE unhappy events of the Queen's persecution and death profoundly altered Brougham's life. Professionally his position was much strengthened. Attorneys flocked to call upon the man who had fought these great forensic battles. Although for another seven years he was forced to remain a member of the junior Bar, he was assured of a large income, and all the work which he needed. He was never a great " case-winning barrister." His contemporaries say that he " lacked *nisi prius* tact," but for the next ten years he shared the leadership of the Northern Circuit, first with Scarlett and then with Pollock. His success proved a considerable embarrassment to his circuit. Being retained to lead in so many cases, he put out of employment a number of men senior to him in date of call, though perhaps younger in age. Within a few years there was only one King's Counsel on this circuit, but Eldon remained immovable on this point.

Campbell considered that the Lord Chancellor was playing a double game. He quotes a letter which Eldon wrote to his daughter in 1825. After referring to some attacks made upon him by Brougham in the Commons, the Chancellor remarks, " No young lady was ever so unforgiving for being refused a silk gown, when silk gowns adorned the female forms, as Brougham is with me, because, having insulted my master, the insulted don't like to clothe him with distinction, and honour, and silk." On this Campbell comments as follows :— " Notwithstanding such language, the consummate hypocrite, who tried to deceive his own daughter and himself, was in the habit of sending messages to Brougham, lamenting that no impression could be made upon the King's prejudices." [1] Whatever may have been the truth, the deprivation did not prevent Brougham, or his fellow-sufferer Denman, from making plenty of money at the Bar from 1820 onwards. A year or two later Brougham was reported by Lord Thanet to be " bidding £15,000 for two farms in Westmorland." [2]

In the political arena, where Brougham's chief interests always lay, his standing had not been improved by these happenings. All through the negotiations and the " trial " he had been placed, as a politician, in an equivocal position. His opposing Attorney-General, Gifford, was acting for the King and for the Tories. Brougham was acting for the Queen only, but a portion of the Whigs wanted him to pull the chestnuts out of the fire for them. Both Parties were displeased with the course of events. The Tories felt that they had lost caste, the Whigs had a vague idea that the Government ought to have been forced out of office. Both sides attacked Brougham, the most prominent person in the case. Most of their criticisms cancel each other out. Campbell, a typical careerist, and then, in 1821, a rising young Whig lawyer, quoted with approval Castlereagh's remark about Brougham's " plan to keep the King and Queen both open." Yet this amounted to no more than that Brougham had not wanted Caroline to come back to England, and during the preliminary negotiations was on friendly terms with responsible Ministers. Once

---

[1] Campbell : *Lives of the Chancellors*, viii. 347.
[2] Thanet to Creevey. *Creevey Papers*, ii. 51.

the Bill had been introduced, Brougham deliberately and irretrievably ruined himself with the King. Scarlett, another rival Whig lawyer, thought that Brougham could have easily saved the Queen, and incidentally brought in the Whigs. The "Mountain," if we may take Creevey as typical, thought Brougham was cowardly for not exploiting the Queen's case after the withdrawal of the Bill. "If you had heard him trying to humbug me about the transitory nature of this popular ferment, comparing it to the Duke of York's case and Mrs. Clarke, you would have snorted in his face." [1] But within a month there was a popular reaction, which thoroughly justified the caution not only of Brougham, but of the older Whig leaders.

A possible change in the Government was, as always, the chief preoccupation of the Opposition, but the first years of George IV's reign only emphasized the weakness of the Whigs. Their long period out of office, their divisions and lack of any definite political principles, had not encouraged the younger men to join them. There was little left of the Party except some of the old families—this element being sadly weakened by the defection of the Grenvillites—together with a few lawyers and "professionals" with little influence, and intensely jealous of each other. A change could only come from a split in the Tory ranks, due to the breaking away of the younger men—probably under Canning— from the old leaders, the "Mumpsimus" gang—Eldon, Castlereagh, Sidmouth, etc. This possibility seemed less remote when Canning adopted a line of his own about the Queen's affair. There were certainly conversations, in 1820, about the formation of a moderate Tory admin- istration with Whig backing, but they never went very far. The country gentlemen rallied round the Govern- ment; and the Queen by the beginning of the following year was becoming a political liability rather than an asset. In January the Commons defeated, by a majority

[1] *Creevey Papers*, ii. 2.

of over 300, a Whig resolution that the Queen's name should be included in the Liturgy. Some of Canning's associates in the Lords voted against the third reading of the Bill of Pains and Penalties, but none felt it necessary to follow his example and resign. The old gang had been badly shaken, but were not defeated, and Canning made up his mind to accept the Governor-Generalship of India, which then, as now, was considered amongst politicians to be almost a " dead end."

Conscious of the King's enmity, and consequently of his own ineligibility for any political office, Brougham seems to have reverted to his old method of working for reforms as a free-lance, and depending on support outside Parliament. His Education Bill came up for its second reading during the excitement of the Queen's affair.[1] The story of Brougham being discovered redrafting its clauses during an interval in the " trial " must be considered apocryphal, but it is evidence of the manner in which his name was identified with the cause of education, and of his own concentration upon the subject. The general ferment may have helped towards the defeat of the Bill in the committee stage, but so long as the " Mumpsimus " group were at the head of affairs it was a thankless task being a reformer, and except for a speech on the state of the country, which roused the anger of Ricardo, he took little part in politics during the twelve months following the Queen's death. Then occurred an event which had a profound effect on English, and possibly on Indian, history.

Castlereagh's suicide completed the work of disintegration amongst the old-fashioned Tories, which had been begun by Peterloo and the Queen's " trial." At first its full significance was not appreciated either by Canning or Brougham. The two happened to meet at a circuit dinner in the following week. " I had a good deal of talk with him about Castlereagh," wrote

[1] See above, Chapter VI. Brougham's speech on the second reading of the Bill was on June 28, 1820.

Brougham, "and he spoke very properly. Neither of
us canted about the matter, but he showed the right
degree of feeling. I don't think he is going to be sent
for, and am pretty sure he will go to India." [1]   A fortnight later Canning was writing to Huskisson that he
had heard nothing, but finally Lord Liverpool persuaded
the King that his Ministry needed a broader basis.
Canning went to the Foreign Office, and became Leader
of the House of Commons. The colourless Lord
Amherst succeeded the Marquess of Hastings in Calcutta,
at a time when a man of Canning's weight and liberal
ideas would have had an immense influence on the future
of India.

The older Whigs cannot have liked this new development. Grey had a strong personal antipathy to Canning,
dating from the days of Fox, and would never have
agreed to form a coalition with him except under great
pressure. He must have now foreseen that Canning
would either liberalize the Government, in which case
the Whigs would be in danger of losing their identity
and their *raison d'être*, or else that the Tories would split
—the ultras against the moderates—and then the King
might be forced to call in Grey to form a Ministry.
The latter prospect aroused Grey to unusual activity,
for he had no wish to be head of a central Party containing Canning. He must, therefore, have someone in
reserve who would be capable of dealing with the great
orator. In those days a Party did not require a large
number of speakers. Debates were more like those
Homeric encounters in which the leaders fought their
duels, but the struggles of the lesser fry were of little
importance. These could talk during the dinner hour,

---

[1] Brougham to Creevey, Aug. 21, 1820. *Creevey Papers*, ii. 45.
Canning and Brougham must have accepted their invitations to
dinner before Castlereagh's suicide, when there was no suggestion
of Canning not going to India. Yet Sir Walter Scott seems to
have suspected that Canning had arranged a meeting " to quicken
movements elsewhere." Scott : *Familiar Letters*, ii. 150.

to the accompaniment of loud conversation and occasional animal noises, but convention demanded that two long set speeches should be made before a vote was taken. Grey knew that Brougham was the only man on the Whig benches of the House of Commons, who would be a worthy opponent to Canning.

" The possible event (as it certainly is) of, either now or some months hence, a negotiation being begun " led to a correspondence between Brougham and Grey, in which a future Whig Ministry is discussed with considerable frankness. In a letter of September 5, 1822, Brougham again suggested the need for a Whig " programme " in which he puts the " Catholic question, Irish tithes, and putting down that vile Orange junta " as the first essentials. After sketching the outlines of a foreign policy, he advocates certain domestic reforms —the remission of taxes, repealing the Press laws, stopping prosecutions for libel, revising the criminal law, abolition of flogging, etc. The omission of parliamentary reform shows that it was intended as an emergency policy which all Whigs, and some Tories, might support. As regards personnel, he recommends the omission of Denman, as well as himself, both being hopelessly compromised with the King.

Grey replied immediately, making it clear that if a Whig Administration should ever come into existence, the " management of the House of Commons " would be in Brougham's hands. He was not afraid of Brougham going over to the Tories, but of his accepting one of those absurdly over-paid legal appointments with which it was customary to silence formidable opponents who had some distinction as lawyers. Eight years later Grey attempted, unsuccessfully, to quiet Lord Lyndhurst in this way. Some tentative offers of this kind had already been made to Brougham since the affair of the Queen's trial. The temptation to accept was considerable, for up to that time " professionals " were hardly ever admitted to administrative posts in the Cabinet. The

Tories had relaxed that rule a little, but never the Whigs. Grey now made it clear that he could not form a Whig Administration without Brougham in office.

> " After thinking much upon the subject, I am satisfied that the lead there must *really and effectively*, if not nominally, be in your hands; and this it can only be by your being a member of the Government. I should be the last person to advise you to give up the splendid and, what is more, the certain advantages which you must command in your profession. No advantage to a new Government could justify me in urging such a sacrifice. But it is not necessary. Lord Mansfield, Thurlow and Wedderburn were all in succession the chief supports of the Administration with which they were connected. But in office you must be, or the Government, I am persuaded, could not go on. Nobody disapproves more than I do—though I am not sure I may not at times have fallen into the same error myself—the language of those who talk of the impossibility of forming an Administration in the House of Commons." [1]

These proposals were to remain entirely hypothetical. Events turned out as badly as possible for the Whigs. Canning took over the Foreign Office and the leadership of the Commons without any serious split in the Party. He did not get rid of the " old gang "—Eldon, Bathurst and Westmorland retained their posts—but Sidmouth had already given way to Peel at the Home Office, Robinson succeeded Vansittart at the Treasury, and Huskisson took the Board of Trade. This meant that the reformist element had the four key positions in the Cabinet, and during the course of the next five years they achieved a minor revolution in English political life. The old Tories' bark was worse than their bite. They

[1] This important correspondence is given in Brougham's *Memoirs*, ii. 440-58.

might protest and intrigue, but they would not break up the Government. The old guard dies but never resigns, and Lord Liverpool managed to keep his mixed team together. From 1822 onwards the Administration was so superior to its predecessors that the Whigs found their occupation gone. They suffered the common fate of all " left wing " movements. Having partially converted the country to their views, they had to watch their opponents putting some of their ideas into practice and the men, who had fought them most strenuously and derided their proposals, remaining quietly in office.

Peel, at the Home Office, may have been, in Disraeli's phrase, " a burglar of other men's ideas," but ideas are common property. He was certainly an adept at talking Tory and acting Whig. The whole system of repression, connected with the names of Castlereagh and Sidmouth, was quietly dropped. With it went the iniquitous use of police spies, like the notorious Oliver. Sir James Mackintosh's long struggles to reform the criminal law at last bore some fruit, and over a hundred capital offences were abolished. Pitt's Combination Acts were repealed in 1825, and for a time Trade Unions were allowed a remarkable freedom, which was subsequently curtailed. The Government also repealed the laws against the emigration of artisans. The formation of a properly organized police force came after this period, and was at first considered a reactionary step, but it was really part of this eminently Liberal term of office.

Huskisson, who shared with Peel the credit of relieving the Trade Unions, initiated a series of reforms which were very much along the lines suggested by Brougham in his earlier speeches. Huskisson was an empirical free trader, encouraging the flow of foreign trade by simplifying the tariff, substituting moderate for prohibitive duties, but not opening the ports to uncontrolled dumping. He amended the Corn Laws, introduced the principle of the sliding scale, and modified the Navigation Laws, which contained a number of obsolete provisions dating back to our naval struggles with the Dutch. Robinson, as Chancellor of the Exchequer, followed the inefficient Vansittart, and was chiefly occupied in restoring some order to the national finances, but he worked loyally with Huskisson. It is more doubtful how far Canning was an innovator in his department. Recent investigations suggest that Castlereagh's foreign policy was more liberal, though his repression at home was even less defensible, than was commonly supposed. But Canning was more open in his dislike of the Holy Alliance, in his objection to interfering with Governments because of their " Liberal " tendencies, and in his encouragement of the new Governments of South America. It was a movement in the direction towards which the Whigs had been pressing, and left them with no alternative policy.

Brougham's speeches on Canning's Spanish policy, in the spring of 1823, were great oratorical efforts, but did little more than support the Government policy in less diplomatic language than could be used by the Foreign Minister. During the next two or three years there was another reason why many Whigs were on Canning's side. George IV had begun, about 1824, to intrigue against his Foreign Minister. This was the time of the famous " Cottage Coterie," to which Count Esterhazy had access. In this intrigue Lord Liverpool loyally backed up his Minister, but the Duke of Wellington was on the King's side, and appears to have informed Esterhazy about the Cuba guarantee. Canning stuck to his guns, and won—partly by the simple expedient of appointing Lady Conyngham's son to a post in the Foreign Office.[1] This squalid story, in which mistresses and diplomats are inextricably mixed, is important because it explains why Lansdowne and Brougham felt they were fighting the King's undue influence when they

[1] H. W. V. Temperley : " *Canning, Wellington and George IV*," *Eng. Hist. Review*, April 1923.

were supporting Canning, and why Wellington was always so bitterly antagonistic to Canning.

The Radicals were delighted at this change. They had always suspected, with some reason, the sincerity of the Whigs as reformers, or the likelihood of their achieving anything in office. They now saw a Tory Government actually passing reforms and setting up new standards for the Opposition. As Francis Place put it, " the more the present Ministers do, the more must be done by any set of men who may succeed them." They were content, therefore, to apply an occasional spur, but they had no desire to replace the Liverpool–Canning Government, and were only afraid that it would break up of itself in a year or two.

The Whigs, as a Party, were frankly unhappy, though they may have personally appreciated some of the changes which were taking place. They found themselves despised by the Radicals, their reformist thunder had been stolen by the Tories, and Lord Grey, their nominal leader, was still obsessed by his old personal feud against Canning, who, on most questions, was at least as advanced and as liberal-minded. The only distinctive Whig policies which remained to them were full of difficulties and dangers. There was the old question of parliamentary reform. On this there was little agreement inside the Party, only a few sharing Lord John Russell's enthusiasm. More urgent was Catholic emancipation, which was Canning's most vulnerable spot. But it was a dangerous subject, being one of the few about which the politicians were, as a whole, in advance of public opinion. Brougham would have emphasized the importance of his special interests —elementary education and the abolition of slavery—but members of the House of Commons would not accept these as major questions.

The difficulties in which the Whigs found themselves account for the comparative ineffectiveness of Brougham as a parliamentarian during the early " twenties." The natural Party tactics were to drive in a wedge between the reformist element amongst the Tories and the reactionaries. He wrote to Lansdowne, towards the end of 1822, suggesting that their policy was "to increase (Canning's) differences with his colleagues, and not to commit ourselves on our points of difference with him. My solution is abstinence from needless attack for a while."[1] But even this method had its dangers. Owing to Grey's attitude towards Canning its effect might be to split their own Party, and to some extent this occurred. Grey, after 1825, withdrew himself from active politics, and a Whig group, led by Brougham and Lansdowne, gave a limited support to Canning, attacked Eldon, and pressed for Catholic emancipation. The remaining Whigs, who followed Grey in unrelenting opposition to Canning, became known later as the "Malignants." Creevey belonged to this small minority, a fact which discounts many of his attacks on Brougham, whom he begins to describe as the Arch-fiend, Wicked-shifts, or Beelzebub.

Brougham's line of action was probably best for the country, and in the long run for the Party, as the Whigs were obviously incapable of providing an alternate Government. Lord Liverpool was in poor health, and his resignation would either mean the return of " Eldon and Co.," or a central Government under Canning. The former would have been a tragedy, to be avoided at all costs, but " non-factious " opposition was not the type of parliamentary work for which Brougham was suited. He made some good speeches on foreign questions, he exposed the scandals of " planter " rule in the West Indies, but Russell noted, towards the end of Canning's term as Foreign Secretary, that "Brougham is not so brilliant as usual, very moderate and conciliatory. But a man who pounces and claws like an eagle cannot coo like a dove."[2]

[1] Brougham to Lansdowne, Dec. 18, 1822. Lansdowne MS., quoted in Dr. Aspinall's *Lord Brougham and the Whig Party*, p. 130.
[2] *Early Correspondence of Lord J. Russell*, i. 246.

This restraint, combined with the bitter feelings roused by the Catholic question, led to a curious and unhappy personal quarrel between Brougham and Canning, in which the former stigmatized Canning's acceptance of office without guarantees about emancipation as " the most incredible specimen of monstrous truckling, for the purpose of obtaining office, that the whole history of political tergiversation could furnish." Canning took this oratorical extravaganza with unnecessary seriousness, and shouted " It is FALSE." According to the curious conventions of the time, Canning's rejoinder necessitated a duel. The most extraordinary insults and innuendoes often passed unnoticed, but " the lie direct " meant a duel, just as in the army two privates will bandy epithets of the most lurid nature, but a hint of illegitimacy entails a fight. At that time political duels were usually circumvented by placing the principals under preventive arrest, especially when the dispute occurred in the House. Sir Robert Wilson prevented the incarceration of the two leaders by suggesting that the offending words had been used in a " parliamentary " sense, and Brougham made a withdrawal along these lines. Campbell has suggested that this inspired the incident of the quarrel between Pickwick and Blotton, but Dickens was only twelve at the time, and it was another ten years before he became a Parliamentary reporter. These scenes were not uncommon in the last years of duelling, and this particular quarrel was chiefly interesting because it added to the legend about Brougham's refusal to resent an insult. " The easy lubricity," wrote Bulwer Lytton about this time, " with which our gentlemen glide out of a duel is an understood thing with us; and neither party considers it a disgrace to the other." [1]

---

[1] *England and the English*, Chap. IV. Lytton coined the word " epeaphogy " or word-swallowing to describe the shifts by which duels were habitually avoided during these last years before the custom was abolished.

N

In this connection it may be worth mentioning two other incidents which occurred during this period. In 1824 Brougham was attacked in the House of Commons by a man called Gourlay, who was detained for a period as insane. Campbell, with even more than his usual malignity, suggests that this was only a subterfuge, and that Gourlay was quite normal.[1] What evidence survives is sufficient to show that Gourlay was a completely unbalanced person. After losing an estate in England, he went to Canada, ran foul of the authorities, and was imprisoned. He returned home full of grievances, to plague the life of every Radical who would listen to him. Cobbett was no friend to Brougham, but sympathised with him on this point, describing Gourlay as " one of the most malignant devils that I ever knew anything of in my life." [2] An equally wanton attack came from a fellow known as " Dandy " Raikes, who was put up, probably by some members of the Lowther family, to insult Brougham in Brooks's Club. Creevey gives a long but not very conclusive account of this affair, which occurred immediately after Lord Liverpool's retirement, and was perhaps connected with it. It would seem that Brougham sent a challenge through Wilson, but Spring Rice (afterwards Lord Monteagle) intervened, and Brougham was arrested and bound over. His conduct seems to have satisfied his fellow-members of the club.[3]

The comparative quiescence of party politics allowed Brougham sufficient leisure to give more time to his two favourite subjects, the abolition of slavery and popular education. He put in much spade-work, which was to bear fruit after the Reform Act. The first brought him back into the company of the " Saints," amongst whom Zachary Macaulay was his closest ally. The young " Tom " Macaulay's first speech was made at an anti-

---

[1] Campbell : *Lives of the Chancellors*, viii. 343.
[2] *Rural Rides*, G. D. H. Cole's edition, ii. 385.
[3] *Creevey Papers*, ii. 106–9.

slavery meeting in London, when "Orator" Hunt got up to call attention to the worse state of people at home, and Brougham had to deal with this awkward interruption.

A rising in Demerara provided Brougham with a concrete example of "planters' rule." A missionary, the Reverend John Smith, was accused of "misprision" in having encouraged the negroes to revolt. His chief offence seems to have been that he "taught the slaves the religion of peace, and consoled them for the cruel lot inflicted by the crimes of this world with the hopes of mercy in the next." He was tried, found guilty, and sentenced, quite illegally, to death. He died before the sentence was carried out. Brougham collected evidence with his usual energy. "Many thanks for your supplies of stories," he wrote to Zachary Macaulay, "but I want other description of ammunition—in reference to official or other authentic accounts of the Insurrection. If you cannot, let me have the accounts themselves—also accounts in newspapers of the trial of the negroes, and especially of Jacky, into whose mouth they evidently put a confession."[1]

When his case was complete, Brougham brought a motion before the House of Commons. On the first occasion the House was counted out, the appearance of a balloon over Westminster assisting the efforts of the West India faction to kill the discussion. On June 1, 1824, Brougham brought forward his motion again in a very powerful speech. The Government was severely shaken, for the case was almost indefensible. Canning made a "heathenly and planterly and almost slave-trading speech" with curious references to the early Christian martyrs. After an adjourned debate the motion was defeated by 193 to 146, but the unfortunate John Smith did not die in vain, for the scandal of this case did more for negro emancipation than any other exposure of planters' methods.

[1] *Life and Letters of Zachary Macaulay*, p. 418.

Amongst the majority were three prominent members of the next Whig Government—Lord Palmerston, William Lamb and Charles Grant, the future Lords Melbourne and Glenelg. As Brougham commented bitterly in his preface to his speeches, written after the break up of the Whigs in 1835, they thus gave " to the country an early pledge of those principles so hostile to colonial liberty, on which they have since acted." [1] To Brougham such questions as these were the essence of the Liberal Party which he was trying to build up, and some of these early votes by future Whig leaders must be remembered in connection with the events which led ultimately to Brougham being ousted from the Cabinet.

The question of popular education, even more than that of emancipation, marked out Brougham, and the few who thought with him, from the bulk of the governing classes. In order to emphasize the difficulty of his position and the novelty of his ideas it may be worth recalling the famous passage which, twenty years later, Disraeli was to introduce into his *Sybil*. Such a public avowal of a dangerous truth was even then considered very bold. England, said Stephen Morley, was " two nations; between whom there is no intercourse and no sympathy; who are as ignorant of each other's habits, thoughts and feelings as if they were dwellers in different zones or inhabitants of different planets; who are formed by a different breeding, are fed by a different food, are ordered by different manners, and are not governed by the same laws." When Egremont interposed a question, he was told that the two nations were THE RICH AND THE POOR. Disraeli's own capitals suggest that he knew that he was enunciating a startling theory.[2]

Most of the men with whom Brougham had to deal, including many of his political Party, unconsciously accepted this division. They considered that they owed their first loyalty to the nation to which they belonged, only they would probably have given it a

[1] Brougham : *Speeches*, ii. 46.   [2] *Sybil*, Chap. V.

more dignified name than THE RICH. On the other
side were many who would equally have held that their
loyalty was due to THE POOR. Brougham had not got
this class conception. He recognized an aristocracy of
intelligence, but believed that a man could raise himself
out of the uneducated class into the educated, and could
see no objection to the educational ladder being made as
easy and as accessible as possible. Such a ladder, he
believed, would make democracy effective. Hobhouse
recalls a conversation with him in 1824.

> "Brougham and I walked home together. He
> differed from me in thinking that the people would
> never have spirit or power to procure a fair Govern-
> ment, and thought that Mechanics' Institutions and
> other establishments for instructing the lower classes
> would work out the cure for all political evil, and
> make the people too strong for the Government." [1]

After the defeat of his Education Bill in 1820,
Brougham concentrated upon work outside Parliament,
though he introduced another measure in 1826 which
met the same fate as the first. He began an attack upon
three lines—elementary education, cheap educational
literature for adults, and a new University. In regard
to the first he was active as ever in the British and
Foreign Schools Society, and made a special study of
infant schools. Robert Owen had started an infant
school at New Lanark, and Brougham, borrowing one
of his teachers, founded one in Westminster. This was
a notable experiment, for Owen's school was attached
to the mills, while Brougham's was not connected with
any institution, but in the middle of what was then a
poor and crowded area.

Miss Berry, writing in 1825, describes Lord Dudley

> "riding to Banbury, at my recommendation, to see
> the infant school, and I hope he will subscribe some-
> thing handsome towards it; for it is the very best

[1] Broughton : *Recollections*, iii. 51.

institution possible; and Brougham would deserve to be immortalized, if he had done nothing else, for setting this going as he has done by the Westminster school for infants from two to seven years old. This one at Banbury is an imitation of it, and when I tell you that they have contrived to make the multiplication table a source of happiness to children, you will allow they have done wonders! My brother asked the clergyman why those schools were not more generally adopted, and he answered, ' *Because it was invented by Mr. Brougham.*' All Tory as he is, my brother did not consider that a sufficient reason, and has therefore subscribed largely to it." [1]

Brougham's next enterprise was to supply the growing class of artisans with lectures and cheap literature. With Birkbeck he helped to found a number of institutes to which workmen would subscribe, and in connection with these various technical journals were published. J. McCulloch, the economist, noted in 1824 that politics seemed to be on the wane.

" The Ministers are exceedingly popular, and the populace are seeking excitement in the formation of Mechanics' Institutions, and in the purchase of periodical publications. The number of these in circulation is quite incalculable. The *Mechanics' Magazine* sells about 16,000 copies a week, the *Chemist*, 6000, and so on. I was the other night at the Mechanics' Institute, and met there with Brougham. There were more than 800 persons present, and I never saw a more orderly and attentive audience. There are about 1500 workmen subscribers, at the rate of a guinea a year each. The applications for admittance are numerous, and it is estimated that in two or three years there will be six Institutions —four in London and two in the Borough." [2]

[1] *Journals and Correspondence*, iii. 51.
[2] McVey Napier : *Correspondence*, p. 39.

The politicians of the Whig " Mountain " were dragged to these functions. Creevey dined with Brougham " for the purpose of attending an evening lecture upon Mechanics to the rising young world of the lower order. A job of Brougham's own, for what purpose he knows best." [1] He had more encouragement from Lord John Russell, one of the few young Whigs with the same kind of constructive energy as himself. With the help of William Allen and Dr. Lushington, Brougham's old colleague of the " Queen's trial," they founded the Society for the Diffusion of Useful Knowledge, which published a number of sixpenny pamphlets. Brougham had already published, in 1825, a pamphlet, *Practical Observations on the Education of the People*. This emphasized the need for cheap accessible literature. The Society, which began to function two years later, had a remarkable success, and considerably perturbed those people who thought that knowledge should be a monopoly. Readers of Peacock will remember Dr. Folliott's cook, " taking it into her head to study hydrostatics in a sixpenny tract, published by the Steam Intellect Society, and written by a learned friend who is for doing all the world's business as well as his own. . . . My cook must read his rubbish in bed, and, as might naturally be expected, she dropped suddenly fast asleep, overturned the candle, and set the curtains in a blaze." [2]

In 1833 appeared the first numbers of the *Penny Cyclopaedia*, which found its way into so many middle-class homes, and from which, some twenty years later, the little Edmund Gosse learnt of pemmican, peonies, and pepper.

The Society produced a series of scientific tracts for farmers, the same which were read by Job Thornberry. The comments of the young man's father and Mr. Ferrars, the Tory, are interesting. *Endymion* was,

[1] *Creevey's Life and Times*, p. 194.
[2] *Crotchet Castle*, Chap. II. Dr. Folliott discourses at length on Brougham's iniquities.

of course, written fifty years later, when Disraeli could
look back philosophically at his former colleagues and
the troubles of an old order rapidly changing.

> " ' He is a good farmer, too, is Job, none better;
> a little too fond of experimenting, but then he is
> young. But I am very much afraid he will leave
> me. I think it is the new thing the big-wigs have
> set up in London that has put him wrong, for he is
> always reading their papers.'
>   ' And what is that ? ' asked Mr. Ferrars.
>   ' Well, they call it the Society for the Diffusion of
> Knowledge, and Lord Brougham is at the head
> of it.'
>   ' Ah, he is a very dangerous man,' said Mr.
> Ferrars.
>   ' Do you know, I think he is,' said Farmer
> Thornberry, very seriously, ' and by this token, he
> says a knowledge of chemistry is necessary for the
> cultivation of the soil.'
>   ' Brougham is a man who would say anything,'
> said Mr. Ferrars, ' and of one thing you may be
> certain, that there is no subject which Lord
> Brougham knows thoroughly.' " [1]

The Broughams of this world suffer much during their
lifetime, and more in their reputation, from the great
clan of Ferrars, who write so many books, find their way
into so many Government offices, teach so many of the
young. Brougham was essentially a positive man;
inspiring action when, as often, he was right; provoking
discussion when, as sometimes, he was wrong. Nowadays every arable farmer can discuss the comparative
effect of using sulphate of ammonia or nitrate of lime,
and is the better for using his intelligence to acquire
that knowledge, but the Ferrars's had their usual deaden-
ing influence, and many a Job Thornberry gave up the
land in disgust.

[1] *Endymion*, Chap. XIII.

Of all Brougham's educational activities during this period, the one which most upset the educated classes was the foundation of London University. Brougham had, in 1825, become Rector of Glasgow University, and his own upbringing made him loth to accept the claims of Oxford and Cambridge to a monopoly of English University life. There is some dispute about the origin of the London scheme. Thomas Campbell claims to have suggested the idea of a non-sectarian college, but William Frend, Edward Irving and others had also been thinking along those lines. At any rate the proposal was taken up by many of those with whom Brougham usually co-operated, and he became an enthusiastic supporter. The first Council, appointed in 1825, contains a number of familiar names—James Mill, George Grote, Lord John Russell, Joseph Hume, Zachary Macaulay, as well as Brougham himself. The religious question was all-important, for they depended largely on Nonconformist and Jewish support. The Council, divided between " exclusion or comprehension," decided on the former policy. Brougham was very active in collecting funds, and persuaded the reluctant Lord Grey to take a share by remarking that " Lord Fitzwilliam takes five." [1]   A site was found in Gower Street, and in 1829 the new University College held its first session.[2]

Opposition to the " God-excluding seminary " was immediate and vocal. The *Quarterly Review* and the Tory press scolded the founders " for setting up labourers as a separate or independent class." The country gentlemen felt instinctively that it was a dangerous innovation. " The only thing that Sir Christopher Mowbray does not exactly comprehend is the London University. The affair really puzzles the old gentleman, who could as easily imagine a county member who was not a freeholder as a university which was not at Oxford or

[1] Brougham : *Memoirs*, p. 469.
[2] The site was the Field of the Forty Footsteps, where two brothers fought a duel.

Cambridge." [1] Five years later, when Brougham was returned for Yorkshire, he was to upset the other convention.

The older Universities made no pretence of welcoming a rival. They had grown used to Radical politics and proposals, but this was something concrete, and it cut nearer the bone. Mackworth Praed's " Lament of a Don " did not much exaggerate their attitude.

> " Let Mackintosh battle with Canning and Vattel,
>   Let Brougham be a friend to the ' niggers,'
> Burdett cure the nation's misrepresentations
>   And Hume cut a figure in figures;
> But let them not babble of Greek to the rabble,
>   And teach the mechanics their letters;
> The labouring classes were born to be asses,
>   And not to be aping their betters.
>
> 'Tis a terrible crisis for Cam and Isis.
>   Fat butchers are learning dissection;
> And looking-glass makers become sabbath breakers
>   To study the rules of reflection. . . ." [2]

The College was known as " Brougham's Patent Omnibus "—from its motto *Patens Omnibus Scientia*—or else as " Stinkomalee." [3] Barham of the *Ingoldsby Legends* joined in the attack on the " Godless College of Gower Street," with a new version of Canning's " University of Gottingen," which he sent to *John Bull*. In this, Brougham was, as usual, treated as *fons et origo malorum*.

> " To crown the whole with triple queue,
>   Another such there's not in town,
> Twitching his restless nose askew,
>   Behold tremendous Harry Brou-
>   —Am! Law Professor at the U-
>   niversity we've got in town,
>   niversity we've got in town." [4]

---

[1] *Vivian Grey*, Chap. XIV.
[2] *Morning Chronicle*, July 19, 1825.
[3] A. D. Waller : *Short Account of Origins of the University of London*.   [4] *Life of Barham*, i. 145.

The institution survived this fusillade, and was so successful that the " Saints," who chiefly objected to its lack of religion, were driven to set up a rival—King's College.   To-day London University stands as the finest monument to Brougham's energy and contempt for ridicule or abuse.

If the University made Brougham unpopular amongst the " Dons," it was also the cause of disputes with men outside the conventional academic circles.   A new and unrecognized institution is likely to have difficulties about collecting a staff of professors.   Filling the Chair of Literature gave Brougham a lifelong enemy, who did much to injure his reputation.   In 1827 Carlyle was little known in London, and Brougham, who had never met him, can hardly be blamed for failing to recognize Jeffrey's thirty-two-year-old Scotsman as a genius.   There were other applicants, including Thomas Campbell, whose open letter to Brougham, in 1825, is sometimes taken as the genesis of the Gower Street College.   Brougham hesitated over Jeffrey's suggestion, but, as Carlyle wrote, he was " alarmed at my German predilections," or possibly felt that a more conventional appointment would be better suited to a College which was so open to attack.[1]   Unfortunately, this rebuff was followed four years later by the curious suggestion that Brougham, then Lord Chancellor, should make Carlyle one of the Registrars of the new Bankruptcy Courts.[2]   This also came to nothing; " the Whig Ministry will have nothing in any shape to do with me," and Carlyle, who on general grounds disliked the Benthamites, never missed an opportunity of sneering at the Lord Chancellor—" no ray of genius, and even a considerable tincture of insincerity . . . a politician truly, and *nothing* more."   He also attacked his educational work, especially the Society for Diffusion of Knowledge—" they treated literature as if it were a *tabula rasa,* whereas good books already existed

[1] D. A. Wilson : *Carlyle to the French Revolution,* p. 29 *et seq.*
[2] *Id.,* p. 255.

in abundance." Brougham's oratory he compared with a " hurdy-gurdy." Finally, in 1862, when Brougham was eighty-four, the National Portrait Gallery was offered the picture which is now hanging there. Carlyle was a trustee, and successfully moved against the acceptance on the grounds that Brougham was still alive, but he went out of his way to add, " and when he is dead he will be speedily forgotten." [1] Brougham's multifarious activities involved him in many of these one-sided feuds, which discount much of the criticism to which he was exposed after he left office.

[1] D. A. Wilson : *Carlyle to Threescore and Ten*, p. 476.

CHAPTER XI

> Peace ! impudent and shameless Warwick, peace,
> Proud setter-up and puller-down of kings.
> *King Henry VI*, Pt. III.

THE most complicated and obscure phase in Brougham's political career began in February 1827, when Lord Liverpool had an apoplectic attack and retired from public life. For some weeks it was not clear who was to succeed him. In the formation of Canning's short-lived Government, and of the even shorter Goderich Ministry, Brougham played a decisive part, which earned him the sobriquet at the head of this chapter. As his motives have been much impugned, it is necessary to consider his general position at the time of the crisis.

Brougham was now a man of forty-eight. He was still a member of the Junior Bar, and had never held any Government office. For twenty years he had been in the Whig Party, struggling to give it a consistent liberal policy, to interest its members in social questions, and, by example and precept, to make them more effective in the Commons and outside. All through this long period his work had been stultified by certain factors, which were incompatible with the Whigs having any great future as a reformist party. The family tradition remained as strong as ever. " Damn the Whigs," said Melbourne some years later, " they're all cousins." Brougham was not a " cousin." Although he had married into the fringe of the patrician circle, he knew that he never would be a " cousin." Although he had been for many years the most active and prominent Whig in the Commons, he owed the position entirely to his own ability and to Lord Darlington's continued support. If he had lost his seat, it was doubtful whether the Whig leaders would find him another, and it would have been almost impossible to buy one for himself.[1] If some chance brought the Whigs into office, it was unlikely, even apart from the King's objections, that they would break with tradition and place him in the Cabinet, where he would have some voice in the Party's policy. Probably he would have to be content with a "professional" job, such as the Attorney-Generalship, which had been suggested in his correspondence with Lord Grey five years before.

He thus found himself tied to the Whigs, with their archaic ideas of patrician rule, with their inability to attract new talent, and having, as their titular head, a leader who took no part in current politics, but would occasionally descend from Northumberland to make a speech in the House of Lords. It was natural for him to take stock of his prospects, political and professional. He had a great reputation in the country, which had been considerably increased by his various educational activities. His income from the Bar was more than enough to make him financially independent, and he had not yet taken over his brother John's horde of children. He must have felt, like many middle-aged men, that what was good in his position was due to his exertions, and what was bad was the result of his connection with his political party.

The younger Whigs had little reason for any personal loyalty to the Party. The Fox tradition was nearly dead, and they would look back, with less composure than Lord Grey, upon a long period of political futility. It

[1] By the 'twenties, when Brougham might have been able to buy a seat for himself, the traffic in "closed boroughs" had almost ceased. For legal and other reasons it was nearly impossible to buy single seats during the ten years before the Reform Bill. Otherwise Brougham might have followed Romilly's example and made himself independent.

was natural that a considerable group were inclining towards an alliance with the Canningite Tories, whose outlook was in many respects modern and progressive, and it was to these that Brougham found himself drawn. Many Whigs felt they were losing ground. What was then called a " factious opposition " was not part of the political convention of the time, and they had no definite set of principles to oppose to those of Canning. If Lord Grey had come out strongly in favour of the " long-term policy " for which Brougham had pressed so often, he might have rallied the Party. There could be little enthusiasm for a leader who was continually talking of retiring, nor was it easy to take seriously his revived interest in parliamentary reform, while he still held the most out-of-date ideas about the class of people who should carry on the government of the country.

Lansdowne, who as Lord Henry Petty had been at Edinburgh with Brougham, was the leader of those Whigs who were generally well disposed towards Canning, though they were critical on certain points, and were continually pressing for a further measure of Catholic emancipation. Tierney, Abercromby and Scarlett were prominent in this group, and also that queer quixotic soldier Sir Robert Wilson, who, after a distinguished record in the army, had been imprisoned in Paris in 1816, dismissed from the service in 1821, and was now Member for Southwark. The " Malignants " in 1827 would have claimed a considerable proportion of the Whigs. They remained frankly hostile to Canning, either from loyalty to Grey or from a desire to maintain the separate identity of the Whigs. Althorp was, perhaps, their leader, but many of his followers drifted over when the Coalition Government was formed, and Grey later in the year talked about being " unconnected with anybody but the very few who took the line I did in the last session."

To Brougham's realist mind, the only alternative to joining the first group must have been to become an independent Radical. From some points of view his place was with them. For years he had worked with men like Francis Place and James Mill to improve popular education, and with Zachary Macaulay for the emancipation of slaves. But he had little sympathy with the Radicals in the House of Commons. They were a few very wealthy men, most of whom had bought their own seats—as Burdett, Hume, and Ricardo had done. Brougham found them obsessed by economic theories with which he often disagreed, and they had no cohesion amongst themselves. His long experience of radicalism outside Parliament had not been fortunate, and had set him violently against " Orator " Hunt and the demagogues. If Brougham had decided to take a line of his own he would have had to leave Parliament and built up a party of his own, a futile and almost impossible undertaking. He certainly would not have co-operated with any existing group of Radicals, a point which he makes very clear in an important letter written to Lansdowne in March 1827. In this he explains his general ideas about the future of the Whig Party. He can see no advantage in an alliance with the Radicals,

> " a set of drivellers who call themselves a kind of
> *doctrinaires*, and hold opinions subversive of all
> liberty, as that the Minister is never to be blamed,
> but only the system, and that you are bound to
> exact impossibilities from men out of place, and be
> thankful for a mere nothing from men who have the
> power to give you all you have the right to or wish
> for. These men have much of the Press in their
> hands, which makes them look bigger than they are.
> They are in their religion intolerable atheists, in
> their politics bloody-minded republicans, and in
> morals somewhat gross, and most selfish lati-
> tudinarians." [1]

[1] Most of this letter from the Lansdowne MS. is reprinted in Dr. Aspinall's *Lord Brougham and the Whig Party*, p. 145.

It was not a very happy way of describing the " left wing " politicians of that time, but Brougham had suffered much from them during the previous five years. The letter helps to explain his determination to continue working with Lansdowne, giving general support to Canning, and pressing for a coalition with the moderate Tories if the High Tories should try to form a Government or go into opposition. He knew that so long as George IV was on the throne there was little hope of any personal advancement for himself, either politically or professionally. His main object was to " lock the door on Eldon and Co.," but after twenty years of opposition he probably felt he would like, for a change, to be supporting Ministers in office, and helping in the preparation rather than the criticism of new measures. He may have thought that a little experience on the ministerial side would give the Whigs more balance. Apart from Grey and Lansdowne there was no one in the Party who had ever held high office. Tierney had only had a minor post in the 1806 Ministry. If Grey was to have his way, and keep the Party in " factious " opposition, there was a grave danger that the Whigs would become a little family faction, like the Grenvillites, incapable of forming a Government, and unlikely to become the representatives of that growing middle-class Liberalism to which Brougham looked for the ultimate accomplishment of his reforms. It seemed better to get a centre party into power, and use its dependence on Whig support as a lever to get some measure of Catholic emancipation.

The Catholic and Irish questions had continued to vex English politics up till the end of Lord Liverpool's tenure of office. In 1825 Brougham had bitterly attacked the Government's Bill for suppressing the Unlawful Societies of Ireland. His defence of the Catholic Association, as the only organ through which Irish public opinion could make itself heard, and his remarks on the Duke of York's anti-Catholic declaration, had driven

o

Canning to protest that he was alienating those members who were favourable to the Catholics. This was a little too ingenuous, but Canning was in a very difficult position. The Commons were, as a whole, sympathetic towards the Catholics, but not towards the Irish. A few months later Burdett's Relief Bill passed the Lower House, and nearly wrecked the Ministry, for it was, of course, thrown out by the Lords, and might have provoked a crisis with the Crown. Eldon was threatening to stampede the " country "—or rather the tiny section which had any voice at elections—by raising the cry of " No Popery," still a potent threat to a generation which had not quite forgotten the Gordon riots. The question of the proper tactics to pursue in this crisis marked out the division in each Party. Littleton attempted to appease the Lords, and ease Canning's difficulties, by introducing a Bill to raise the Irish franchise qualifications. Lansdowne and Brougham supported this on the grounds that emancipation was worth a sacrifice. The Radicals and the " Malignants " opposed, seeing no reason to help Canning, and holding that parliamentary reform was more important than emancipation.

The General Election of 1826 did not materially alter the balance between the various groups. A strong contingent of the High Tory Party still sat behind the Treasury Bench, and, as Palmerston said, formed the real Opposition in the Commons. " On the Catholic question; on the principles of commerce; on the Corn Laws; on the settlement of the currency; on the laws regulating the trade in money; on colonial slavery; on the Game Laws, which are intimately connected with the moral habits of the people—on all these questions, and everything like them, the Government find support from the Whigs and resistance from their self-denominated friends." [1] In the Lords the old Tories were in an overwhelming majority. It was a situation which

[1] E. Bulwer Lytton: *Palmerston*, i. 172.

could only be handled by a master of compromise, and by a man of sufficient standing to be considered indispensable by both sections.   When Lord Liverpool went, the whole fabric of the Government collapsed.

The Duke of Wellington, who had a strong personal antipathy to Canning, always contended that the latter opened negotiations with the Whigs before Lord Liverpool's illness.   Probably some overtures were made from the Whig side, but there is no evidence that Canning gave any reply.   For some weeks the question of Liverpool's successor was left open.   The King, who was at the time annoyed with the High Tories, would have preferred a " mixed " Ministry under Peel or Wellington, but neither had sufficient support in the Commons. Canning was standing out for an important constitutional principle, which is partly why Brougham was keen on supporting him.   As Huskisson wrote in April, Canning " does not wish to do anything which might be misconstrued into an attempt to canvass in support of the King's right to name the individual who is to be at the head of the Administration.   It is against this right that the present effort is directed." [1]   Canning and Huskisson, neither of whom were really " patricians," were fighting against two eighteenth-century ideas—the first was that the King could choose his own Ministers without reference to the majority of the Commons; the other, equally objectionable, was that they should be only drawn from certain " patrician " families.   In this struggle Brougham was wholeheartedly on Canning's side as against Wellington and Grey.   Lord Lansdowne, the patrician, though inclined to support Canning, did not see things in the same light.   To Brougham the attack on the old tradition far transcended in importance such minor questions as the introduction of certain measures for Catholic relief or parliamentary reform, measures which were certain to be defeated in the House

[1] Huskisson to Croker, April 12th, 1827.   L. Melville: *Huskisson Papers*, p. 220.

of Lords. This explains Brougham's tactics, and why
he, with Wilson, Spring Rice and other non-patricians,
were sometimes at cross-purposes with Lansdowne.

George IV opened negotiations with Canning towards
the end of March, and Brougham wrote an important
letter to Sir Robert Wilson, who acted as his political
confidant when he was away from London on the
Northern Circuit. It was sent from Lancaster on
March 18th.

> " I have heard nothing from you. Is it possible
> Canning can dream of safety for six weeks, if he
> thinks of taking office with the ultras and no
> arrangement ? Or is it possible he can doubt our
> entire and cordial support if he holds out ? For my
> part I will only say that I am prepared to back him
> in whatever way he himself would deem most
> effectual. It is our duty, and we should all be found
> at our posts. But so should we if he were to give
> in and throw his good principles over." [1]

The substance of this letter was shown to Canning, and
at his request Brougham followed it with a more formal
letter on March 26th.[2] There were also some indirect
communications between Canning and Lansdowne.
Brougham's second letter was probably the decisive
factor when Canning had his final interview with the
King. This was Brougham's own view, and it receives
support from Greville's account, given some years
later.[3]

[1] Add. MSS. 39115, f. 36.
[2] Printed in full in Stapleton's *Official Correspondence of George
Canning*, ii. 300.
[3] Broughton : *Memoirs*, iv. 7. Account of dinner with
Brougham in 1830 in which " he told us of the King's remark,
when Mr. Canning showed him the letter in which he (Brougham)
had offered to support the Government without office. ' Does not
your Majesty think that very magnanimous ? ' ' Very magnanimous,' said the King; adding soon afterwards, ' Take him at his
word.' "

"I told (Melbourne) that I believed the Tories were aware of Canning's communications with Brougham. Brougham wrote to Canning, and made an unqualified offer to support. When the King asked Canning how he was to obtain support to carry on the Government, he pulled the letter out of his pocket, gave it to him, and said, 'Sir, your father broke the domination of the Whigs; I hope your Majesty will not endure that of the Tories.' 'No,' said the King; 'I'll be damned if I do,' and he made him Minister." [1]

Whatever may have happened behind the scenes, on April 10th Canning kissed hands as First Lord of the Treasury and Chancellor of the Exchequer. Most of the High Tories refused to serve under him. Wellington, Peel, Bathurst, Melville and Westmorland resigned. Lord Eldon, at long last, gave up the Chancellorship. This wholesale clearance was in itself a considerable achievement. It meant the temporary displacement of the old gang, who for a generation had done their best to repress political freedom and block every reform. It was like a series of exchanges at chess. It opened up the game, but it did not leave Canning in a strong position. There were no young Tories of outstanding ability to strengthen his Cabinet. He was hopelessly weak in the Lords. Copley, as Lord Lyndhurst, became Chancellor, and together with the feeble Robinson, as Lord Goderich, was sent to lead a forlorn hope. They had to face the combined attacks of Wellington and Grey, who were drawn together by their personal hatred of the new Premier and their distrust of new men and new ideas.

Obviously Canning would have to demand something more definite from the Whigs than their benevolent neutrality, always an asset of doubtful value in politics. Towards the end of April some rather confused negotiations began, with the object of bringing one or two Whigs

[1] Greville: *Journal*, iii. 141.

into the Cabinet.   Lansdowne wished to lay down precise conditions; an early Catholic Relief Bill and Repeal of the Test Act.   He also objected to the appointment of anti-Catholics to the Irish offices.   Canning refused to tie himself on either point.   The first meant an immediate conflict with the Lords, the second with the King. Lansdowne broke off the negotiations, but Brougham called a meeting of the Party which he described in a letter to Creevey.   (The opening sentence is interesting. Brougham apparently did not know that Creevey was a keen " Malignant," and was now habitually referring to him as the " Arch-fiend."   It suggests that grouping inside the Whig Party was not very definite.)

" As I am sure by instinct that you are with the true and faithful servant of the Lord in this time of our trial, and not with the vain and foolish Malignants, I write to say that the negociation was off last night, and we had a row at Brooks's (which I own I created) and the negociation is on again to-day, with a fair prospect of success.   These difficulties come from some of our friends being still in the year 1780. . . . My principle is—*anything* to lock the door for ever on Eldon and Co.   I have the easier pushed this great matter because I can have no sort of interest in its success.   My crimes (which I prize as my glory) of 1820 are on my head;   and by common consent the King is to be gratified." [1]

Lansdowne, though he afterwards blamed Brougham for his interference, acquiesced in the arrangements which were then made.   On July 16th he took the Home Office without making any terms.   Scarlett became Attorney-General, Lord Carlisle took the Privy Seal, Tierney the Mint.   Brougham, with the Lansdowne group, and also a number of the former " Malignants," crossed the floor of the House.   Only a few Whigs, under Althorp, remained in Opposition.   As Brougham sat in Pitt's

[1] Brougham to Creevey, April 21st.   *Creevey Papers*, ii. 114.

old seat, the " Hill-fort," with his " knees in Canning's back," he must have looked with some misgivings on the Ministry he had done so much to create. It was a non-patrician Government, forced upon the King, but its hold on life was so weak. It was seed thrown on stony places. The Coalition began life on July 16th, Canning died on August 8th. " What a world this is ! And how does fortune banter us ! "

In theory the Coalition was sound enough. It marked an important constitutional advance, and a breach in the system of government by the great " tax-eating " families. Metternich shrewdly recognized that Canning was the embodiment of a new political force : " M. Canning," he wrote at the end of April, " a pour lui ce que les cent mille trompettes du jour appellent sa FORCE; cette force est le fait incontestable que ce Ministre est le Repré-sentant véritable de l'Esprit du temps."[1] The High Tories saw their old prerogatives crumbling. Some, like Wellington and Grey, hated Canning's foreign policy, but the main attack came from Lord Londonderry, who cheerfully attacked the Coalition as " a state of disgusting concubinage." He had a personal grievance against Canning. After drawing £160,000 for ten years of not very strenuous diplomatic work he had applied for a pension. Canning had referred the matter to Lord Liverpool, whose endorsement, " This is too bad," became public property. Londonderry led the revolt of the " tax-eating " families, and they pursued Canning in Parliament with a vindictiveness only possible from those whose pockets have been touched.

At first Canning seemed to have the country behind him, but his " Hundred Days " were not a happy experience for himself nor for his supporters. They

---

[1] See H. W. V. Temperley's *Foreign Policy of Canning*, p. 430. For fuller accounts of the formation of the 1827 Coalition see H. W. C. Davies's article in *English Historical Review*, Oct. 1923, together with Dr. Aspinall's *Lord Brougham and the Whig Party*, Chap. VIII.

were attacked by Tories, " Malignants " and Radicals.
Every measure was held up by the Lords. The King
was playing a doubtful game. Inside the Cabinet there
were difficulties. The two groups did not work well
together. Huskisson was troublesome, and the Whigs
retorted by keeping their separate party organization.
Above all, it must be confessed that Brougham added
considerably to Canning's troubles. " Ten dervishes
can sit on one mat, but two kings cannot share one
throne." The personal rivalry between them had always
been very keen. Canning had, perhaps, too much
regard for Brougham's omniscience and oratorical
prowess. " Brougham will find me out. Nothing
ever escapes him," he once remarked when thinking of
using a rather dubious quotation from Clarendon's
History.[1] With Brougham sitting behind him, he must,
at times, have felt uncomfortably like a puppet.

The Whigs had come into the Coalition without
making any terms, and Brougham began to press their
point of view upon the Government. His exclusion
from office added weight to these representations, but
it also led, almost inevitably, to some personal complications and difficulties. His old enemy, Lord Lowther, was introduced, quite unnecessarily, into the
Government. The King, now that Eldon was gone,
promptly gave way on the question of the " silk gown,"
but accompanied the concession by the intimation that
he would prefer Brougham not to kiss hands on the
appointment. The position placed a very heavy strain
on Brougham's magnanimity, and he probably felt that
Canning was not sufficiently strenuous in overcoming
" the very unworthy womanish prejudices in certain
quarters " which he mentioned in his original letter to
Sir Robert Wilson.[2] This suspicion must have been

[1] Le Marchant : *Lord Althorp*, p. 217.
[2] Letter of March 26, 1827. " I shall not easily, if at all, be
induced to be more than a warm friend to any good government.
I know there are womanish prejudices in certain quarters, and I
don't want to thwart them." Add. MSS. 30115, f. 36 *et seq.*

increased by the fact that Canning offered him, presumably with the King's consent, the post of Chief Baron of the Exchequer.   It would have meant an income of £7000 for life, but would have excluded him from the House of Commons.   For a man who had never been in office it was a magnificent bribe to withdraw from controversial politics, and very few people in Brougham's position would have refused it.   The future of the Whig Party was not very bright—the Coalition never looked like having a long life—and Brougham's own prospects, even if the Party revived, were far from certain, but he had a strong sense of social duty which continually prevented him following the easy path which is usually offered to the man who has successfully made himself a nuisance to the governing classes.

One of Brougham's finest qualities was his resilience. A defeat merely roused him to fresh activity.   Within a week of Canning's death he was busily planning to avert the return of " Eldon and Co.," which would have been fatal after such a very short interlude.   The longer the High Tories were out of office, the more certain was the ultimate breach between them and the Canningites—Huskisson, Palmerston, Sturges Bourne, Grant, Lamb and the rest.   Brougham wrote at once to Lansdowne to hearten that very cautious Whig.

> " I can answer for myself *now*, not only because I have tried the experiment of supporting Government without any official connection with them, and found myself quite comfortable in what had appeared an anomalous position, but furthermore, because I am sure any little difficulty, which might be before, exists no longer, for I never could for a moment feel annoyed by giving all kinds of aid to Huskisson or Sturges Bourne, or whoever might be the leader." [1]

He had visions of a wider coalition which should

[1] A. Aspinall : *Lord Brougham and the Whig Party*, p. 154.

bring in the two men whose enmity to Canning had been chiefly personal, Lord Grey and the Duke of Wellington. The latter he never, at any period, considered as a typical High Tory. " I hope due advantage will be taken of the only benefit this lamentable calamity has brought with it, namely, removing the objection to Lord Grey joining, and to Wellington being Commander-in-Chief." To Wilson he wrote on August 11th : " Canning's death a severe blow, but nothing in reality to alarm us. . . . Give W(ellington) the army, and join Lord Grey, if you can; if not, defy them, and all Malignants."[1] Now that Canning was gone, he saw that the Whigs could and should lay down certain principles, and aim at a " united government on the great Irish question." To Grey he wrote on August 13th. The letter has been much criticized, and Grey's rather chilly reply has been taken as a well-deserved snub. This criticism is only justified on the assumption that Grey was a single-minded gentle-man, striving his utmost to keep the Whig Party and Whig " principles " intact, while Brougham was the rather seedy " professional " intriguing for a place. This is history as seen from patrician drawing-rooms. Actually Lord Grey had done very little to help his Party or keep it together during the last ten years. He was " bone lazy " as a politician, and had only been stirred to a little " factious opposition," and to a virtual alliance with the Tory Duke of Wellington, by his personal resentment against Canning's Premiership. For years he had resisted any attempt to provide the Party with a definite policy. Brougham was not a " cousin," but he was a man of great erudition, high up in his profession, and he had just refused a very dignified and lucrative post. His offence was that he would never recognize the aura which surrounded members of the governing caste. If he had approached Lord Grey apologetically, as an erring subordinate, the great patrician might have unbent. The correspondence is printed in Brougham's *Memoirs*.[2] It merely shows Grey preferring to follow

[1] Add. MSS. 30115, f. 118.   [2] *Memoirs*, ii. 485-9.

his own line, which three years later was to result in his becoming Prime Minister, not as the head of the strongest Party in the Commons, but as the choice of the new King, on the recommendation of the Duke of Wellington.

The Goderich Ministry, without any new access of strength, was not destined to survive for more than a few months. Lord Holland helped to keep the Coalition Whigs together, but the King now took a hand, and pressed for the appointment of Herries as Chancellor of the Exchequer. From every point of view this was distasteful to the Whigs. Herries was a strong Tory with a shady financial past, against whom there were grave accusations of making money by the misuse of official information. With the feeble vacillating Premier in the House of Lords, Herries was likely to become virtual leader of the Commons. It seemed impossible to resist the appointment, and the only question was whether the Coalition Whigs should resign. Lansdowne would have taken this course. Brougham felt it best to let the moribund Government carry on for as long as possible, so long as Herries could clear himself of the accusations brought against him. Writing to the Duke of Devonshire, he put his point of view with cynical force.

" We cannot certainly have this *stockjobber* crammed down our throats, if he does not fully and frankly and immediately clear himself by disclosing how he got his wealth, whether by marriage, lottery ticket, highway robbery, cheating at cards, horse-racing at Doncaster, or any other legitimate mode of amassing wealth. But if he does deny most thoroughly that he ever made a farthing directly or indirectly in any manner of way, if he denies this satisfactorily, then our objection ceases, and we may safely take the dose, for as to the manner of giving it to us by the King, I care little for that. . . ."[1]

[1] Letter of Aug. 26, 1827. See Aspinall, *loc. cit.*, p. 157.

The older Whigs were prepared to condone any
amount of political jobbery, of sinecures and pensions,
such as had built up the fortune which Lord Holland
inherited, but Herries was something of a portent.   In
the end Lansdowne swallowed the insult, and the new
Ministry was launched.   Brougham had got what he
wanted, another session with the High Tories out of
place, and himself as a free lance.   Until George IV was
swept away it was the most that he could hope for, and
it was helping to break up the old monopoly of power.
He wrote a remarkable, half-ironical letter to Spring
Rice, who had helped to bring the Coalition into being,
and was Lansdowne's Under-Secretary.

> " I am sure Lord Lansdowne does far more good
> to his principles by giving way, when the matter is
> so pressed and on such grounds, than by gaining a
> victory dangerous to the victor and galling to, and
> never to be forgotten by, the vanquished.   Nothing
> can be better, and I look forward now to amity and
> courtesy and, I hope, kindness prevailing with the
> King and our friends.   They should not be out-
> rageously proud and dignified, but think how much
> good on momentous questions they may do by
> gratifying the King and his friends in trifles.   All
> other modes seem resorted to of furthering great
> objects, this alone we neglect.   I have some half-
> dozen reforms in our law and policy well matured,
> for I must avail myself of the influence my singular
> position gives me in the House to do permanent
> good; viz. all the weight of being out of place
> (both weight with King and country) and the
> favour of the old Tory opposition, who I do not
> think will attack me rashly." [1]

Brougham had certainly got a weak Government,
amenable to outside influence, but it did not last for the

---

[1] W. M. Torrens : *Memoirs of Lord Melbourne*, i. 125.

year or so which he had hoped. The battle of Navarino, where Admiral Codrington destroyed the Turkish fleet, was a fatal blow. Brougham rejoiced. "I am for seeing the Turk out of Europe even if Russia is to have Turkey (the Greeks the Morea of course). It will bring the Tartar into Europe and make him amenable to the common law of Europe." [1] But few, even amongst the Whigs, were prepared for such an anticipation of Gladstonian policy. The Tories were dismayed. The Cabinet broke up into little warring factions; Huskisson against Herries, and Lansdowne pressing for Lord Holland at the Foreign Office. Goderich collapsed under the strain. He was dismissed at the beginning of January 1828, and the King, on the advice of Lord Lyndhurst, sent for the Duke of Wellington to form a Ministry.

From Brougham's standpoint the advent of some such Ministry, though premature, was fully expected. His manœuvres of 1827 had been so far successful that it was not a High Tory Government. "Eldon and Co." did not come back to office. A new Middle Tory Party was in existence, under Peel's leadership. What Brougham did not expect was the ease with which Wellington won over the Canningites. Having never been in office, and having his own professional interests, he was inclined to under-estimate the tenacity with which a Palmerston or a Grant would cling to some kind of Government employment. Their defection made the Opposition a very feeble affair, for the two sections of the Whigs did not settle down very happily. Grey continued to refer to the "Lansdowne Party," and for the next three years kept out of their councils. So close was his connection with Wellington that his inclusion in the Cabinet was seriously considered, but the King's objections, dating presumably from 1820, were too strong.[2]

[1] Add. MSS. 30115, f. 126.
[2] Grey heard of these difficulties through Lauderdale. *Creevey Papers*, ii. 151.

Brougham's relations with the " Malignants " were not
improved by an unfortunate dispute with Grey, which
Creevey seems to have done his best to foment, and of
which we have only his account.[1]   The quarrel cannot
have been very serious, and by the end of 1828 the two
were again corresponding amicably, but the Whig Party
was far from being a happy family.   It was riddled with
intrigues, and neither Tierney, Althorp nor Brougham
could pull it together.   Edward Ellice, the " Bear," a
business man with large Canadian interests, became very
prominent behind the scenes.   He was a brother-in-law
as well as a keen supporter of Grey, and was apparently
anxious to bring both him and Brougham into the
Wellington Government.

Brougham, in Opposition, returned at once to the
building up of a Liberal programme, and to his old
interests—legal reform, education and the abolition of
slavery.   These had kept him in touch with men like
Bentham and Place.   The octogenarian law reformer was
prodigal with schemes and advice, accompanied by
letters presumably intended to enliven a dull subject.
This, for example, was sent in October 1827, when
Brougham was already collecting material.

> " Dear Sweet Little Poppet—If it continues,
> *unus bonus puer*, it will toddle hither immediately
> upon its return ; and besides some more pap, made
> in the same saucepan, it will get fed with some of its
> own pudding ; for a dish there is, which in the
> vocabulary of Q.S.P. goes by the name of ' *Master
> Brougham's pudding*,' though if an indictment for
> stealing it were named by the name of pudding,
> defendant prisoner would be acquitted, had the
> whole army of martyrs kissed their thumbs in proof
> of the act. . . ."[2]

Brougham brought forward his proposals for legal
reform on February 7th, within a month of the fall of the
Goderich Ministry.   His six-hour speech, covering the

---

[1] *Id.*, ii. 149–50.   [2] Bentham : *Works*, x. 576.

whole field of legal administration, is sometimes considered as his greatest oratorical effort. His case was so overwhelming that there was little reply, except promises to remedy certain abuses, and the appointment of two Commissions. These did something towards clearing away the eighteenth-century rubble which blocked the course of justice, though they hardly fulfilled the ideals laid down in Brougham's famous peroration. After referring to the boast of Augustus, " that he found Rome of brick and left it of marble," he continued : " But how much nobler will be our Sovereign's boast when he shall have it to say, that he found Law dear and left it cheap; found it a sealed book and left it a living letter; found it the patrimony of the rich, left it the inheritance of the poor; found it the two-edged sword of craft and oppression, left it the staff of honesty and the shield of innocence." Bentham was not satisfied. " Mr. Brougham's mountain is delivered, and behold !—the mouse. The wisdom of the reformer could not overcome the craft of the lawyer." [1] But the Reformers were sad people to please. Brougham achieved all he could possibly have done in opposition. He brought new hope to the common people of England, then suffering under the law in a way now difficult to appreciate.

The same year, in which Brougham sowed the seeds of many legal reforms, saw another of his schemes coming to fruition. In October 1828, when writing to Grey about Ireland, he mentions the successful opening of London University. " The entry of students at starting exceeds anything before known in London at the opening of a course—namely 54. The professors and all concerned are therefore in the highest spirits, and we may consider the *medical* school as fairly launched. The general department will be much benefited by this success. . . ." Grey's reply emphasizes the part which Brougham had played in fighting " Stinkomalee's " first battles against the unbelievers.

[1] *Id.,* p. 588.

" I had previously read in the newspapers of the successful opening of the London University. It must afford the truest satisfaction to everybody who thinks, as I do, of the public benefit likely to arise from such an institution. But to you it must be peculiarly gratifying, for *you* have been the creator of this establishment, and your name will be for ever united with the improvements which may spring not only from this, but from the rival college, which never would have existed but for the success of your exertions." [1]

Meanwhile the Wellington Ministry was steering a curiously erratic course, blown hither and thither by the growing opposition in the Commons. Within a few months, Lord John Russell, strongly supported by Brougham, had forced the Government to accept the repeal of the Test and Corporation Acts. The Canningites, who had unwillingly voted for the Government against repeal, resigned in a body, after a rather trumpery quarrel between Wellington and Huskisson over the latter's vote on the disenfranchisement of East Retford. In the summer Wellington was forced to accept a Corn Law embodying the principle of a sliding scale, almost identical with the Bill which, a year earlier, he had defeated in the Lords. But stranger events were to follow. Vesey Fitzgerald, who followed Grant at the Board of Trade, had to stand for re-election in County Clare. He was opposed and defeated by Daniel O'Connell, a Catholic and the greatest figure in Irish politics. The difficulty of excluding O'Connell from Parliament, the growing excitement in Ireland, and the fact that there was a majority in the Commons favourable to emancipation, were sufficient to persuade Peel of the need for some measure of relief. Gradually the Duke himself was won over. With his eighteenth-century views of a Minister as the servant of the Crown, he saw no reason why Peel should resign, as he threatened to do.

[1] Brougham : *Memoirs*, ii. 500.

If concession and repression was the best policy for Ireland, the Duke felt prepared to undertake the task in the same spirit as he had undertaken the premiership. He needed Peel, and he persuaded Peel to remain and pilot the Emancipation Bill through the House of Commons. The Bill was drafted on generous lines, opening not only Parliament, but nearly every post to Catholics. It easily passed the Commons, and Wellington drove it through the Lords as the only alternative to civil war in Ireland. Then, in the manner of English Governments, it was followed by an Act disenfranchising a very large number of Irish Catholic voters, and undoing the conciliatory effect of Emancipation.

Again Brougham had to sit on the Opposition benches and watch hostile Ministers passing measures which he had advocated for years, and which they had bitterly attacked. Two important principles were involved. Should ministers remain in office when they have changed their views ? Brougham, on this point, did not press the Ministers, but merely congratulated them on overcoming their prejudices. The future Lord Shaftesbury, then a young Tory Member, changed with his leaders, but privately took the view that Peel and Wellington "should have said to the Crown, ' it is a measure that must be passed, but it should be passed by those who agree with it. We are not the men to do it ! ' " [1] It is a question which has not yet been settled, and it would have been interesting to hear Shaftesbury's verdict on the events of 1931. But behind this, which is chiefly a matter of individual conscience, lay the deeper constitutional problem, whether Wellington was the servant of the King or of the country. The danger of a military dictatorship was always present, with Wellington in command of the army and sharing the King's views of prerogative. It hung over Wellington's first Ministry, it was to become acute again during the Reform Bill crisis. Brougham in Parliament, and men like Joseph Parkes, Attwood and Place outside, were always building

[1] E. Hodder : *Lord Shaftesbury*, p. 48.

P

up public opinion against this threat. From the first days of Wellington's Government, Brougham had stressed this point, and in doing so coined a phrase which had considerable influence during the next ten years.

" The noble Duke may take the army, he may take the navy, he may take the mitre, he may take the Great Seal. I will make the noble Duke a present of them all. Let him come on, with his whole force, sword in hand, against the Constitution, and the energies of the people of this country will defeat his utmost efforts. . . . There have been periods when the country heard with dismay that ' The soldier is abroad.' That is not the case now. Let the soldier be abroad—in the present age he can do nothing. There is another person abroad— a less important person in the eyes of some, an insignificant person, whose labours have tended to produce this state of things. THE SCHOOLMASTER IS ABROAD. And I trust more to him, armed with his primer, than I do to the soldier in full military array, for upholding and extending the liberties of his country." [1]

These are brave words, and the basis of much Liberal philosophy. Our generation has learnt that education is no sure shield against dictatorship, but Brougham did England a good service when he helped to persuade his countrymen that their future prosperity and liberty lay with an educated democracy.

" The schoolmaster's abroad, you see;
    And, when the people hear him speak,
They all insist on being free
    And reading Homer in the Greek;
The Bolton weavers seize the pen,
    The Sussex farmers scorn the plough;
One must advance with other men;
    And so, I'm not a Tory now." [2]

---

[1] Speech on the Address, Jan. 29, 1828.
[2] Mackworth Praed : *Why and Wherefore.*

CHAPTER XII

DESCENT TO THE WOOLSACK

THE last year of George IV's reign was disturbed and menacing. A comparative lull had followed Castlereagh's death and Canning's accession to office. This was partly the result of a wiser and more conciliatory policy, partly due to a revival of trade. After eight years business was again bad, agriculture depressed, and new forces, economic and social, were coming into play. In the North the workers, helped by the repeal of the Combination laws, were gradually organizing themselves industrially, and there was vague talk, to grow louder in a year or two, about a National Union of the Working Classes. In the South the agricultural labourers were being driven to desperation. It was the old story of landlords, farmers and parsons raising their standards of living during a war and then, when prices fell, attempting to maintain those standards at the expense of the farm hands. The " Speenhamland " system of subsidizing wages from rates provided the machinery by which the agricultural worker was sweated, and allowances had now sunk below the rate at which they provided enough to buy food. Throughout the country there were ominous warnings, presaging the Luddite riots and rickburnings, which were to be such a feature of the next two years.

In some ways the position resembled 1819, but there was now a stronger middle-class Radical element in the country, not too sympathetic with the working-class demand for higher wages, but determined to acquire some voice in the government. With all these movements the politicians, Whig as well as Tory, were almost

completely out of touch. Perhaps there had never been
a time when the poor, especially in the villages, were so
completely isolated.[1] Similarly, the governing classes
lived in a different world from those engaged in trade
or manufacture, the Church folk had little communication with Dissenters. A few Whigs like Brougham
and Lord John Russell, had made and maintained contacts
with Radical elements in London and the North, mainly
through their educational work. Most of the older
Whigs, and nearly all the Tories, except Peel, were totally
ignorant of this new England which had developed
since the Industrial Revolution. Nobody in Parliament,
even amongst the Radicals, had much knowledge of
working-class grievances and ambitions outside London.

The stirring of new life which the politicians did not
understand added to the atmosphere of unreality hanging
over Westminster. No one was very anxious to displace Wellington. It was felt that he could manage the
impossible George IV, and the passing of Catholic
Emancipation showed that he was amenable to pressure.
Grey spent his time at Howick, almost out of touch with
politics. " Having lost my old correspondents," he
told Princess Lieven, " I have not endeavoured to culti-
vate any new ones. From Brougham I have had one
or two letters since I have been here. The last remains
unanswered. I have also heard, once I believe, from
Lord Holland, and from no other person except the
Duke of Bedford." [2] He then goes on to discuss the
far more absorbing subject of the Burke and Hare
murders. While Grey thus remained studiously aloof,
and the High Tories grumbled and fought against Peel
and Wellington, the Opposition began slowly to weld

[1] It is impossible in this biography to deal adequately with the
economic problems which form the background of any history of
these times. The reader may be referred to J. L. and Barbara
Hammond's trilogy, *The Skilled Labourer*, *The Village Labourer*,
The Town Labourer. All deal with the period 1760 to 1832.

[2] G. Le Strange : *Correspondence between Lord Grey and Princess
Lieven*, i. 212.

itself together. The Canningites, so long as Huskisson was alive, retained their own organization, but the death of Tierney, the nominal Whig leader, made it possible for the " Lansdowne group " to choose a more effective successor. The initiative came partly from the Duke of Devonshire. " I quite agree with you," he wrote to Russell towards the end of 1829, " in trusting Althorp and Brougham; but till there is some strong feeling to unite our friends in one general interest, to prevent their following their own devices, we shall never be worth much as a Party." [1]

Portman, Member for Dorsetshire, was responsible for the meeting of forty or fifty Whigs at the Albany, who asked Althorp to take over the leadership. Portman had been roused by a Tory's remarks— " You're a mere loose bundle of sticks, and will be always beaten." [2] It was fully in the English tradition to invite a pleasant and very diffident " amateur " to captain the team as soon as there was a prospect of playing a serious match. The other possible leaders, Brougham, Graham and Lord John Russell, were sounded by Althorp before he accepted the post, and they all acquiesced. Brougham knew that he would remain leader *de facto* while the Whigs were in Opposition, and Lord Spencer's son had the standing and force of character to keep the " ear-wigs " in order, even though, as Campbell remarked, " there is a better speaker in every vestry in England." Althorp, when Parliament reopened in 1830, was able to speak about " we of the Opposition," at which, we are told, Peel gave a visible " start."

Tierney's death affected Brougham in another way. After fourteen years of comparative amity, his relations with his patron were now very strained. Lord Darlington had become Marquis of Cleveland, and for dynastic or other reasons was inclined to support the Duke of

[1] *Early Correspondence of Lord J. Russell*, i. 300.
[2] Le Marchant : *Life of Viscount Althorp*, p. 246.

Wellington. In January 1830 he definitely threw in his lot with the Government. Brougham was placed in a difficult position. Like the other Lansdowne Whigs he was not then in " factious opposition " to the Duke, but the time was clearly approaching when they must claim a share in the Government. From this embarrassment Brougham was relieved by the offer of Tierney's seat at Knaresborough, the gift of the Duke of Devonshire. Grey strongly approved of this trans-action. "I received . . . a full statement from Brougham of what has passed with respect to the change of his seat. I think he has done right. But it will be taken as an unequivocal symptom of hostility to the Government." [1]

So long as George IV was alive, Brougham could see no point in pressing the Government too hard. Writing to Creevey about the first session in 1830, he asks : " What do you say of the first day ? Are you of those lunaticks who are angry that we did not go ding-dong at the Beau (Wellington) and turn his Govt. out ? That is, displace him without an idea who would get in ; or, in other words, put things in a state from which nobody but the Tories and King could have profited ?" [2] The summer proved the wisdom of patience. From June onwards events marched rapidly.

On June 26th, " Prinney " was " really dead—on a Saturday too, as was foretold." He had encumbered the earth too long. His death was a general relief, and the prelude to the shaking of many new patterns in the kaleidoscope. The new King was a genial, well-meaning man, indiscreet but not unpopular. Neither Brougham nor Lord Grey had had any personal quarrel with William IV when he was Duke of Clarence. There was no political issue, now that Emancipation had been passed, which would make the Crown a barrier to the Whigs taking office. They might also hope to win some seats at the General Election which would follow

[1] *Corr. of Grey and Princess Lieven*, i. 428.
[2] *Creevey Papers*, ii. 208

an accession.   It was time to take the offensive, and
Brougham returned to the attack with the pent-up
combativeness of two years in muzzled opposition.

The object of Brougham and the Lansdowne Whigs
was to force Wellington to accept enough Whigs and
Canningites to form a middle party Government, with
a strong Liberal element, and prepared for certain reforms, parliamentary and economic.   If Wellington
refused, then they hoped to form a Ministry with the
help of Huskisson and the Canningites.   Brougham's
first onslaught, delivered within a week of George IV's
death, rather overshot the mark, with its references to
the " mean fawning parasites of the Duke " who occupied
the opposite front bench.   It enabled Peel to make an
effective rejoinder, but it probably helped to let the country
see that something was happening at Westminster—no
easy task in those days.   Brougham was now " in full
force," at the beginning of a great campaign.   Following
his old tactics he inspired, if he did not write, a pamphlet,
The Country without a Government, and followed up the
attack with an article in the *Edinburgh Review*.   He made a
great speech on the emancipation of slaves, just before
the close of the session, which roused the Nonconformist
and Quaker elements of the North, and obtained for him
the signal honour of an invitation to stand for Yorkshire,
as the man upon whom had fallen the mantle of their
leader Wilberforce.   It was an offer not without its
embarrassments, for it might mean fighting the seat
twice, if he accepted office, and county seats were a very
expensive luxury.   He seems to have come to some
arrangement with the Duke of Devonshire about keeping
open the Knaresborough seat, and within a month of
George IV's death he was nominated for Yorkshire.

While Brougham was doing his utmost to revive the
fortunes of the Whigs, events on the Continent were
strongly encouraging a political " swing to the left."
The Revolution of July, the fall of Charles X, the failure
of Polignac, the subsequent August revolution in Belgium

were followed with great interest in England. Probably
M. Halévy is correct in emphasizing the vague but general
suspicion that Wellington was in close touch with
Polignac, and would have liked to have imitated him if
he had succeeded.[1]   Another important factor was the
effect of the 1830 revolutions in effacing the memory
of 1789, which had always hung, like the Old Man of the
Sea, round the necks of English reformers.   There is a
parallel, too close to need stressing, between the propagandist value of the earlier French Revolution to the
Tories, and that of the Russian Revolution to the modern
Conservatives.   By 1830 the argument had been used
for forty years, and was wearing a little thin.   A successful
middle-class revolution, not followed by atrocities,
completely exorcised the memory of the earlier happenings.   The revolution in Belgium also suggested that
regular troops were not necessarily invincible against a
popular rising—a tradition that has unfortunately survived on the Continent after changes in equipment have
destroyed any validity it may have possessed.   The
early activities of the Birmingham Political Union, which
began its work for Reform in 1830, shows how the
Radicals of the North were thinking in terms of an
orderly revolution on the French model.   One of their
first functions was a dinner, at which three thousand
attended, to celebrate the overthrow of Charles X.

The importance attached by Brougham to the French
Revolution is illustrated by a dispute which occurred
between him and the young Macaulay, the beginning
of an unfortunate estrangement.   Brougham had done
his best to launch Zachary Macaulay's son upon the world.
In 1827 he had written to the new Chancellor, Lord
Lyndhurst : " Let me strongly advise you to give an
early token of favour to young Macaulay.   He is the
greatest genius now coming into the profession.   Make
him at once a Commissioner of Bankruptcy." [2]   Lynd-

---

[1] E. Halévy : *Histoire du Peuple Anglais au XIXe Siècle*, iii. 2.
[2] *Life and Letters of Zachary Macaulay*, p. 442.

hurst obligingly consented. Three years later, there was a little trouble, because Lansdowne brought Macaulay into Parliament, when Brougham thought that Denman ought to have had the seat. Then came the French Revolution, and Macaulay, who had gone over to Paris, prepared a great article for the *Edinburgh Review*, only to find that Brougham, more interested in the English political situation, insisted on dealing with the subject himself. Macaulay was grievously offended, and that long-suffering editor, Macvey Napier, received an effusion in which " Tom's snip-snap " style is employed in castigating Brougham's " intolerable dictation," and his " wish to domineer in any association, literary or political." [1] The incident is only worth recalling because Macaulay was never quite reconciled to Brougham, and always tended to " write him down "; and also because it shows how Brougham, with his political enthusiasm and drive, would leave behind him a trail of jealous detractors.

With every factor in their favour the Whigs strengthened their position considerably during the summer. At the election they won some of the open seats, and Brougham, after a hurricane campaign, was returned, on August 6th, as one of the four Members for Yorkshire. This was considered a great portent, for he had to face the opposition of the " silly, impotent, superannuated landed dons," Whig as well as Tory. They objected violently to such an innovation as the election of a man who possessed no property in the county. There does not, however, seem to have been more than the usual ill-feeling. Brougham, following an ancient custom, solemnly rode round York girt with a sword, and with long spurs attached dangerously to his long legs, but the ceremony passed without mishap. It was the beginning of a year which marked the summit of Brougham's personal ascendancy in England, and, as usual, success

[1] Letter of Sept. 16, 1830. *Selected Correspondence of Macvey Napier*, p. 89.

roused him to further activities. He was always a man to use every inch of sail with a following wind. Pamphlets, articles in the *Edinburgh Review*, a remarkable congratulatory letter to the Duc de Broglie on forming a Government under Louis Philippe, all built up the popular conception of Western Europe throwing off the shackles of the eighteenth century, and the rise of a new order, progressive, middle-class, unfettered by the Church or the threat of militarism. Grey was swept along, half protesting, in the general movement. He described one of Brougham's pamphlets as

"powerfully and bitterly written but not very prudent in some particulars. His calculations on the result of the election (a gain of some thirty votes) I believe to be generally right; but there are some evident mistakes, and it is, after all, not very wise to stake too much on results which may disappoint you from a thousand causes, of which nobody can well estimate the effects till Parliament has met. . . . " [1]

Grey, however, began seriously to consider the formation of a Whig Ministry in alliance with the Canningites, based on parliamentary reform and a reversal of foreign policy. Negotiations were carried on during September and October with Lambton, who was now Lord Durham, as one of the principal intermediaries. The Government's intentions were still uncertain. Would Peel and Wellington try to repeat their tactics of 1829, and " dish the Whigs " by introducing a Reform Bill of their own ? This was very generally expected. Brougham, writing to Dr. Chalmers about negro emancipation, said : " I congratulate you sincerely on the favourable prospects of those great causes on which we feel interested in common. Really slavery cannot now expect much longer protection from a Government so weak that it is even about to give Parliamentary Reform as a sop,

[1] *Corr. of Grey and Princess Lieven*, ii. 95.

and to save itself for a few months." [1]   It is possible that the death of Huskisson was the deciding factor. This accident, at the opening of the Manchester and Liverpool Railway, on September 15th, removed not only the strongest but also the most definitely Tory of the Canningite group, and probably ended any idea of their reconciliation with the Wellington Government.

With the possibility of office, the old Whig clannishness became as marked as ever. Brougham was never really admitted into the inner counsels where Lord Grey, Lord Holland, Lord Durham, Lord John Russell, Lord Althorp and Lord Lansdowne slowly came to terms with Lord Melbourne, who, after Huskisson's death, was the leader of the Canningite group. In these titled circles Brougham had no place. Only Durham, with his streak of real Radicalism, had sufficient understanding to see that Brougham, the outstanding Whig of the moment, was certain to take a line of his own if he was excluded from real co-operation, and would do so, not because he was a careerist, but because he wanted to see some results from twenty years' work. " I do not believe," wrote Durham to Grey in October, " that Brougham's activity originates in a desire to make himself leader, but in extreme anxiety to overthrow the present Government. . . . I know your ladies are no friends of Brougham's. I wish to keep everything as smooth as possible; he is an extraordinary man, difficult to manage as an ally from his wild eccentricities, and dangerous to an almost fatal degree as an enemy." [2]

The last sentence shows well enough the " family " view of Brougham. He was not one of themselves, only a dangerous erratic star to which the Party wagon had somehow got hitched. There was no other Whig commoner of any standing, and apart from him it would have been easy for Grey and Wellington, still good

[1] W. Hanna : *Life of Dr. Chalmers*, iii. 289.
[2] Letter of October 4, 1830. Quoted in G. M. Trevelyan's *Lord Grey of the Reform Bill*, p. 221.

friends, to arrange with the King for a transfer of offices from one group of landed gentlemen to another. The rampageous Brougham was a disturbing factor, with his Jacobin ideas of a Party forcing its leader on the Crown, but he could not be ignored. " He is, next the King, the most popular man in England. There is no other man whose entrance into any town in the kingdom would be so certain to be with huzzaing and taking off of horses." [1] So, a year later, wrote Tom Macaulay to his sister. Brougham was every whit as powerful in the autumn of 1830. The Whig managers were terrified about the independent line which he might take when the session began. On the same date that Durham was urging his father-in-law to take a more broad-minded view, Althorp was writing to Brougham with the obvious intention of quieting him.

> " I am inclined to ground our opposition to the Government mainly, if not entirely, on their total inefficiency. I think the greatest danger . . . is giving people an opportunity of saying that we were very moderate and mealy-mouthed as long as there was a chance of the Duke of Wellington taking us in, but that now we despair of this we are more violent. . . . I think we ought to be cautious how we urge anything against the Ministers which might have been equally well brought forward last session." [2]

It is not certain whether Wellington, when Parliament met again, deliberately rode for a fall, or whether he believed that by rallying the ultra-Tories he could carry on the Government. Brougham continued his policy of bringing independent pressure on the Government by giving notice of a motion on Parliamentary Reform. The Duke, on November 2nd, explicitly denied any intention of making the least concession

---

[1] G. O. Trevelyan : *Life and Letters of Lord Macaulay*, i. 189.
[2] Le Marchant : *Life of Lord Althorp*, p. 252.

on this question, but the older Tories were still bitter about Catholic emancipation, and were not to be won over by a negative policy.   The end was hastened by the unnecessary postponement of the King's visit to the City; from fear of a disturbance, which if it had occurred would only have been aimed at the Duke.   Within a fortnight (November 15th) the Government was defeated on the question of the Civil List, and the King, on the Duke's advice, asked Lord Grey to form a Ministry.

The Whig families continued to meet in secret conclave.   Their main difficulties were the filling of the law offices and the management of Brougham.   The other appointments were simple enough.   They would be distributed amongst the four or five leading families, and amongst those of the Canningites, like Melbourne, Palmerston and Goderich, who had already held office. Hobhouse, writing two years later, describes the atmosphere in which these preliminary preparations were made.   " At the meeting of Lord Grey's friends at Lansdowne House, it was discussed who was to be Lord Chancellor. Lord Lyndhurst ? ' No.' Brougham ? ' Oh, no, no.'   Everybody was against him, and when he was subsequently selected, Lord Holland said, ' Then we shall never have another comfortable moment in this room.' " [1]   It was always Brougham's fate to upset the complacent comfort of the Whigs.   He was now fighting almost alone against the eighteenth-century system.   The King, of course, saw matters in the same light as Wellington or Grey.   The latter wrote to Lord Holland on November 16th, the day on which he went to see William IV.

" Brougham is the difficulty, and it is really the only one with the King.   Peace, Reform and Economy, the acknowledged principles of the new Government.   Carte blanche as to all offices both in Government and the Household, but

[1] Broughton : *Recollections*, iv. 256.

Brougham. You will have heard his speech to-night. I saw him in this morning, and he positively refused the Attorney-Generalship. What is to be done with him? You could do more than anybody." [1]

In spite of Brougham's great standing in the country, it was extremely difficult for him to hold his own inside the Whig Party. There were very few independent Whig members outside the leading Whig families and the small group of Canningites. Most of the remainder were sitting for closed boroughs, or were of the genus Taper and Tadpole, only desirous of getting some minor office after so long a period in the wilderness. In the reformed House of Commons Brougham would inevitably have built up his own Party from amongst the representatives of the northern industrial towns, but the intense excitement caused by his return for Yorkshire emphasizes his loneliness in the 1830 Parliament. For this reason Grey could afford to leave him out of those meetings at Lansdowne House which decided how the next Cabinet was formed. Lansdowne himself was not excluded, as the place of meeting shows, although he had led the group which had defied Grey and joined the 1827 coalition.

From the first there was no question of Brougham receiving an ordinary Ministerial appointment. That would have been too great a departure from Whig tradition. There were only three possible legal posts. Grey offered him, not too tactfully, the Attorney-Generalship. This he naturally refused. Apart from the fact that it involved him in a very hazardous and costly bye-election, it would have placed him in a position inferior to a number of untried men, whose measures he would have to defend. There is little doubt that Brougham would have liked to have been made Master of the Rolls. This would have left him in the House of

[1] Letter of November 16th, 1830. Printed in Trevelyan's *Lord Grey of the Reform Bill*, p. 241.

Commons, have given him some recompense in dignity and emoluments for the work he had done, and left him free to advocate the reforms, social and legal, which he had at heart. Such an arrangement might have been admirable for the country, but would have been extremely uncomfortable for Whig Ministers, who wanted a quiet life. Brougham would have been little more tied than if they took him at his word, and allowed him to remain as an independent Member without office. Lord Althorp felt that either would make his position impossible. He could not face an unmuzzled and critical Brougham in the Commons. Wellington is reported, on rather doubtful evidence, to have advised the King against allowing Brougham to take the Rolls without a peerage; certainly the offer was never made. There remained only the chancellorship.

Campbell, in a letter to his brother, describes a conversation with Brougham on November 17th. It is interesting as showing the kind of pressure being brought to bear upon Brougham to make him take office.

" It is said that Brougham is troubling everything. I had a long and serious conversation with him to-day, and gave him some sound and serious advice. But he says he cannot take office without losing Yorkshire. His object is to lead the ' Mountain.' I told him that if he did not place his glory in bringing about a revolution, he ought to go into office. He said he supported Canning though not in office. . . . He says the Great Seal is the only thing he could take, and it would then be thought his conduct was sordid. I suspect he would like to be Chancellor; but he is so pledged about Education, Slavery, District Courts and Parliamentary Reform that Grey can hardly place him on the woolsack without endangering the Government. However, Brougham at present professes a fixed determination to take no office whatever." [1]

[1] *Life of Lord Campbell*, i. 489.

The 19th of November was the crucial day in Brougham's life. He was offered the Chancellorship by Grey, at first wanted to refuse, and then, under great pressure from the Whigs, accepted. Grey assured him " the whole treaty was up " if he did not concur. Althorp insisted that he would not take office if Brougham remained as an independent Member, or had an irremovable office like Master of the Rolls. " If Brougham is left in Parliament," he told Grey, " the Ministry will not last three months, and I certainly will not belong to it." [1] Old friends like Sefton and Duncannon pressed him to take the Seals. According to Brougham's own Memoirs, Althorp said to him, " I have not a word to say against your reasons and your feelings, and therefore there's an end of the matter; and you take upon yourself the responsibility of keeping our Party out of power, and the loss of all the great questions which will follow, instead of their being carried." [2] His brother James Brougham, and his old friend Denman, who now became Attorney-General, seem to have had the last word, and persuaded him to make what he afterwards recognized was a great mistake. The whole business was settled in the intervals of arguing a case before the House of Lords, surrounded by Whigs all eager for office. It was too big a decision to be made in that atmosphere of bustle and excitement. He should have withdrawn for a few days from the cajolery of Whig aristocrats scheming to keep their old privileges, from the importunities of minor politicians yearning for office, and the advice of lawyers for whom politics were an interest secondary to their professional career.

The lives of many keen political reformers fall into a certain pattern. Up to the age of fifty or thereabouts they are quite content " to be in the right with two or three "; they endure the great moral strain of supporting a definite point of view against the dead-weight of

[1] Le Marchant: *Life of Lord Althorp*, p. 261.
[2] *Memoirs*, iii. 79

hostility and indifference. Then in later middle age, when they have, perhaps unknown to themselves, deeply affected the outlook of a new generation, they become weary of well-doing, they long for some concrete recognition, for a " label " and a place in the world. Sometimes they begin to suffer from that last infirmity of noble minds—social ambition—and fall to a title or the smiles of a duchess. Sometimes the old acquisitive instinct, long suppressed, comes out in a keenness to amass a fortune. Often they find themselves at variance with the younger men who have followed their lead. Few masters like being surpassed by their pupils. All these factors encourage a more worldly view of life and politics. A decline in zeal and combativeness are so normal that it is the variations from type which are interesting. Those truculent Radicals of Brougham's generation, Burdett and Hobhouse, ended their careers, the first as a member of the Conservative Party, the second as a Peer.

Brougham at fifty was undoubtedly affected by all of these influences. He probably felt, though perhaps unjustifiably, that his political views had prevented him having an established position in his profession. He certainly was not free from a queer kind of snobbishness, which led him into an exaggerated eulogy of aristocratic government, shortly before he took office. This alone can account for his adopting the title Vaux as well as Brougham when he became Chancellor. The second title was based on some fantastic family claim to an ancient barony by descent through the female line. He made no serious attempt to substantiate the claim, and it was, of course, the subject of innumerable jokes about Vauxhall, and the Vaux and Grapes. The best was " that Henry Brougham has destroyed himself, and was now *Vaux et præterea nihil.*" Another consideration, far more pardonable than this weakness shown by his desire to be a member of the aristocracy, was the temptation of a large income and comfortable pension. Ac-

Q

cording to Greville, Brougham had about this time " lost
an immense sum of money by being security for his
brother who had failed as a wine merchant," [1] the
brother John who died in 1829, and whose nine children
he educated.   All these were factors influencing his
choice, but they would scarcely have prevailed apart
from the appeal to his Party loyalty, and Althorp's
plea that he would be ruining the prospects of the Whigs.
" At that," writes Professor Trevelyan, " he yielded,
and there is no reason to think that he did not yield
mainly on public grounds." [2]

Within a few years Brougham had bitterly repented his
acceptance of the Chancellorship, and it is almost certain
that if he had escaped for a few days from London he
would have made a different decision.   As a politician
he drew his strength from public opinion outside Parliament, and that strength, which was so troublesome to
Whig and Tory alike, he must gradually lose as a member
of the House of Lords.   That he recognized his position
is shown by his reply when Canning offered him the Chief
Barony and observed that it was only one stage from the
Chancellorship.   " That is true," said Brougham, " but,
out of Parliament, where am I to get post-horses to
take me that stage ? " [3]   In 1830 his position was far
stronger.   Whether Whigs or Tories took office—
and Althorp's refusal might not have been fatal—a
Reform Bill would probably have been introduced within
a year or two, and Brougham would ultimately have been
the first great Liberal leader, having behind him a section
of the Whigs and a larger element of the new " Radicals,"
who came in for the industrial constituencies as soon
as they were enfranchised, and contained many who were
more moderate and more in sympathy with Brougham's
outlook than men like Cobbett or Hunt.   But while

[1] Greville : *Journal of the Reigns of George IV, etc.*   Under date
Nov. 17, 1834.
[2] *Lord Grey of the Reform Bill*, p. 244.
[3] Wellington : *Despatches, Correspondence and Memoranda*, iv. 182.

some people must have thought like this, there were few who could advise him. Two, we know, did. One was John Allen, the crabbed honest old doctor who held such an anomalous position at Holland House. The other was his mother, who, in Brougham's words, " warned me against giving up the substance of power for a name." " If, as is probable," she wrote to him, " office is offered you in the new Government, pause before you accept it; do not be tempted to leave the House of Commons. As Member for Yorkshire, backed by all you have done for the country, you are more powerful than any official that ever existed, however high in station or in rank. Throw not away the great position you have raised yourself to—a position greater than any that could be bestowed by King or Minister." [1] For four years Brougham held his ground precariously. For the remaining thirty-four years of his life he was left to meditate upon the fate of Antæus, like Brougham a mighty wrestler, who allowed himself to be lifted off the ground from which he drew his strength.

Few appointments can have caused such general rejoicings amongst politicians. The Whigs never felt sure that Brougham would not force them to live up to some inconvenient principle, or lead them into some uncomfortable adventure. He had now placed himself at the mercy of the Whig family circle. " Brougham is Chancellor," wrote Lord Sefton to Creevey; " it is supposed he will be safer there, because, if he don't behave well, he will be turned out at a moment's notice, and he is then powerless." [2] Hobhouse describes the scene at " Brooks's, where our friends were handing about a list of appointments. Brougham Lord Chancellor ! Reform of Parliament, Anti-Slavery, Law Reform, Useful Knowledge Society, *Edinburgh Review*, Sublime Society of Beef-steaks, hail and farewell ! ! But it is believed, and people seem glad to get rid of my learned friend from the House of Commons. He

[1] *Memoirs*, iii. 80.   [2] *Creevey Papers*, ii. 214.

came. We set up a shout and he soon went away." [1]
Their opponents were equally content. They took the
conventional view which Princess Lieven hastened to
send back to Russia. " Lord Brougham, Lord Chancellor.
Democrat transformed into an aristocrat, a tiger whose
claws are cut, of wise resolve, though at first apparently
violent. He will be dangerous no longer." [2] The
older Tories were pleased that their cyncial view of reformers was confirmed. " I have known *four*-and-
twenty leaders of revolts." The younger were relieved
at their escape from what seemed a formidable danger.
Greville's views are worth quoting at length, for they
show the impression which Brougham had made upon
the Conservative elements in the country during the
first fifty years of his life, as well as expressing the general
feeling that Grey and Althorp had tricked him out of
a great, if dangerous, career.

> " At 12 o'clock yesterday everything was settled
> except the Great Seal, and in the afternoon the great
> news transpired that Brougham had accepted it.
> Great was the surprise, greater still the joy at a
> charm having been found potent enough to lay the
> unquiet spirit, a bait rich enough for his restless
> ambition. . . . I was persuaded that he had made
> to himself a political existence the like of which
> no man had ever possessed, and that to have refused
> the Great Seal would have appeared more glorious
> than to take it; intoxicated with his Yorkshire
> honours, swollen with his own importance, and
> holding in his hands questions which he could
> employ to thwart, embarrass and ruin the Ministry,
> I thought he meant to domineer the House of Com-
> mons and to gather popularity throughout the
> country by enforcing popular measures of which

[1] Broughton : *Recollections of a Long Life*, iv. 74.
[2] Princess Lieven : *Letters during her Residence in London, 1812–24*,
p. 277.

'Hush!—— How astonished he'll be
when he awakes.'

HB

SAMSON AND DELILAH
From a sketch by H. B. Doyle.

he would have all the credit, and thus establish a sort of individual power and authority which would ensure his being dreaded, courted and consulted by all parties. He would have then gratified his vanity, ambition and turbulence; the Bar would have supplied fortune, and events would have supplied enjoyments suited to his temperament; it would have been a sort of madness, mischievous but splendid.

" As it is, the joy is great and universal; all men feel that he is emasculated, and drops on the Woolsack as on his political death-bed; once in the House of Lords there is an end of him, and he may rant, storm and thunder without hurting anybody." [1]

With Brougham on the Woolsack Grey had no further difficulty about making up his Cabinet. In the cant of modern politics it might have been described as a National Government. It was made up of men holding widely different political views, who had been in opposition to each other before, and within a few years would again be on opposite sides of the two Houses of Parliament. Between them they could claim a large amount of support in the country, but only because they were temporarily united in a project for some measure of parliamentary reform. Their reasons for advocating such reform were not those which would have gained them much support; for nearly all the Ministers, except perhaps Brougham, believed that a change of electorate was the only chance of preserving the rule of the landed aristocracy. In the homelier phraseology of those times, it was a Broad-bottomed Administration, and as such was not likely to have a very long life.

[1] Greville : *Journal*, November 20th, 1820, ii. 67.

CHAPTER XIII

THE REFORMING CHANCELLOR

Nothing is more common than for men to wish, and call loudly too, for a reformation, who when it arrives do by no means like the severity of its aspect. Reformation is one of those pieces which must be put at some distance in order to please. Its greatest favourers love it better in the abstract than in the substance.

BURKE.

" IF Brougham had not accepted the Chancellorship " must remain one of those interesting conjectures with which historians sometimes amuse themselves. Greville's predictions were not immediately fulfilled. The next four years were, perhaps, the most interesting and important in Brougham's life. He accomplished much between the beginning of 1831 and the end of 1834. He initiated a number of important legal reforms, and as a member of the Cabinet he successfully pressed forward his old demands for the emancipation of slaves, and State aid for popular education. During the first two years he took a leading part in the passing of the Reform Bill, the " Revolution of 1832." For the sake of clearness, it will be best to deal with these two fields of activity in separate chapters. Neither Brougham's position nor the personnel of the Whig Cabinet were altered when the first " reformed " Parliament met in the beginning of 1833, though the introduction of a large Radical element into the House of Commons probably enhanced Brougham's relative importance. It is possible, therefore, to consider the first years of Whig rule as a period of continuous activity, in which Brougham worked away for certain reforms, and took his share in the great constitutional changes.

Although in the long run his mother and Greville were right, Brougham had no intention of letting the Woolsack become his "political death-bed." In spite of the unhappy lapse about his second title, he does not seem to have been overwhelmed by the pageantry of his new office. He kept his sense of humour. Three days after his appointment he was "in excellent spirits" at dinner, when Sefton "quizzed him" unmercifully, and "walked out before him with the fire shovel for mace."[1] He did his best to keep on his old footing with those with whom he used to work. He surprised Hobhouse by turning up, a week later, to the committee meeting of the Society for the Diffusion of Knowledge, where he "transacted business, as usual, with much speed and accuracy. The company, consisting of some of the most scientific men in the land, seemed proud of their patron. Indeed it is somewhat a wonderful sight to see such a man in such a place."[2] In those days a lord was a lord, and Brougham set a new example by refusing to sign his letters by his title. For the rest of his life he used his old "H. B.," and answered fully if illegibly an enormous personal correspondence, sometimes two hundred letters a day. He had always been considerate and unaffected in dealing with his juniors. Le Marchant, who became his principal secretary, described how he was not "changed in this respect by his elevation to office, although he must have been tried by the homage at first paid to him. On the day he took his seat on the Woolsack at Westminster, Prince Leopold, and the Dukes of Sussex, Gloucester and Devonshire, and many noblemen and foreign ambassadors, attended to do him homage. The gallery and court were crowded with spectators, and the oldest lawyers admitted that there was no instance of such an assemblage on a similar occasion."[3]

[1] Greville : *Journal*, ii. 72.
[2] Broughton : *Recollections*, iv. 74.
[3] Le Marchant : *Life of Lord Althorp*, p. 268.

Brougham's Chancellorship was in itself a portent, terrifying to the propertied classes, and arousing that excited expectation of change which has such a powerful liberalizing effect. The first Labour Government offers a parallel. When Mr. Ramsay MacDonald decided, against the advice of many supporters, to form a minority Government, his chief argument was that it meant a break with tradition, and a change in the tone of the Administration. In 1830 a Reformist Chancellor, even in a Whig " family " Government, was as great an innovation as a Labour Prime Minister in 1924. It would not appear in the same light to the country at large as to politicians or to officials, like Greville, who appreciated better the Conservative bias of the constitution. " I do not know," wrote Lord Dudley, " what effect the appointment may produce now, but I am perfectly sure that a few years ago it would have seemed like the beginning of a revolution, such was the terror and aversion that his name inspired. As it is, I cannot but think that the clergy in general, and a large part of the landed gentlemen, will regard him with an evil eye." [1]

It was in this spirit, as the forerunner of a peaceful revolution, that Brougham began his work. There is no reason to doubt the sincerity of his valedictory address to his Yorkshire constituents. " The thing which dazzled me most in accepting office was not the gewgaw splendour of the place . . . but the field for more extended exertion." During the first two unhappy decades of the century Lord Eldon had made the Chancellorship seem to be the key-stone, locking the whole edifice of Tory reaction. He helped to kill every legal and social reform, let his own Court of Chancery remain a bye-word for delay and injustice, and allowed the English criminal courts to be a subservient instrument in the political repression connected with the names of Castle-reagh and Sidmouth. To reverse this tradition seemed

[1] *Letters to " Ivy,"* p. 356.

a fitting and sufficient task even for a man of Brougham's genius. Though many of his reforms miscarried, or were blocked by politicians and by the great legal trade union, yet his coming was like the opening of shutters and windows in rooms long closed to light or fresh air. Sydney Smith, in a speech on the Reform Bill, described the changed atmosphere.

> "Look at the gigantic Brougham, sworn in at twelve, and before six o'clock has a Bill on the table abolishing the abuses of a court which had been the curse of England for centuries. For twenty-five long years did Lord Eldon sit in the court, surrounded by misery and sorrow, which he never held up a finger to alleviate. The widow and the orphan cried to him as vainly as the town-crier cries when he offers a small reward for a full purse. The bankrupt of the court became the lunatic of the court; estates mouldered away, and mansions fell down, but the fees came in and all was well; but in an instant the iron mace of Brougham shivered to atoms this house of fraud and delay." [1]

Something must be allowed for Sydney Smith's exuberance in the unaccustomed rôle of political speaker. Brougham, though inexperienced in Equity practice, managed to work off most of the arrears in the Chancery Court. He sat late into the evening, and far into the vacation. He once even held his court on Good Friday. This last gesture grievously offended the young Gladstone, then a young Tory at Oxford, and he "repeated with deep complacency a saying of Wetherell, that Brougham was the first judge who had done such a thing since Pontius Pilate." [2] Brougham's schemes for the

---

[1] Lady Holland: *Memoir of Sydney Smith*, p. 36.
[2] John Morley: *Life of Gladstone*, i. 71. Neither the action nor the comment were original. Crabb Robinson in 1817 tells the story of Lord Mansfield proposing to sit on Good Friday, and Serjeant Davy protesting "there has been no precedent since Pontius Pilate."

permanent reform of the Chancery Court were less successful. Although he got rid of many sinecures, he was unable to abolish the Masters in Chancery, who were the principal cause of delay. The Court was still a scandal in the 'fifties when Dickens wrote *Bleak House*, and the chief effect of Brougham's term of office was that he showed the way to a cheaper and more expeditious kind of justice, and made the first real breach in the fortress of eighteenth-century Law and of legal vested interests.

No feat of arms could have been more generally popular. Contemporary literature is full of illusions which show the fear not only of criminal but of civil courts. One of Brougham's earliest decisions was to release a man who had been in gaol for fifteen years for contempt of court. He had been summoned before Lord Eldon for marrying a ward in Chancery without permission, and when the Chancellor said something about men of low family, he replied, " My family is ancient and opulent, and were neither coalheavers nor coalheavers' nephews." It was a bad remark, but it hardly justified a life sentence, for Lord Eldon, in spite of apologies, had shown no signs of relenting. This feeling explains Wellington's unexpected remark that he was " glad Brougham is Chancellor. He is the only man with courage and talent to reform that damned Court." [1] General L'Estrange, returning to England, asked the pilot for news. " Oh," said the sailor, " Brougham is doing wonders in the Court of Chancery. He has decided more causes in the last three months than Eldon did in as many years. There never was such a man." [2] Countrymen coming to London used to include a glance at Brougham in the Chancery Court as one of the sights, to be taken after " mounting the Monument and visiting the lions at the Tower." Brougham was not a great judge, certainly not a great

[1] *Creevey Papers*, ii. 218
[2] Le Marchant : *Life of Lord Althorp*, p. 289.

Equity judge.   His quick mind revolted from the formality and reiterations of the Chancery lawyers, most of whom were violently hostile to the new spirit which the Chancellor was introducing into their court.   Matters were not improved by the constant opposition of Sir Edward Sugden, the leading Chancery barrister, who had quarrelled bitterly with Brougham when they were both in the Commons.[1]   They wrangled continually, and Brougham seems to have countered Sugden's forensic verbosity by dealing with correspondence and working out mathematical problems.   Brougham's decisions are not landmarks in Equity law, but judicial procedure had reached such a pass that justice would have been better served by the tossing of a coin, and the popular instinct was right in its support of the Chancellor's methods.

In other fields Brougham's legal reforms met fierce opposition and achieved only partial success.   He did much administratively to make justice cheaper and speedier.   He showed the country that the " Law," which had for so long been a bad master, might in time become a good servant.   He could not, however, realize more than a portion of the great programme which he had sketched out in 1828.   Although he lived long enough to see many of his ideas put into practice, he was continually thwarted during his term of office.   His Local Courts Bill may have contained faults in drafting, but it was blocked for other reasons by a group of Law Lords.   They saw, in the scattering of legal business, the end of a lucrative monopoly, and many, like Lord Lyndhurst, were glad to defeat anything of Whig origin.

---

[1] Greville ascribes Sugden's personal quarrel with Brougham to an interjection by the latter when Sugden, " speaking of Fox, said he ' had no great respect for his authority '; on which Brougham merely said, loud enough to be heard all over the House, and in that peculiar tone which cuts like a dagger, ' Poor Fox.'   The words, the tone were electrical; everybody burst into roars of laughter.   Sugden was so overwhelmed that he said it was with difficulty he could go on, and he vowed he would never forgive this sarcasm."   *Journal*, iii. 23.

Lyndhurst, although a Tory, had been appointed Chief Baron by Lord Grey, but he was not won over by this gesture. He first delayed the Bill and then persuaded the Lords to throw it out, on the ground that the appointment of the County Court judges would give too much patronage to the Chancellor. So England had to wait till 1846 for the " County Courts," which would enable small men to enforce small claims or collect small debts cheaply and expeditiously.

The same objection about the creation of new patronage was raised by Wetherell and Sugden against Brougham's Bankruptcy Bill. In this case the Opposition was not successful, and his scheme was passed for regulating and simplifying the procedure in cases of bankruptcy. This jealousy about the power of appointment to new offices acted as a break upon many schemes of reform. To some extent Brougham countered it by abolishing sinecures attached to his office, and amounting to over £17,000 a year. He also got rid of that venerable nest of jobbery, the Scottish Court of Exchequer. This was a considerable achievement at a time when the Cabinet as a whole was doing very little to redeem its " economy " pledges. Apart from Brougham the new Government was almost entirely a Whig " family " affair. It was not merely a question of nepotism, though Grey did introduce a considerable number of his own relations—Lord Durham, his son-in-law, became Privy Seal; Lord Howick, his son, an Under-Secretary; Ellice, a brother-in-law, was made Secretary to the Treasury, and Barrington, another son-in-law, Lord of the Admiralty. The rest of the Government was drawn from a few families. The Cabinet consisted of fifteen members—thirteen peers or sons of peers, one baronet, and one untitled commoner. The men in the lesser offices were mostly of the same type, with eighteenth-century traditions of living at the expense of the country. Below them again were the old retainers, lean and hungry after twenty-five years, and longing for the

" £1200 a year " jobs. This sum was exactly what Creevey received, when at the mature age of sixty-two he entered the Civil Service as Treasurer of the Ordnance.

When men like Creevey, who had been noted for his attacks upon jobbery, could fall so easily into the system, it is not surprising that Grey and the Canningites did little towards removing the old abuses. There was a difference, both in practice and theory, between Brougham and the rest of the Government. Brougham not only did far more to abolish useless officials than did any of his colleagues, but he fought and was defeated upon the principle of compensation to the holders of sinecures. It was an expensive decision by the Cabinet, for it became a precedent for large payments of public money whenever any future Government ended such abuses, as, for example, the purchase of army commissions. In this, as in so many other matters, Brougham was in advance of conventional Victorian opinion. He also departed from the usual custom, in allowing the Bishops to make most of the Church appointments which are in the Chancellor's gift. One of the few exceptions was the offer of a living to Dr. Arnold, which was declined. Two other appointments are interesting. " I am in high good humour with him," wrote Macaulay in December 1830, " he has given my brother a living of £300 a year in Warwickshire, without the least solicitation, direct or indirect. It was the first living he had to give, and nothing could be done more handsomely." [1] Brougham also gave a living to Connop Thirlwall, who had been forced to resign his tutorship at Cambridge for writing a pamphlet in favour of admitting Dissenters. The *History of Greece* was one of the fruits of the leisure which the holder of a country benefice was then expected to enjoy.

Returning to Brougham's judicial reforms, some of his most important and valuable work was of a rather technical nature. He abolished the antiquated system of

[1] Macvey Napier : *Correspondence*, p. 99.

" fines and recovery," and thus began the great task of simplifying the conveyance of land. Many famous lawyers, including Lord Birkenhead, have continued the process, which is still far from complete. Brougham would have liked to institute the system of land registration, and drafted a Bill to this effect. He arranged for its introduction in the House of Commons by his brother William, but Lord Althorp would not sponsor it, and Brougham, like his successors, found he was opposed by one of the most powerful vested interests in the country. He had less trouble in founding a new Court of Appeal—the " Judicial Committee of the Privy Council." This took the place of the Court of Delegates, a cumbrous survival from the sixteenth century. The ecclesiastical jurisdiction of the new Court did not remain unchallenged, but as the Empire grew and communications became easier, the Committee acquired its modern importance as an imperial court of appeal. According to Greville, who was adversely affected by the change, Brougham " smuggled his Privy Council Bill through the House of Lords without the slightest notice or remark," which suggests that by 1833 he was learning the most effective method of dealing with obstruction.[1]

Peel had already done much to humanize the criminal law, but Brougham was able to continue the work with the help of his old friend Denman, who had become Attorney-General. The death penalty had been abolished for a number of offences against property, and the list was extended to horse-stealing, burglary and forgery. Then the Lords, faithful to their tradition, took alarm and insisted on retaining capital punishment for the falsification of wills, and some other felonies. Brougham's reforms may seem a light harvest for a man with his great backing in the country, but he was like a farmer taking over land which is neglected and sour. His great achievement was in showing his generation that legal reform was possible, just as Lord Grey showed

[1] Greville : *Journal*, ii, p. 370.

that the constitution could be altered.   But in the legal world Brougham had to face a more subtle and effective resistance than was roused by the most far-reaching changes in industrial or social conditions.

Outside his special sphere of legal reform, Brougham found his influence was limited.   In the House of Lords the Whigs, though weak in numbers, were strong in debate.   Grey, Durham, Lansdowne, Melbourne, Holland and Goderich were Cabinet ministers of some standing and ability.   Brougham would occasionally be called upon to defend his own legal measures, or to speak upon some question of foreign policy, such as the Methuen Treaty or the Russian-Dutch Loan, but he missed the cut-and-thrust of the Lower House.   For the first two years the Reform Bill brought periods of great excitement, but normally there were only a few comatose figures, half lost in the gloom of the old Upper Chamber, with, perhaps, the Iron Duke, deaf but persistent, ready to shake an admonitory finger if the Chancellor upset the deadly decorum of the Lords.   Sometimes the Chancellor attempted to bring a little life into that assembly, but the only result was to involve him in acrimonious and futile disputes with a group of old Law Lords, who watched his every step with jealous and hostile eyes.   A year after his appointment Brougham gave evidence before the Committee on the Reduction of Official Salaries.   He seems to have spoken in that ingenuous way, which confounded his friends and enemies, about the disadvantages of being a peer.

" He told us that his colleagues in the Cabinet had obliged him to change his mode of living.   He had wished to continue in his house in Hill St., but had been forced to move into Berkeley Square; and also that instead of one chariot, he had now two coaches and two chariots, in spite of his earnest remonstrances.   When speaking of the retiring pensions given to ex-Chancellors, he said that he

wished to God he could be *dispeered* by Act of
Parliament, and return to his profession; but as that
could not be, he had thought of a scheme for
increasing the retiring salary, and giving the
ex-Minister something to do." [1]

Time did not ease his nostalgia for the fierce delight of
battle with his real peers, the opposition in the Commons
and the opposing counsel in the Law Courts. His
position was made more difficult by the popular enthusiasm which was roused by the Reform Bill struggle,
and which tended to concentrate upon Brougham as the
most remarkable and picturesque figure in the Government. His old connection with the Press brought him
the most embarrassing encomiums, which only added to
the excitement. Campbell describes the atmosphere in
which he lived outside the House. "Dedications, attempting to describe his virtues, were showered down upon
him by all classes, particularly the clergy; strangers
flocked to London from all parts of the kingdom to look
at him; the Court of Chancery, generally a desert from
its dullness, as often as he sat there was crowded to
suffocation; when his carriage drew up in a street a
mob of admirers gathered round to see him get out,
cheering him as he passed by; and the Italian image
boys gave orders for grosses of Lord Brougham in plaster
of Paris faster than they could be manufactured. In this
palmy state he could not be accused of 'high-blown
pride,' for he was good-humoured and courteous and
kind to everybody, and seemed to regret that he could
not all times enjoy social intercourse with old acquaint-
ances in a footing of perfect equality."

Inevitably Brougham made mistakes. He had been
forced into the life of a modern celebrity without the
safeguards of a modern office staff, telephones, card-
indexes and Press agents. He made promises of
patronage and support which he forgot to fulfil. His

---

[1] Broughton : *Recollections*, iv. 84.

A GREAT *ACTOR* PLAYING TO *EMPTY* BENCHES

From a sketch by H. B. Doyle.

Sept. 14, 1832.

exuberant vitality got him into trouble inside and outside Parliament. Careless or challenging statements which would pass almost unnoticed in the give-and-take of the House of Commons, would in the House of Lords re-echo like some ill-timed jest uttered in a mausoleum. He is supposed to have grievously offended the legal fraternity by remarking, in connection with the Warwick Disenfranchisement Bill—

> "It will be necessary for the House to name the counsel by whom it is assisted; if not, all Westminster Hall may be let in upon us. There is now an order generally that counsel may be heard, and any one gentleman, or score of gentlemen, on the look-out, may come dropping in under cover for the purpose of being engaged as counsel."

Then there was the absurd incident of his "forcing the guard." His coach was held up at the archway of the Horse Guards when he was on his way to the Queen's Reception. The officer was probably under a misapprehension, because he had just allowed the Speaker to go through. It is no longer worth discussing whether the footman did not understand Brougham's order, or what he told the coachman, which made the latter push on. The affair is only of interest because the importance then attached to it, the hullabaloo in Press and Parliament showed how every slip was magnified. The Marquess of Londonderry, that disgruntled pension-hunter, seized the opportunity for one of those personal duels with the Chancellor which recur with unnecessary frequency in the pages of *Hansard*.

Another violent quarrel, this time with Sugden, who was in the Commons, arose out of Brougham's characteristic weakness. He never quite accepted the contemporary view that the State was just a corporation from which as much should be got as possible, and that public money should not be saved at the expense of those in public life. Amongst the sinecures which Brougham

R

abolished, one was vacant. It had to be filled temporarily, and Brougham knew that any holder, under the
vicious system accepted by the Cabinet, would claim
compensation. He put in his brother James, as a person
whom he could trust not to make such a claim. If it
had merely been a straightforward piece of nepotism,
nobody would have much minded, but it was like his
offer to go act negotiator with America in 1812, and his
suggestion to Lyndhurst, which caused so much annoyance in 1834. It was an offence against the spoils
system as then operating.

Inside the Cabinet Brougham must have felt rather
isolated. Grey and Lansdowne had come to terms with
the Canningites without consulting him, and both
sections belonged to a social sphere in which Brougham
was never fully accepted as an equal. Amongst the
fifteen members he was like a stranger in a company of
people calling each other by their Christian names.
Cabinet secrets were then fairly well kept. There was
much gossip, recorded in correspondence and diaries,
but not that direct revelation of confidential statements
upon which future historians will be able to draw when
describing political events in post-war England. Certain
differences about parliamentary reform were brought to
light during the dispute between Durham and Brougham
in 1834, but most of the dissensions, which must have
occurred in Grey's rather patchwork Ministry, stayed
within four walls. It is, therefore, difficult to assess
Brougham's personal share in the flood of legislation
which followed immediately after the Reform Bill and
occupied the first years of the " reformed " House of
Commons. Amongst the most important measures of
1833, which he defended in the Lords, there were two
which were intimately connected with his previous
career—the abolition of slavery and the first educational
grant.

Brougham had always retained his close personal
connection with the " Saints," and with the movement

for Emancipation. His Yorkshire candidature was chiefly due to his great speech advocating abolition, and there is abundant evidence in his correspondence of his intimate relations with Zachary Macaulay and Fowell Buxton. Under Buxton's instigation, Canning had issued a circular in 1823 about the better treatment of slaves, but this had done little more than rouse " planter " opposition, and much talk about " Independence." The totally indefensible case of the missionary Smith, which Brougham had ventilated in the Commons, did much to keep the question alive during the later 'twenties. The Grey Cabinet considered it was useless to work through the Jamaican Assembly, and decided upon immediate emancipation. Stanley, who had fortunately succeeded the incompetent Goderich at the Colonial Office, had charge of the Bill in the Commons. Brougham was its chief protagonist in the Lords. As finally amended the Bill abolished slavery in 1834, ordered that all small children should then be entirely free, but that others should be bound by a system of " legal apprentice-ship " which was to last for seven years. The sum of £20,000,000 compensation was paid.

This was a signal triumph for the Liberal element inside the Cabinet, for there is little doubt that several members were indifferent, and others, like Melbourne, were hostile. " They would have their fancy," Melbourne is reported to have said, " and so we've abolished slavery, but it's great folly." [1] It may be remembered that the eight years before all Canningites had voted against Brougham's motion for an inquiry into the case of the missionary Smith, and Hobhouse quotes a conversation at Holland House shortly before the introduction of the Abolition Bill. " We talked about Lord Mulgrave's dissolution of the Jamaica Assembly, and Brougham read Mulgrave's speech aloud. We agreed that it was a very good speech for the purpose; but Lord

[1] Archbishop Whately's Table Talk. *Life and Correspondence*, p. 417.

Melbourne rose, and as he was going away, said, 'By
G—d, you are ruining your empire.' 'Yes,' said Lady
Holland, 'and there is the chief sinner,' pointing to
Brougham." [1]   The division on this subject was typical
of that cleavage within the Whig Party which was to
lead to its disruption in 1834, and the long eclipse of
its more advanced wing.

Brougham's speech in the Lords on the Slavery Abolition Bill was memorable for his attack on the Duke of
Cumberland.   The " Butcher " had joined Lord Londonderry and the other ultra-Conservatives in the dangerous
game of baiting the new Chancellor.   There had already
been what the modern newspaper delights to call
" scenes," and Brougham could not resist the opportunity of a little lecture to their Lordships on the equality
of British subjects, and at the same time indulging in a
well-turned sarcasm at the expense of the Duke.   The
Bill, he explained, " would give the man of colour as
clear a right to sit in that house (if his Majesty should so
please) as either of the illustrious Dukes now present
(Wellington and Cumberland), whether the illustrious
Duke who is illustrious by his deeds, or the illustrious
Duke who is illustrious by the courtesy of the House."
So far Brougham's prediction has not been fulfilled, and
it was ninety years later that the first Indian peer was
appointed.

In the same year as the passing of the Abolition Act,
Brougham persuaded the Cabinet to make their first
grant for elementary education.   It was a very small
beginning.   A Treasury Grant of £20,000 a year, to be
administered by the two Societies—the National Society
and its Nonconformist rival the British and Foreign
School Society, with which Brougham had been intimately connected for many years.   The State took no
responsibility, and Brougham, after the failure of his
Bill in 1820, seems to have become reconciled to the
voluntary system.   " I am of the opinion," he told the

[1] Broughton : *Recollections*, iv. 280.

Lords, " that the only safe course which we can take for the supplying of the lamentable deficiency which I have described is to furnish the great towns with the funds now wanting, and to apply this public aid so as not to interfere with the exertions of individual zeal or cut off the supplies of private munificence." [1]   He continued to work for elementary education long after he had ceased to have any connection with the Whig Government under Melbourne, but circumstances forced him to become an opportunist striving to pick up what crumbs he could in the way of a normal school, or the proper allocation of charitable funds.   From this first meagre grant of £20,000 was to develop, very, very slowly, the system of State education which he had promulgated in 1820; the grant led to supervision, supervision to control, and control to responsibility.   Indian State education has developed in the same way from the first grant of £10,000 a year, which was made, curiously enough, twenty years earlier than the English grant.

Brougham's great energy led him to take an active interest in some of the minor responsibilities of his office.   Following Lord Lyndhurst's example, he went into the question of the many lunatics who were under his care, and produced a new scheme for their proper management.   " The Chancellor's idiots " had been one of the minor scandals of Lord Eldon's time.   He even found time to consider the question of literary patronage, and began a correspondence in 1831 with Southey. Brougham seems to have suggested a " Guelphic Order " to encourage authors, but Southey, remarking that he would then prefer to be a Ghibelline, concentrated on the thorny subject of the Copyright Act. [2]

[1] *Parl. Deb.*, 3rd Series, xxvii. 1319.
[2] Greville : *Journal*, ii. 115.

CHAPTER XIV

LAUNCHING THE REFORM BILL

From Sam, " the Chancellor's motto "—nay,
    Confound his puns, he knows I hate 'em;
" Pro Rege, Lege, Grege "—Ay,
    For King read " Mob ! "   Brougham's old erratum.
                                            Ingoldsby Legends.

BROUGHAM's lack of an organized political following has led to some misunderstanding of the part which he played in the extremely complicated struggle preceding the passing of the Reform Bill. From the orthodox Whig standpoint his conduct can easily be made to appear anomalous and unworthy, and it will be necessary, therefore, to consider the position of the Whig Party, and of Brougham himself, during the first month or two of Lord Grey's Ministry. Parliamentary reform had been one of the three points on which the Whigs had fought the election of 1830, but in those days of pocket boroughs and of counties dominated by landed interests, political programmes were not taken very seriously. One important section of the new Government, the Canning-ites, were not pledged to reform, and never showed the least enthusiasm for it. Many of the Whigs were known to be hardly more enthusiastic than Palmerston or Melbourne.

In the country Brougham was probably considered as the leading Whig exponent of Parliamentary Reform. Alexander Somerville, in his *Autobiography of a Working Man,* describes how he heard of the fall of the Wellington Ministry when quarrying in Scotland. " We took off our hats and caps, and loud above the north wind, and the roaring sea, shouted ' Henry Brougham for ever.'

At that time we knew little of Earl Grey." [1] In political circles Grey, Durham and Lord John Russell had a reputation as parliamentary reformers, but a series of unsuccessful motions, brought forward at intervals, did not show any great uniformity in Whig ideas on the subject, and Grey had been at pains, as recently as 1827, to disclaim any marked leaning towards " democracy." " If there should come a contest," he said in the Lords, " between this House and a great portion of the people, my part is taken, and with that order to which I belong I will stand or fall." [2]

There seem to have been three main causes for the sudden impulse which drove the Whig Ministry to bring forward an extremely drastic Reform Bill during the early months of 1831. The first was the disturbed state of Southern England and of Ireland, which led to repressions so severe that they were bound to alienate Radical opinion. The second was the rapid development of the middle-class movement for reform. It was specially strong in Birmingham under the leadership of Thomas Attwood, Joseph Parkes and the local " Political Union," but powerful all over industrial England. The third reason, which possibly has not been sufficiently emphasized in many standard works, was the complete failure, in nearly every department, of the new Ministry during the first month or two of office. These were the chief considerations which encouraged Grey to attempt the familiar political manœuvre of " dishing the Radicals " by an unexpectedly far-reaching Reform Bill, just as thirty-five years later Disraeli was to play the same trick on the Whigs.

The new Government inherited part of their troubles from the Duke of Wellington's hapless Ministry, but matters were made worse by two unfortunate appointments. The quick-tempered Conservative-minded

[1] A. Somerville : *Autobiography of a Working Man.* Quoted in J. R. M. Butler's *The Passing of the Great Reform Bill*, p. 156.
[2] *Hansard*, N. S. xvii. 1261.

Stanley, as Chief Secretary for Ireland, was not likely to ease conditions in that disturbed island. The lethargic Melbourne, as Home Secretary, was a palpable misfit in any reformist Government. Twelve years before he had supported the repressive policy of Sidmouth and Castlereagh. He had been reared in the traditional fear of the *sans-culottes*, had recently served under the Duke of Wellington, and it was a political arrangement rather than any change of view that had brought him into Grey's Cabinet. Directly he took office he had to deal with the agricultural disturbances, the " last labourers' revolt," which had broken out in the southern counties towards the end of Wellington's term of office.

The tragedy of this repression remains one of the most unhappy chapters in English history. Lord Grey and the whole Whig party must bear some share of responsibility for the lamentable Winchester Assize—only comparable with Judge Jeffrey's Western Circuit—and for the transportation, after the first panic was over, of 457 farm-workers and others to a living hell in Australia. Brougham, like Grey, allowed himself to be persuaded that this miserable abortive rising of half-starved labourers constituted a threat to the Government far more serious than the Yorkshire Luddite riots with which he had had so much to do. The early reports must have been very exaggerated, and Brougham, like so many Radicals, was more ignorant, and therefore more afraid, of the countryman than of the northern industrial worker. Even Cobbett allowed that " with all his half Scotch crotchets " Brougham " has at any rate no blood about him," but he was swept away by the universal feeling against the labourers, just as were the two leading Radicals, Burdett and Hobhouse. He attempted to justify himself in a letter written about this time.

> " People forget *now* what alarm they were in, and how they called on Government to pacify the country. *It is pacified*, and now the selfsame people

cry out against the very means by which peace has been restored. If the worst criminals escape the burnings, etc. will begin again, and far more punishments will be necessary from ill-judged lenity now. It is true mercy to make timely examples, not going beyond what is necessary. In 1813 seventeen men were hanged at York by the Special Commission, yet all the Luddite riots were over months before. Fourteen of these were for cases of no blood and very little violence, mere burglaries and robberies. Here, though the disturbances have been infinitely greater, only three suffer." [1]

But in this wretched affair " the chief shame attaches to Melbourne, who let the judges do their worst." [2] He made no attempt to inquire into the destitution, which in December 1830 was driving men to excesses, and in the summer of 1831, when the " revolt " had been suppressed, irretrievably damned himself by proposing to allow landowners to use spring-guns " under licence," though this had been made a misdemeanour under an Act of 1826. Melbourne in England, and Stanley in Ireland, effectually destroyed any claim on the part of the Whigs to be more humane or to have a better understanding of the poorer classes than the Tories. The unsuccessful prosecution of Cobbett, when he was able to call Whig Ministers, including Brougham, as witnesses for the defence, was only another stage in the process by which the Whigs lost the respect of working men and women.

More serious from the immediate political standpoint was the threatened alienation of the middle-class Radicals. Their conscience had not been much disturbed by the happenings in the South. Like all the comfortable classes at that time, they were obsessed by ill-digested Malthusian theories, and they looked with some alarm

[1] Add. MSS. 34615, f. 13.
[2] Mr. and Mrs. J. L. Hammond: *The Village Labourer*, p. 290 *et seq.*

and no great sympathy on certain working-class move-ments—syndicalist rather than socialist—which were developing in the industrial areas. " The nonsense to which your Lordship alludes," wrote James Mill to Brougham, " about the right of the labourers to the whole produce of the country, wages, profits and rent all included, is the mad nonsense of our friend Hodgskin which he had published as a system, and propagated with the zeal of perfect fanaticism. These opinions, if they were to spread, would be the subversion of all civilised society, worse than the overwhelming deluge of Huns and Tartars." [1]

But the threat to the Radicals from this side only made them the more critical of the complete failure of the Whigs to redeem their economic pledges. Althorp was a poor Chancellor of the Exchequer, and his first budget had to be withdrawn in February 1831. The most damning point was the failure of the Whigs to abolish sinecures and cut down the swollen pension lists, which many of them had been denouncing for some years past. The real obstacle was that the whole aristocratic system had been built up by grants of public money, and the Cabinet was full of men whose families had been great " tax-eaters " in the past. " Those damned pension lists," wrote Creevey, " are a cursed millstone about the neck of the Government. Grey was almost *crying* when he talked to Sefton of the difficulty and misery of de-priving so many people of their subsistence." [2] Some-how Grey could never be brought to envisage sinecures as a serious evil. He went into " fits of laughter over the leathering of Jimmy " in *John Bull*.[3] " Jimmy " was Sir James Mackintosh, who had accepted a post in the India Office, though he had quite recently voted for its abolition as a sinecure. Men outside the magic circle found the joke less mirth-compelling. It was certainly

1 A. Bain : *Life of James Mill*, p. 364.
2 *Creevey Papers*, ii. 218 .
3 J. Gore : *Creevey's Life and Times*, p. 337.

not the spirit in which " Old Corruption " would be destroyed.

Althorp was the most notable failure, but there was an equal lack of drive and enterprise in most of the other departments except the Lord Chancellor's Office. Brougham was in a very difficult and isolated position. For years he had been almost alone in urging the Whigs to accept a policy of social reform, and when they at last reached office, he had a sheaf of plans for the future, of which parliamentary reform was only one.   Within his own limited sphere he could begin operations at once.   Not only did he introduce a number of new measures within the first two months, but he began an active campaign against those sinecures which were under his jurisdiction.   The value of this early individual effort was appreciated by reformists in the country, but Brougham must have been fully aware that, apart from the question of parliamentary reform, there were no prospects of any similar activities by other Ministers. Even his own attempts at cutting down useless officials had been nullified by Althorp's insistence on the principle of compensation.   It was at this period that Brougham was accused of starting a Press campaign to liven up the Government.

A short digression is necessary upon Brougham's relations with *The Times*, and its editor, Thomas Barnes. The recent publication of " *The Thunderer* " *in the Making* has thrown some new light upon a friendship which began when the lawyer and the journalist were both trying to help Leigh Hunt and the *Examiner* through the difficult years from 1812 onwards.   Barnes became editor of *The Times* in 1817, and for the next fifteen years Brougham was his most valuable " contact " in the political world. After Lord Liverpool's death a kind of working arrange-ment seems to have developed whereby Brougham supplied information, and Barnes seconded many of his political activities.   There is no evidence that Brougham ever wrote leaders for *The Times*, or inspired the paper as directly as is suggested by Maclise's sketch.[1]   The feeling against barristers and politicians writing for the daily press was still very strong.   " As for Lord Brougham," wrote Bulwer Lytton in *England and the English*, " the bitterest accusation ever made against him was that he wrote for a certain newspaper."   Barnes himself would have objected to such an arrangement, but " how closely he was in touch with Brougham at this time is proved by letters which, by a rare exception, have survived.   They enable the inspiration of Brougham to be illustrated from leading articles in *The Times* on the Test and Emancipation questions, and on the Duke of Wellington's difficulties in forming a Cabinet at the beginning of 1828." [2]

In 1830 Barnes lent his general support to Lord Grey's Government, but, like Brougham, tended to criticize its supineness, the composition of the Ministry, and its lax ideas about sinecures.   Barnes and Brougham " breakfasted together frequently," and a regular contact was established through William Brougham and Denis Le Marchant.   Their object was to prevent any retreat on the question of Parliamentary Reform, and to press for certain other measures.   The Whig aristocracy bitterly resented this kind of pressure, which was almost a new experience for them, but they had only themselves to thank.   Brougham owed them no personal loyalty. They had excluded him from the inner counsels of the Party before the Ministry was formed; they did their best to force him into a subordinate position outside the Cabinet; they were now, from Brougham's standpoint, failing to redeem their pledges to the country.   It was a time of crisis, with thrones tottering all over Europe, and Brougham, finding his counsels disregarded in the Cabinet, began to organize opinion outside.   There

---

[1] The reference to Brougham's contributions in Dasent's *Life of Delane* is probably due to a confusion with William Brougham, who worked on the paper for a time.

[2] " *The Thunderer* " *in the Making*, p. 256.   The letters show that Brougham only supplied information and hints of probable developments.

British Museum.

SKETCH OF BROUGHAM REPUTED TO BE BY MACLISE

is no evidence that he wished to replace the Prime Minister. It was not a campaign like that of 1915, but only one, for which there are several modern parallels, to " ginger up " a feeble Government.

A letter from Lord Sefton to Creevey shows how these activities appeared to the patricians. It incidentally fathers a useful modern word upon Brougham.

> " . . . There is a systematic attack upon Grey and panegyrics upon Brougham, with a comparison between them to the prejudice of the former. Brougham's late advancement of Masters in Chancery is selected as a case in point.   ' The Lord Chancellor it is said, had two brothers lawyers, but he thinks it is his duty to give this patronage to the old practitioners in his Court. How unlike the *Nepotism* of Lord Grey.' Now you must know, Barry, that this word Nepotism as meaning relationship is known to be Brougham's *own word*, and it is equally known that William Brougham, the youngest brother and a clever chap, is a regular writer in *The Times*. Under these circumstances Lord Grey is deeply impressed with the idea that these attacks come from Brougham himself. . . ." [1]

The suspicion led to a bitter dispute between Brougham and Lord Durham, who was quite capable of bullying his father-in-law, but strongly resented anyone else doing so. This was the beginning of a personal quarrel which was to last for the rest of Durham's stormy career.

Brougham's campaign was important because it undoubtedly helped to frighten the Cabinet, until, scared by the rising tide of discontent, the Ministers decided that the only way of retrieving their position was a strong measure of parliamentary reform. Grey, who had a keen theoretical interest in a certain type of reform, was thus able to give Lord John Russell a free hand.   It was

[1] *Creevey's Life and Times*, p. 338.

sound political strategy.   Besides appeasing the Radicals, a struggle with the Crown and with the Lords might provide an effective counter-irritant to the many economic troubles which had been the cause of such alarming disturbances throughout England.   A good constitutional quarrel would rally the middle classes, and might make poorer men forget they were hungry.

Grey's own point of view is interesting.   He undoubtedly looked upon parliamentary reform as the only method of saving aristocratic rule.   The pocket boroughs had gradually been bought up by the type of men whom Grey most disliked—the stockjobbers, the war profiteers, the Indian " nabobs," the new rich who had been freely raised to the peerage by Pitt.   Grey felt that the scales had been unfairly weighted against the old Whig governing classes.   The " closed boroughs " prevented the natural swing of the pendulum between the two parties. This was made evident in the years after the Napoleonic wars, when the Whigs might normally have expected to gain a majority.   Grey's main object, therefore, was to get rid of the " closed " boroughs, of which at least two-thirds were held by Tories.   He knew that in the counties and the " open " constituencies, the old Whig landed families would still have every prospect of success, owing to their experience and local connections.   He was fortunate to have, in Lord John Russell, a young Whig of good family, who also combined a strong theoretical belief in democracy with a full belief in the necessity of having good aristocrats at the head of affairs.   Princess Lieven, who for all her cleverness never really understood the English, wrote regretfully about Grey that " under the most haughty and aristocratic manners he is a thorough democrat."   Really he was at heart as thorough-going an aristocrat as could be found amongst the Tories or the older Whigs.   This was the basis of his hatred of borough-mongering, which few of his Parliamentary followers really shared.   Many of the rank and file knew that they could never afford to fight an open constituency, and reform was their political death-warrant.

Brougham did not see this question of reform in the same light as the patricians. He was the only member of the Cabinet with any real experience of " open " constituencies. He had contested Liverpool, and been defeated because of the limited nature of the franchise. He had fought Westmorland three times, and knew that it was almost as useless for an outsider to stand against the Lowther interest as to put up for a closed borough. He knew that wealth was an important factor even in the one or two " democratic constituencies " like Westminster or Southwark. Yorkshire, it is true, had provided him with a seat under very easy conditions, but normally he would have had to pay his own expenses, and these were prohibitive for anyone without capital upon which to draw. Brougham fully recognized that the urban and industrial areas of the North and Midlands must have their members, but he had less enthusiasm than Grey for the immediate and wholesale abolition of the pocket boroughs, which did at least enable a few unmoneyed men to find their way into Parliament. He saw that the only chance for the " professional " against the landed aristocracy and the very wealthy would be to give the new seats a wide electorate and the ballot.

In order to understand the contest which went on inside the Whig Party it is necessary to remember the main points at issue. (1) How many of the depopulated privately-owned boroughs should be disfranchised? There were, of course, degrees of " rottenness." A very bold measure would abolish about sixty double-member boroughs, and take one member from another fifty. (2) Ought the borough-owners to be compensated? The Whig leaders, except Brougham, had been in favour of compensating the holders of sinecures, even though there had been little pretence of their performing any public service. The borough-mongers could claim that they had paid good money for their rights. (3) What should be the new franchise in counties and boroughs? The former had remained unchanged for four centuries, though the real value of the " forty-shilling freehold " had altered. The borough franchises were a mere lumber-room in which the early efforts at self-government had been allowed to decay. Some uniform system was essential for the new boroughs, but what should be the basis, and should vested interests like those of the " pot-wallers " of Taunton, be recognized and preserved? (4) Should the ballot be introduced? The Radicals were strongly in favour; the Whig patricians, who still hoped to maintain family influences in the " open " constituencies and the counties, were generally against the secret ballot. (5) Finally, as there were bound to be difficulties, both with the King and with the House of Lords, the Government would have to decide which were the most essential points.

On all these questions there would be some difference of opinion between Brougham and other members of the Cabinet. Grey handed over the drafting of the Bill to a Committee of Four, from which Brougham was pointedly omitted. The first choices were Lord John Russell and Durham, which showed that Grey was determined upon a far-reaching measure, at least in regard to the " pocket boroughs." The other two were Sir James Graham, who represented Althorp's views, and Lord Duncannon, who had special knowledge of Ireland. The preparation of the Scottish Reform Bill was entrusted to Jeffrey, who, after consulting with the Committee, went to Westmorland to draw up the Bill with Brougham's help. Apparently Scotland could be left to the professionals.

Lord John Russell, the future introducer of the Bill, held the key position, and this narrowed down the points of difference. Though Brougham undoubtedly resented his exclusion from the Committee, he had much in common with Russell. " Don Giovanni " was an old friend, and could be trusted to recommend the

June 6, 1831.

British Museum.

THE TRICOLORED WITCHES

"*Black Spirits and White,*
Yellow Spirits and Grey,
Mingle, Mingle, Mingle,
You that mingle may."

Shakspeare.

abolition of pocket boroughs without compensation. He wished, however, to do away with the nomination system at once, and pass a Bill which would settle the franchise and the distribution of seats once for all. It was the attitude which later earned him the nickname of "Finality Jack." Brougham would have preferred a series of measures by which "rotten boroughs" would be transferred, but he did not want the Whigs to begin their term of office by staking their existence on a single Bill. Russell wished to establish a uniform electorate, based on a fairly high property qualification. Brougham was almost the only prominent Whig, except Lord Durham, who demanded household franchise.

The main recommendations of the Committee of Four were the total disenfranchisement of some sixty double-barrelled constituencies—these were listed in the famous "Schedule A"; a smaller number of "pocket boroughs" in more populous places were to lose their close franchise, and also one of their two Members; the borough franchise would be based on a minimum £20 rateable value; finally, and surprisingly, the Committee proposed the introduction of the ballot. Grey accepted the first two proposals. The Cabinet lowered the qualification to £10, a figure which had been discussed by the Committee, but refused the suggestion of the ballot—probably because the King would not have permitted the introduction of a Bill containing such an innovation.

The boldness of the attack upon the borough-mongers swamped, as it had been intended to do, all other considerations. Brougham put before the Cabinet his alternative scheme for a piecemeal abolition of nomination boroughs and a wider franchise, but he was placed in the anomalous position of defending abuses. Yet his attitude was logical enough, and was justified by subsequent events. England was not ripe for a permanent settlement of her electoral question. Her population was still growing rapidly, and drifting towards certain centres. Tavistock, for example, under Russell's Bill,

s

received the same number of Members as Manchester. Only a few constituencies and large cities had any democratic organization. The Bill would create a small privileged class, whose support in many areas would be as readily purchasable by the wealthy as were the old pocket boroughs. A series of reform Bills, continually reducing the nomination boroughs, would have been a more satisfactory solution, and would have presented no great difficulty, once rid of Burke's old dogma that the British constitution could not be changed. But as a piece of political strategy the Reform Bill had obvious advantages. The borough-mongers were an easy target, and introduced the personal objective which is so valuable, but the natural fruits of the Reform Bill were Chartism and also that intensification of corruption which was caricatured in the *Pickwick Papers* and Warren's *Ten Thousand a Year*.

Looking back on the constitutional struggle of the next fifteen months, Brougham agreed that " it was Schedule A that finally carried the Bill."

> " Although I had a great tendency towards retaining one member, I could not resist Grey's view of how impossible it was upon principle to give a single person, because he happened to be the proprietor of a borough, the power of naming a representative of the people. I gave up with reluctance my household suffrage for the ten-pound franchise . . . but I succeeded in altering the twenty-pound, which was the sum the Committee had fixed. I was certain that this would create many small constituencies, and on this being stoutly denied by the Committee, I obtained returns, which proved it to demonstration. One town with 17,000 or 18,000 inhabitants had not twenty persons who would have been entitled to vote. In that town there were not even three hundred rated at ten pounds." [1]

[1] Brougham : *Memoirs*, iii. 92.

Brougham argued his case in the Cabinet with his usual vigour, and seems to have worried the leaders. "The measure on the whole was well received, Brougham alone dissentient and disposed to carp by raising little points when he could find no real objections, and very much inclined to defend the Nomination Boroughs."[1] All this was, however, *inside* the Cabinet, and is only known because Durham was away, and letters were written to him explaining what was happening. Once the main lines of the Bill had been accepted, Brougham gave it his full support, and in due course became its sturdy defender in the Lords. It was Palmerston, Lansdowne and Richmond who wished to modify the measure after it had been introduced, and pressed their views upon Lord Grey. Brougham's misgivings were partly appeased by the enthusiasm with which the Bill was received by the Radicals and the country generally. It was a moment when a bold gesture was needed. Whig stock was very low. "The Finance schemes of Ministers," wrote Hobhouse at the end of February, "are universally decried, and were it not for Brougham's Chancery Reform and the expected parliamentary reform, would turn them out."[2]

The gesture came when Russell, the "little fellow not weighing above eight stone," read out the list of sixty boroughs in Schedule A, and proposed to sweep away, without a penny of compensation, "vested interests" worth about a million. The weaknesses of the Bill—the high electoral qualifications which in some constituencies would disfranchise men of the class who already had votes, the dropping of the ballot, the anomalies in distribution of seats—these were for the time disregarded by working-class and middle-class Radicals alike in their joy at the "first great inroad in the accursed system." Hunt, the one working-class Member, was guarded in his approval, but Francis Place

[1] Graham to Durham, January 25, 1831. *Passing of the Great Reform Bill*, p. 185.

[2] Broughton: *Recollections*, iv. 86.

seems to have assumed that once the " constitution " had
been changed, further reforms would follow easily.
Cobbett was equally optimistic, and the contagion
spread.　Burdett and Hobhouse went to a meeting at the
famous " Crown and Anchor " tavern, thinking that
" our Westminster friends would oppose the £10
qualification; but we were wrong, for we found all our
supporters delighted with the Bill." [1]

Brougham, with a better knowledge of the Whigs,
knew that a Bill on these lines would become part of a
new constitution almost as difficult to change as the old.
Grey and Russell had won their first strategic victory over
the Radicals as well as the Tories, but it was a continuous
gamble.　Peel might well have had the Bill thrown out,
if he had moved for its rejection as a revolutionary
movement, immediately after Russell had finished his
speech.　The three weeks' respite before the second
reading showed that there was an unexpected amount of
popular support, but this was not reflected in the Commons, and the second reading was only carried by one
vote.　The risk helped to make the Bill popular.　The
Englishman loves a victory to be " close-run," and the
sporting instincts of the country were now thoroughly
aroused.　Questions of general policy were forgotten
in the excitement of a struggle against the borough-
mongers and the Lords.　In those days the King was
supposed, on very slender grounds, to be in favour of
reform.

The victory of March 22nd, though so close as to make
a defeat in the Committee stage almost certain, was of
great importance.　It would immensely strengthen Grey
in his later demand for the dissolution, which was the
only hope of getting a working majority.　The Tories
recognized the seriousness of their accidental defeat.
Luckily Macaulay was there to describe the scene.
" And the jaw of Peel fell; and the face of Twiss was
as the face of a damned soul; and Herries looked like

[1] *Id.*, iv. 92.

Judas taking the necktie off for the last operation." [1]
If the Bill had been defeated on the second reading, the
King would probably have asked Wellington to form a
Ministry, and some of the waverers, who were against
reform but afraid of their seats, would have taken
courage.   The first Whig Government for a generation
would have disappeared, having achieved nothing except
Brougham's first legal reforms.   Seldom can so much
have depended upon a single vote since the Habeas
Corpus Act passed the House of Lords because a corpulent peer was counted as ten, and the tellers forgot
about their little joke.

Although Brougham disapproved of the Whig leaders
taking risks which seemed unnecessary, he threw himself
into the struggle with his usual energy.   The presenta-
tion of petitions enabled him to make a few preliminary
speeches in the Lords, but his chief activity was in
organizing public opinion outside.   He kept in constant
touch during the next fourteen months with the various
political associations which were springing up all over
the country, and he was responsible, directly and indirectly, for a mass of anonymous pamphleteering and
journalism.   The best known are some imaginary
dialogues in which the rather wooden figures of
Tomkins and Jenkins meditate on politics, and the
very downright pamphlet " What will be done with
the Lords ? "   Both these seem to be Brougham's
own work.

The three weeks between the second reading and the
Committee stage gave Lord Grey time to work upon the
King, who was still unwilling to grant a dissolution.
The process of conversion is shown in the published
correspondence between them, but Grey had not got
any guarantee when a wrecking amendment was passed
against the Government on April 19th, and on the 20th
there was opposition in a committee on the Ordnance

[1] G. O. Trevelyan : *Life and Letters of Lord Macaulay*.   Letter
to Ellis, Chap. iv.

Estimates, which the Lord Chancellor described, two days later, as a " stopping of supplies."

The part which Brougham played in the important crisis of April 1831 has been the subject of some dispute. It is unfortunate that Roebuck in his *History of the Whig Ministry*, written in the 'fifties, gives an inaccurate and highly-coloured account of the dissolution, which he is supposed to have obtained from Brougham, who was then over seventy. There is no evidence that Brougham was responsible for this passage, and the simpler account in his own Memoirs, written also in old age, seems to be substantially correct. The main facts are as follows. Up till April 20, the Ministers did not believe the King would dissolve Parliament, and were prepared to resign. Brougham on that date wrote a memorandum for his successor. On the 21st the King wrote to Grey consenting to a dissolution, and the same evening Lord Wharncliffe gave notice that he would move, on the 22nd, an address to the King against a dissolution.[1] If this had been passed, the King might well have reconsidered his decision. Grey and Brougham accordingly waited on the King next morning. Their object was not, as Roebuck makes it appear, to force a hesitating King to grant a dissolution, but to persuade him to go down in person that very afternoon, before Lord Wharncliffe's motion. Brougham describes in his Memoirs how he first hustled the Cabinet and Lord Grey into approving the visit to the King, and then the King himself into going.

> " (The Cabinet) met accordingly, and almost all agreed to go on, though one or two, appalled by the increasing difficulties, asked if it was too late to reconsider the whole matter. Here I appealed to the Duke of Richmond, and asked him if he had ever seen a council of war held on the field just before going into action. He said, ' By God !

[1] *Correspondence of the late Earl Grey with King William IV*, i. 231.

never; neither I nor anyone else.' Then, said I, let us go in to the King. Grey and I went in, and stated our clear opinion that it would be necessary for him to go in person, though we were most unwilling to give him that trouble. I took care to make him understand the threatened proceedings of the Lords, and the effect the proposed motion for an address was intended to have on his Majesty's proroguing Parliament. He fired up at this— hating dissolution, perhaps, as much as ever, but hating far more the interference with, or attempt to delay, the exercise of the prerogative; and so he at once agreed to go, only saying that all must be done in the usual manner; and he mentioned several things which he said could not be got ready in time, for it was little more than one hour off, and the House meeting at two o'clock." [1]

The chief requirements were someone to carry the sword of state, an escort, and the state coach. Grey agreed to carry the first, and Brougham had, with some coolness, already sent to the Horse Guards. The King, according to Brougham, " said, ' Well, that was a strong measure ' . . . he ever after, when in high good-humour, used to remind me of what he called my high treason." As for the coach, " the King said he was determined to go, and that anything would do. There was a story about London that he said to Lord Albemarle he would go in a hackney-coach rather than not at all." Brougham hurriedly went back to change, took his seat on the Woolsack, while the House of Lords rapidly degenerated into a bear-garden. It was again a " close-run thing," for Wharncliffe's resolution would have been passed without speeches, and the Duke of Richmond had to waste time by an irrelevant motion, while Brougham harangued the Lords on the necessity for a dissolution after the Commons had refused supplies. It was not a

---

[1] Brougham : *Memoirs*, iii. 115 *et seq.*

dignified scene, with the guns booming in the distance, and Brougham frequently going out to see whether the King had arrived. He came in at last, with his crown slightly awry, and Lord Grey " looking like his executioner " carrying the sword of state. The King prorogued Parliament, and added these important words : " I have been induced to resort to this measure for the purpose of ascertaining the sense of my people." [1] It was a sign of a new era, but was by no means the end of the struggle for the Reform Bill.

[1] J. B. Atlay, in his Life of Brougham in *The Victorian Chancellors*, rightly criticizes Roebuck's account, but adds, " even the simpler story contained in Brougham's Memoirs is without foundation " (p. 304). But such points as the ordering of the Horse Guards, the hasty closing of the Cabinet meeting, and sending to the Earl Marshal, are corroborated in a letter which Brougham wrote to Althorp within five years. Althorp (then Lord Spencer) would certainly have discussed these questions with other members of the Cabinet. They may in time have gained a little by the telling. See Dr. Aspinall, *Lord Brougham and the Whig Party*, 190–1. Lord Grey told Creevey about the hackney-coach on the next day.

CHAPTER XV

THE STRUGGLE WITH THE LORDS

They say Lord Brougham has power to teach
    All sorts of puzzling things,
From alphabets and parts of speech
    Down to the crimes of kings.
If yet, in pamphlets and reviews,
    He loves young minds to drill,
Some day perhaps he will diffuse
    Some knowledge of the Bill.

                  MACKWORTH PRAED.

THE Dissolution and the King's speech, which Brougham seems to have drafted—" I altered the speech, and had it copied by a man I had stationed on purpose in the ante-room " [1]—probably marked the end of an epoch, but the Whigs were still faced by twelve months of strenuous fighting for the Reform Bill. In May 1831 the old electoral system was stretched as far as it could be by popular feeling. The Whigs could make little inroad into the scheduled boroughs. " Bear " Ellice, the Party Whip and Patronage Secretary, managed to buy four seats from Lord Yarborough, who held them as trustee for his niece, but the other gains were in contested seats. A " Loyal and Patriotic Fund " was organized, to which Brougham contributed, and this enabled the Party to fight wherever it was possible. In the counties the freeholders were almost solid for the Bill, and the Tories, for all their landed interests, only saved six seats. Anti-clerical feeling was strongest in the country—tithes, pluralism and the magisterial damnation of the " black

---

[1] Letter from Brougham to Althorp. Quoted in Dr. Aspinall's *Lord Brougham and the Whig Party*, p. 190.

dragoons" were tremendous factors on the side of reform.
Jane Austen's clergymen, like Mr. Elton or Mr. William
Collins, were not too attractive in the drawing-room, they
must have been hated in their villages. The "black
slugs" round the cathedrals also helped to rouse the wave
of resentment against the Bishops, but the Tories usually
could get their men in for the towns, though they had it
forced home upon them, especially in the North, that
they were on the losing side. The crowds were boisterous, unanimous, but except in a few towns like Wigan,
they were not violent. Sir Walter Scott was only one
of the many Tories who learnt to their surprise that they
were unpopular.

> " The day passed with much clamour and no
> mischief. Henry Scott was elected for the last time
> I suppose. *Troja fuit*—I left the borough in the
> midst of abuse, and the gentle hint, *Burk Sir Walter*."[1]

The attitude of the crowd, and their continual demand
for pledges, confirmed some of the doubtful members
who had voted for the second reading. The electoral
system as a whole was just sufficiently elastic to let the
overwhelming enthusiasm swing over about sixty seats;
enough to give Lord Grey a clear majority of over a
hundred in the Commons. This comfortable margin
and the popular manifestation at election time were of the
utmost importance. They enabled the Commons to
claim that they represented the country, and helped to
develop a corporate feeling in the Lower House as
against the Lords. When the second Reform Bill went
into the Committee stage, there was the usual difficult
period of gestation when differences of outlook on the
Government side and anomalies in the Bill itself are apt
to seem unduly important. Popular enthusiasm slackened
during the summer months; the many political unions,
which had sprung up in a night, began to wither, but the
Commons were now " for the Bill, the whole Bill, and

---

[1] J. G. Lockhart : *Life of Sir Walter Scott*, p. 725.

nothing but the Bill." The rank and file of the Party
were more solid and determined than the Ministry, whose
representatives in the Commons were curiously lethargic
and unenthusiastic, leaving all the work to be done by
Russell and Althorp. Fortunately the Tories had a very
weak debating case. Their only argument was that the
Bill would hand over power to a uniform electorate,
whereas the old system allowed a great variety of classes
to make their opinions heard. The high electoral
qualification—£10 rateable value—gave some force to
this criticism, but it was an argument that could only
come effectually from the Radical side, certainly not from
the Party upholding a system under which half the House
was chosen by a handful of wealthy men.

Although Grey had received a magnificent vote of
confidence at the election, and had this fine block of
supporters in the Commons, his position was none too
secure. The struggle in the Lords, or rather against
the Lords, was likely to be complicated and bitter; the
King was growing " uneasy," and men like Palmerston
and Lansdowne had no great stomach for the fight.
Palmerston was already urging the raising of the £10
qualification, Lansdowne suggesting giving way on the
disenfranchisement question. On the other hand,
Brougham strongly objected to the rather feeble attempts
to placate the Tories and delay the inevitable constitutional struggle. " I am quite vexed," he wrote to
Russell, " at the lingering pace of our Bill. But if the
anti-reformers do stop it—at all events be loud on the
grievance—that puts the saddle on the right horse.
Instead of doing so—what are you all about? You
praise the enemy for his candour and fairness! This is
exactly playing his game, and taking on yourself the load
of the blame. Rely on it you are only going downhill
in the country in consequence, and when once you are a
little lower, the *Lords* will take courage and give you and
the Bill the *coup de grâce*." [1] Brougham here showed his

[1] Lord John Russell : *Early Correspondence*, ii. 27.

usual fine sense of strategy.   While Lord Grey canvassed amongst his peers for support, Brougham could see that any sign of weakness would only encourage resistance. Russell was on Brougham's side, and helped to precipitate matters by his reference—in a reply to the Birmingham Political Union—to the opinion of the Lords as " the whisper of a faction."   It entailed an apology to the King, but, like Brougham's anonymous and truculent pamphlet of " Friendly Advice " to the Lords, it probably prevented the Lords thinking they could bully the Cabinet and the Whigs.

Towards the end of September the Bill passed the Commons and went to the Lords.   " Johnny has taken up his child in his arms, followed by a rare tribe of godfathers, and old Brougham approached us with rare dignity, and taking it into his arms carried it to his place, and told their lordships the name given to it by the Commons." [1]   The debate in the Lords was rendered notable by two great speeches : one by Lord Grey, the quintessence of all that was best in the Whig aristocratic tradition, and the other by Brougham, breathing the spirit of a new age intolerant of shams and conventions. He wisely attacked the basis of the Tory case, that the existing system allowed for the proper representation of " Property."

> " That a Peer, or a speculating attorney, or a jobbing Jew, or a gambler from the Stock Exchange, by vesting in his own person the old walls of Sarum, or a few pigsties at Bletchingley, or a summer-house at Gatton, and making fictitious, and collusive, and momentary transfers of them to an agent or two, for the purpose of enabling them to vote as if they had the property, of which they all the while knew they have not the very shadow, is in itself a monstrous abuse, in the form of a gross and barefaced cheat, and becomes the most disgusting hypocrisy when

---

[1] *Creevey Papers*, ii. 237.

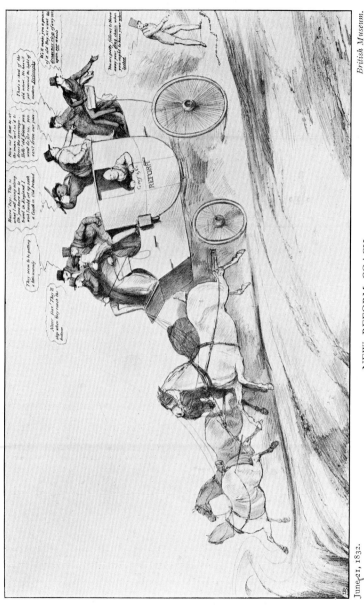

NEW REFORM COACH

Parce puer stimulis et fortiter utere loris.

From a sketch by H. B. Doyle.

it is seriously treated as a franchise by virtue of property. I will tell these peers, attorneys, jobbers, loan contractors, and the nabob's agents, if such there still be amongst us, that the time is come when these things can no longer be borne, and an end must at length be put to the abuse which suffers the most precious rights of Government to be made the subject of common barter, to be conveyed by traffic, pass by assignment under a commission of bankruptcy, or the powers of an Insolvent Act, or to be made over for a gaming debt."

Many of the Lords then present must have remembered another scene, some eleven years before, when a lawyer, defending a Queen, had addressed them with a similar crude disregard for those polite conventions in which it was usual to clothe the anomalies and abuses of the " Old Corruption."   The peroration, also, has more than an echo of that earlier speech in which Brougham succeeded in making an appeal sound suspiciously like a threat.   It was a period when the old histrionic accompaniments of oratory were still in favour, and no one at the time seems to have commented upon the very theatrical ending, " I warn you, I implore you, yea, on my bended knees I supplicate you, reject not this Bill." After this Brougham, according to the *Law Magazine*, " slightly bent his knee on the Woolsack."   Campbell was listening to the speech, and writing to his brother the same day he described it as magnificent, but makes no comment on the peroration.   Many years later, however, when he came to write Brougham's life, he drew on his imagination in order to make a good story.   " He continued for some time in prayer; but his friends, alarmed for him lest he should be suffering from the effects of the mulled port, picked him up and placed him safely on the Woolsack." [1] The story is so much more characteristic of Campbell as an historian than of Brougham as a man, that it can be

---

[1] Campbell : *Lives of the Chancellors*, viii. 398.

relegated to the "legend." It was still an age when alcohol often inspired oratory, and usually helped to mellow or excite the audience. Brougham was not an abstemious man, but there is little contemporary evidence to suggest that drink ever affected his behaviour or his speech.

Whatever may have been the value of Brougham and Grey's oratorical efforts, they probably made few conversions. Most of the peers as well as the Bishops were dead against the Bill. They might yield from fear of a worse fate, or under pressure from the Crown or some Tory leader like Wellington, but not many would be likely to alter their views. Brougham, the political realist, knew this well enough, but Grey seems to have had lingering hopes of winning over some peers and cajoling a few Bishops; he was certainly disappointed when the Second Reform Bill was thrown out by forty-one votes. On this majority were twenty-one Bishops, but amongst these were some of the most violent and intransigent of the anti-reformers, like Dr. Phillpotts, Brougham's old opponent at Durham, who had become Bishop of Exeter.

The rejection of the Bill divided the Cabinet. Brougham, Durham and Holland saw that a struggle with the Lords was inevitable, and were anxious to expedite the next stage, the demand for a creation of reformist peers. Palmerston, Melbourne and the Canningites were prepared to accept the Lords as an equal legislative authority, and wished to modify the Bill to meet their views. Grey, and perhaps Althorp, stood midway between the two groups. The King was a complicating factor. Under the influence of his Household, and especially of the Queen, who was in close touch with Wellington and other Tories, William IV was rapidly losing sympathy with Reform. He began a campaign to stamp out radicalism amongst the many half-pay officers who took some part in politics. He wanted to cashier Colonel Torrens for saying that the

" House of Lords might be placed in Schedule A," and immediately after the rejection of the Bill he proposed to dismiss Colonel William Napier, the historian of the Peninsular War, for a speech at Devizes.   " The affair of Torrens," wrote Grey to Lord Holland, " convinces me that the people who compose the King's private society have had some effect." [1]   The ordinary social relations between the King and his Prime Minister and Lord Chancellor had been very cordial until the autumn, they now became strained and formal.

Besides the King, the Commons, and the Lords, there was a fourth factor, nearly ready in October to engulf all three.   If the disturbances at the time of the General Election were exaggerated by the anti-reformers, those which occurred after the rejection of the Bill were sufficiently severe to justify M. Halévy's use of the word Revolution.   New forces had come into play since the spring.   Cholera appeared in England for the first time in October, spread rapidly through the slums of the industrial North-East, and caused a general terror like the first arrival of bubonic plague in India some sixty years later.   Agricultural distress was again severe over the South, and rick-burning once more became prevalent under the direction of the mysterious " Captain Swing." Miners in the Midlands and weavers in Lancashire came into conflict with Yeomanry and Regular Army.   At Nottingham, where the Duke of Newcastle was specially hated, the castle was burnt.   A new kind of working-class political union, the " low political unions," sprang up, and in some cases began drilling and arming.   Perhaps the deepest impression was caused by the Bristol riots, when a number of buildings, including the Mansion House and the Bishop's Palace, were burnt down when the great anti-reformer Wetherell visited the city as Recorder.

Grey might have resigned after his defeat in the Lords, but, with the strong approval of Brougham, decided to

[1] Trevelyan : *Lord Grey of the Reform Bill*, p. 321.

remain in office without any guarantees from the King. The immediate question was whether to call Parliament. Brougham, who knew that the strength of the Reform movement now lay in the Commons, was pressing for an early meeting. Palmerston and Melbourne were busily intriguing on the other side, a fact which was important in connection with the break-up of the Whigs three years later. The object of the Canningites, and of many patrician Whigs, was to get Grey involved in negotiations with Lord Wharncliffe, and with the few " waverers " through whom it was hoped to come to some agreement with Wellington. Palmerston wrote to Melbourne, on November 20th, just after the decision for an early meeting, showing clearly that they were both working for a surrender to the Lords.

> " It is evident that Brougham has pledged himself in conversation with Barnes and others that Parliament should meet before Christmas, and is determined from vanity to redeem his pledge; and it is also equally evident that he fears that excitement about Reform could not be kept up in its present degree for six weeks longer, and also that these unions would disgust and alarm all well-meaning reformers, and so prejudice the cause. I have no doubt, also, that those out of the Cabinet, who are the most clamorous for an immediate meeting are so because they see that it would prevent all negotiation with the moderate party, and all possibility of coming to an understanding with them. But though these motives may be sufficient for those they actuate, they ought to influence us in a contrary direction. . . ."

About the same date Melbourne's brother, George Lamb, was writing to him in much the same strain, urging the " moderates " to combine, and, accepting defeat, to bring in a truncated Bill next year.

" It seems clear that Grey is for moderation, but if nobody stands firm by him he is sure to give way; and it seems to me that the violent part of the Cabinet are put in continual communication upon this subject, and act in concert. . . . Wharncliffe wants the division into three Bills—disfranchisement, enfranchisement, regulation. . . . It is remarkable that you have decided to call the Parliament at the very moment that the rascally Press had begun to prepare the country for it being put off. There is something at work which we in the country cannot comprehend. In such cases Charles IV of Spain used to say there was a woman in them; I say there is a Brougham." [1]

In this most important struggle Brougham saved the Reform Bill. Parliament met, and the only concession to Wellington and the Canningites was the Proclamation against illegal Unions. Most of the Unions countered this by abandoning their semi-military activities, and Wellington, who believed that the Government had " broken with the Radicals," found that the Cabinet, with the Commons behind them, were not going to surrender. Negotiations with Wharncliffe continued, and had an important influence in the coming year, but the danger of allowing the Opposition to dictate the form of the Bill was now averted.

The Third Reform Bill, introduced in the Commons on December 12, contained certain concessions to the " waverers "—the total number of Members was not to be lowered, and some changes were made in Schedule A —but they were not likely to commend the measure to the Opposition Lords. Peel immediately declared his intention of fighting the new Bill to the last. The Commons would, of course, pass the Bill, and everything now turned on the question of the King's willingness to make new peers and the Cabinet's fortitude in demand-

[1] Viscount Melbourne : *Papers*, p. 142 *et seq.*

T

ing such a creation. Already, in October, *The Times*, probably reflecting Brougham's views, had demanded sixty new peers. Grey was only gradually won over to this point of view. He seems, at first, to have been obsessed by the practical difficulties of neutralising a hostile majority in this way. " Supposing the majority of forty-one to remain unshaken," he wrote to Burdett towards the end of November, " is it possible to counteract it by a new creation ? Who can say how many more would be required ? certainly more than forty-one. For you may be sure that such an attempt would lose us many of those by whom we have hitherto been supported. It is a question then which goes to the absolute destruction of the House of Lords, an event which I certainly did not contemplate in endeavouring to reform the House of Commons." [1]

Mr. Asquith's struggle, eighty years later, showed that nothing is likely to be gained from the House of Lords by men who are solicitous about its future existence, and it was fortunate that Grey was won over by Brougham and Durham to a more belligerent state of mind. On New Year's Day Lord Holland advised a progressive series of creations. " I am an old tennis-player, and like that way of counting, though it seems odd—15, 30, 40, game—but the main point is to hang over our adversary with a *bisque*; and the knowledge we have it will damp their exertions." [2] Grey, writing to Holland on the same day, pointed out the two difficulties, " the concurrence of the Cabinet and the King : from Lansdowne's letter to me I am afraid he will positively oppose; the objéctions of Palmerston are, I hear, scarcely less strong. Melbourne will be adverse." But he had already been won over to making a start. " I enclose letters which I have had from Brougham, Lambton and Coke on the

[1] Letter printed. G. M. Trevelyan : *Lord Grey of the Reform Bill*, App. H.
[2] Printed in J. R. M. Butler's *The Passing of the Great Reform Bill*, p. 329.

subject. The course advised by the first ('twelve at once,' as an earnest of more) is that to which I most incline. But the difficulties I have stated may very likely make it impossible." [1]

Brougham's suggestion was, of course, based on the precedent of Queen Anne's creation of twelve Tory peers. The parallel was not exact, as Grey was at pains to point out, and the creation had been one of the articles of Harley's impeachment. A constitutional question was raised, which was not settled then, nor in 1911, and is likely to become important again. In view of the attitude adopted by the Canningites, there was ample justification for the truculent policy advocated by Brougham, Durham and Holland, but it contained, as Brougham subsequently allowed, an element of " bluff." Inside the Cabinet it was successful, but Grey had to take his own line with the King. In these negotiations with an elderly man of third-rate intelligence, and full of strange prejudices, Grey showed admirable restraint and tact. It is possible that William might have been taken by storm, and " bounced " into a large creation of peers by the methods which Brougham had applied in the previous April. The ultimate effect would probably have been the virtual disappearance of the Lords as a legislative body. Though Brougham and Durham would have taken risks, Grey had no desire to go down to history as a leader of revolution.

The King's objections seem to have turned primarily on the idea of flooding the peerage with new men rather than the proposal to create peers for a specific purpose. Grey went to see him in January. " His Majesty most graciously listened, and stated his decided opinion, that if an addition was to be made, it should be regulated in this manner; . . . first by calling up eldest sons; next collateral heirs; and thirdly Scotch and Irish Peers . . . he trusted that it would not be proposed to raise to the Peerage any of those who had been forward in agitating

[1] G. M. Trevelyan : *op. cit.*, App H.

the country, as nothing could induce him to consent to
the advancement of persons of that description." [1]
This memorandum by Lord Grey is interesting as showing how far the Royal mind had progressed since the
eighteenth century. On January 15th, William made
his definite promise that he would not " deny to his
Ministers the power of acting at once up to the full
exigency of the case." It was part of a tortuously worded
sentence, but it was accepted as a guarantee by Lord Grey.

During the winter the advocates of " peer-making "
in the Cabinet were weakened by the partial withdrawal
of Durham and Brougham. They were both ill, and in
each case the illness was connected with domestic
troubles. Durham lost his favourite son, and Brougham,
according to a letter from Campbell, " continues exceedingly depressed, although I suppose he will rouse himself
and make a great speech. He believes himself that this
depression proceeds entirely from the melancholy state
of his child." Creevey also noted in February that
" Brougham's illness seemed to affect his vigour of mind,
and made him rather jib on this subject; but now he is
himself again, and quite as vigorous as ever in his demand
for new peers." As the Third Reform Bill passed
through the Commons Lord Grey's difficulties grew more
acute. He had to decide when to ask the King to fulfil
his promise. Many leading Whigs pressed him to insist
on the new creations before the Bill went to the Lords.
Grey took the line that the Lords would pass the second
reading, but the crisis would occur in the Committee
stage. At one moment Durham and Hobhouse threatened to resign, and Lord Althorp to shoot himself, but
Grey stuck to his point, and his good luck held. The
Bill went to the Lords, and the second reading was
passed by 184 to 175. The honours of the debate went
to Grey, who succeeded in being conciliatory while not
sacrificing essentials. Brougham made a powerful
speech against the Tory argument that the popular

[1] *Correspondence with William IV and Sir H. Taylor*, ii. 68-73.

demand for reform was a temporary phase due to the French Revolution of July.

Events now followed much the same course as a year before. The small majority for the second reading forecast trouble in the Committee stage, but gave time for Francis Place, Joseph Parkes, Attwood and Grote to organize some of those mass demonstrations which killed the Tory argument that there was no real support for the Bill. The policy of the Lords was to whittle away the Bill by minor amendments, each too small to offer an excuse for withdrawing it. Some unfortunate remarks by Grey seemed to foreshadow and condone such efforts. " I cannot," he said, " consent to *much* advance of £10." To the Radicals any further rise in the qualifications seemed fatal. Parkes, in a pamphlet written at this juncture, showed that in its original form the Bill would only enfranchise some 4500 out of Birmingham's 150,000. " The measure is in so many parts aristocratical and so exclusively based on property that the £10 franchise is the most important and pledged principle." [1]

Fortunately Lord Lyndhurst made a false move. Amongst a host of minor amendments to be moved by Lord Ellenborough and others, he brought forward one, on May 7th, which would have postponed the disfranchising clauses. On the following day Grey and Brougham posted down to Windsor, and asked the King to consent to the creation of at least fifty peers. The King, who had been slowly receding from his position of January, promised them an answer on the following day. It was perhaps characteristic of the personal feeling amongst those immediately surrounding the King, that the two statesmen were not offered any hospitality. " He did not even offer the poor fellows any victuals, and they were obliged to put into port at the George posting-house at Hounslow and so get some mutton chops." [2] Partly because of a cartoon by Doyle the meal became

[1] Jessie K. Buckley : *Joseph Parkes of Birmingham*, p. 96.
[2] *Creevey Papers*, ii. 245.

famous.   Perhaps it was typical of this queerly assorted couple that Brougham, in his eupeptic fashion, insisted on some kidneys being added to the mutton chops, and that Grey, though he said " he cared not for kidneys," yet " ate them when they came." [1]

Next morning the Cabinet received the King's letter, and the " Days of May " began.   William accepted their resignation and relied " upon their readiness to comply with his request that they will respectively continue in the discharge of their official functions until he shall be enabled to make due arrangement for the public services "; in other words, until the Duke of Wellington should be able to collect an alternative Ministry.[2]   It was perhaps typical of the age, and certainly of Grey's attitude to public life, that the King's valedictory letter should confirm the appointment of the Prime Minister's brother to the Bishopric of Hereford, and that he should be allowed to hold this post while retaining the living of St. Botolph in Billingsgate.   Equally typical was the undisguised pleasure with which the Whig Ministers accepted the prospect of a Tory Government coming into office and presumably passing a Reform Bill.   " Althorp, ' with bright eye and radiant smile,' went off to oil the locks of his beloved fowling-pieces, which had been rusting for eighteen months." [3]   Grey was " afraid " that Wellington's effort would fail.   Even Brougham seems to have been infected by the pleasure of the " amateurs."   " Having read aloud (the letter accepting their resignation) to Sefton, Brougham sprung from his chair and, rubbing his hands, declared it was the happiest moment of his life.   I daresay from his late debility that what he said he felt." [4]   Both he and Richmond were asked by the King to remain in office, but refused.[5]

---

[1] Brougham : *Life and Times*, iii. 192–3.
[2] *Correspondence with William IV and Sir H. Taylor*, ii. 396.
[3] G. M. Trevelyan : *Lord Grey of the Reform Bill*, p. 342.
[4] *Creevey Papers*, ii. 245.
[5] Mr. Atlay, in *The Victorian Chancellors*, p. 312, appears to doubt

The efforts of Lord Lyndhurst and the Duke of Wellington to form a Ministry were defeated, partly by the Commons, who passed a vote of confidence in the Whig Ministry, partly by the activities of the political unions, who set themselves to prepare for a peaceful revolution if a Tory Government were formed.   " In the popular demonstrations which carried the day we must count Francis Place, George Grote and Joseph Parkes as chief amongst those who ' ride in the whirlwind and direct the storm.' "   It is difficult now to assess the factors which defeated Wellington's efforts. Radicals did not credit the idea of Tories passing a Reform Bill, and took Attwood's view, that in any case it would mean a victory for the House of Lords which would break the spirit of the people.

All over the North there were unconcealed preparations for a rising, and doubts about the " staunchness " of the Army and Yeomanry.   Place's organized run on the banks—with his famous placard " To Stop the Duke, go for Gold "—together with the widespread refusal to pay taxes, would have also embarrassed a new Government.   But it was probably the attitude of the Commons which ultimately deterred Peel and other Tories from joining Wellington.   By May 15th it was known that the Duke's effort had failed.

The crisis was to continue for another four days, for the King had not yielded, and Wellington refused to call off the opposition in the Lords.   Brougham was present at the Cabinet meeting of the 16th, which demanded either cessation of opposition or the creation of peers. Wellington's speech on the following day showed that

whether such an offer was made.   There seems ample contemporary evidence, apart from Brougham's own statement, that such an offer was made on May 9th.   See Le Marchant's *Althorp*, p. 423, *Creevey Papers*, ii. 246, and the references from the Hatherton MS., made by Dr. Aspinall, *Lord Brougham and the Whig Party*, p. 191. On the other hand, there is only Campbell's remark, written many years later, " it is quite certain that such a preposterous conception never entered the royal mind."   *Lives of the Chancellors*, viii. 408.

he would not grant the former, and on the 18th, when
the Cabinet met and demanded "full and indisputable
security," they were very close to another resignation,
which would have left the King to cope with a revolution.
Brougham and Grey took the Cabinet Minute across to
the King at St. James's Palace, and William at last gave
way. "His Majesty is, therefore, prepared to afford to
them the security they require for passing the Reform
Bill unimpaired in its principles and in its essential
provisions, and as nearly as possible in its present
form. . . ." [1] It was the end of a long struggle, with
many interesting parallels and contrasts to the passing
of the Parliament Bill in 1911.

The King's Secretary, Sir Henry Taylor, who had
played an important and honourable part in these proceedings, let the contents of the King's letter become
known to the Tory leaders. They preferred not to force
the King to create peers, and, on June 4, the third reading
was carried without opposition. The King refused to
give the Royal Assent in person, and it was accordingly
granted by Commission. Brougham, who had done so
much to press the Bill through, sat with Grey, Holland,
Wellesley, Lansdowne and Durham. The Tory benches
were empty, and only the old Duke of Sussex represented
the royal family.

[1] *Correspondence with William IV and Sir H. Taylor*, ii. 434.

S. W. Reynolds.

THE REFORM BILL RECEIVING THE ROYAL ASSENT

Russell.   Burdett.   Stanley.
Althorp.   Hobhouse.   Graham.

The Commissioners : Grey, Holland, Brougham, Wellesley, Lansdowne, Durham.
Standing by curtain : Duke of Sussex.

CHAPTER XVI

THE DISRUPTION OF THE WHIGS

CROMWELL. The heaviest and the worst,
  Is your displeasure with the King.
WOLSEY.   God bless him !
CROMWELL. The next is, that Sir Thomas More is chosen
Lord Chancellor in your place.   *Henry VIII.*

WHEN the first Reformed Parliament met early in 1833 the personnel of the Commons was considerably changed. The average age was older, " full twenty years older than any that has preceded it." [1]   There were more business and professional men, and a few of the older fighting Radicals, like Cobbett, who seated himself on the front Opposition bench.   These replaced the nominees of the aristocracy.   Many rising young politicians suffered the fate of Endymion's father in Disraeli's novel, and found themselves permanently ousted from public life.   The new men did not lead the same kind of life, they belonged to no political club, they attended the House more regularly.   Money counted as much as ever in the selection of candidates, and in fighting many of the boroughs, but it was new money put up by new classes.

Popular feeling, roused by the struggle over the Reform Bill, was sufficiently strong to ensure that many of these new Members called themselves Radical, but their political ideas were rather nebulous.   If Brougham had been in the Commons he might have welded them into a party, strong enough to have a decisive voice in the Government, but with the possible exception of Lord

[1] Opinion of an " old politician." Le Marchant : *Life of Althorp*, p. 451.

John Russell there was no one else with the necessary
political experience and standing to lead them, and Russell
was too deeply involved in the Whig family system.
Grey made no attempt to bring the new Radicals into the
Government, which remained as aristocratic and ineffective as ever. He believed that it would be sufficient to
pass some legislation of a " liberal " nature in order to
appease them. His own interest was mainly in foreign
affairs, and he was an old man with few ideas about
domestic policy. The Canningites, especially Melbourne
and Palmerston, were a passive obstruction to any
Government activity, and Althorp, though vaguely
progressive, was ineffective. " Lord Althorp made a
reply, but, as is almost invariably the case, was perfectly
inaudible in the gallery." [1] Nor had the ordeal of the
last two years purged the Whigs of certain pleasant vices.
They retained their fondness for sinecures, and their
tenderness towards aristocratic pensioners. Lord Auck-
land, for example, a weak Minister who later became a
lamentable Viceroy of India, insisted on retaining the
Mastership of the Mint together with the Presidency of
the Board of Trade.

In spite, therefore, of considerable legislative activity,
the Whigs rapidly lost any popularity they had gained
over the Reform Bill. John Campbell, who had to
fight a bye-election on his appointment as Attorney-
General, found that a single year had been sufficient to
disillusion the workers of Dudley. " Daniel Harvey
Whittle had, a few days before, brought forward a
motion in the House of Commons about the Pension
List, and my iron-hearted operatives asked, ' Why are
the mothers and sisters and children of peers, who have
done nothing for the public, to be maintained at the public
expense, while we are obliged to support our poor
relatives from our hard-earned wages, or see them sent
to the workhouse ? ' " [2] The Whigs and the Tories were

[1] House of Commons Reports, March 11th, p. 34.
[2] *Life of Lord Campbell*, ii. 42.

still able to buy up the tiny " ten-pound electorates " in many of the boroughs, and the contempt felt for their corruption was a most powerful force behind Chartism. Much of the work which Brougham had done for adult education was swept away in this tide of working-class resentment against the Whigs. " The Unionist," wrote Francis Place a year or two later, "will read nothing which the Diffusion Society meddles with—they call the members of it Whigs, and Whig means with them a treacherous rascal, a bitter implacable enemy." [1]   It was Brougham's tragedy that by accepting the Chancellorship he had been uprooted. He could no longer draw strength or inspiration from his old sources. A new generation was growing up and coming into Parliament, which " knew not Joseph."

There is an interesting passage in a letter from Joseph Parkes to Place, in which he laments the failure of three men—Cobbett, Brougham and Attwood—who " in my lifetime have held in their hands omnipotent means of levelling the oligarchy." Each might have succeeded—Cobbett if " gifted with integrity "; Attwood if he had " foresight, and physical courage, and knowledge, of which he has none "; Brougham " if not sucked into the whirlpool of the aristocracy, and if, instead of vanity of doing good, he had worshipped ' good for good's sake.' " [2]   Whatever may be felt about the second accusation, the first is hardly fair. Brougham was never really absorbed into the Whig aristocracy. He had forced them to accept him as one of the Party leaders, and finally to take him into the Cabinet. This much was unwillingly conceded to his ability and his standing in the country, but he had been obliged to accept a position which partly smothered his peculiar talents, and was gradually sapping his general popularity. Inevitably, when too weak to fight for himself, he was

[1] Add. MSS. 35149, f. 281.
[2] Letter printed in J. K. Buckley's *Joseph Parkes of Birmingham*, p. 82.

expelled from the Whig oligarchy, a process which was to be completed within four years of his becoming Lord Chancellor.

Although the Whig Ministry contained only a small reformist element, there was sufficient Radical impetus left over from 1832 for both Houses of Parliament to accept certain measures of the type which was beginning to be called " Liberal "—Benthamite ideas put through the middle-class sieve. Some in which Brougham was specially interested have already been mentioned—the abolition of slavery, modified by a system of enforced " apprenticeship " for seven years; certain legal reforms, strictly limited by the successful opposition of the legal Trade Union; and the first education grant, cut down to the lowest possible " round figure." The pressure of Trade Unions and of Radicals outside Parliament helped Lord Ashley to pass his Factory Act, but the influence of the Whigs made him drop his proposal of a Ten-hour Day, which would have been immediately beneficial, while he was allowed to retain his Factory Inspectors, who were at first bitterly hated by the workmen. Brougham took a prominent part in pushing the Truck Act through the Lords, and this assisted in abolishing the " Tommy-shops," which were one of the worst features of mining and industrial life. New Bills dealing with India, with the Bank Charter, with the reform of Municipalities, and of the Poor Law were all being hammered out during the two years following the Reform Bill. The Ministry was not idle, but it was not adventurous, it was only progressive under compulsion, and it was hopelessly divided.

Melbourne, Palmerston, Stanley, and the Canningites, who had been brought into the Government, were chiefly responsible for the rapid disruption of the Whigs. Even after the Reform Bill had been passed, Melbourne retained his old prejudices, and his tenure of the Home Office made the Government hateful to working men and vulnerable to Radical attacks. His continued if desultory actions against Trade Unions were to culminate, in 1834, in the tragic absurdity of the "Tolpuddle Martyrs," when Dorchester labourers were transported for administering an oath.   Less serious, but politically more harmful, was the prosecution of a Radical news-paper for advocating the non-payment of taxes, until its programme had been adopted—the exact method of propaganda which many Whigs, including William Brougham, had used so effectively in 1832.

Both Durham and Lord John Russell wished to succeed Palmerston at the Foreign Office.   Apart from personal ambitions, they disliked his attitude towards Poland, and the lack of any distinctive Whig flavour in his policy.   A sympathetic attitude towards Polish grievances had been part of the Whig tradition for many years, and Brougham had been in touch with their leaders ever since he had first entered Parliament.   Dis-putes in the Cabinet about foreign policy began during the first year of office.   Lord Sefton describes how "when some document from Palmerston's office was making its round, and had reached Brougham, the latter in forwarding it was pleased to accompany it with some observations of his own in writing, and the most adverse possible to Palmerston; when this came to the ears of the latter you can't be surprised at his flying out, and the notion in the office is that he will resign and Lambton, alias Lord Durham, is talked of as his successor."[1] Late in 1833, Palmerston's insistence on interfering in Portugal caused another Cabinet crisis and nearly brought about the resignation of Lord Grey.

As so often throughout the nineteenth century, the Irish question was the decisive factor.   For forty years the Whigs had proclaimed that coercive measures were a sign of inefficiency and failure.   As soon as they took office they had to face a revival of political excitement in Ireland, just as the advent of a Liberal Government before the War, and of a Labour Government since, has

[1] J. Gore : *Creevey's Life and Times*, p. 345.

usually caused a rise in the political thermometer in India. The Whigs began the traditional policy of "conciliation and repression," but it was complicated by the appointment of the impetuous Stanley, whose essentially Conservative mentality would never accept the idea of conciliation until the repression was complete. In 1831 Lord Grey intervened, and came to terms with O'Connell, using Sir Francis Burdett as an intermediary. The "Tithe War" began that year, but though Ireland was disturbed by agrarian troubles, there was a political truce during the Reform Bill period. It ended in February 1833, when Stanley insisted on bringing in his Coercion Bill. This very nearly upset the Whig coach, especially as Durham and Hobhouse resigned, the first on the question of the ballot and the "finality" of the Reform Act, the second on the military estimates. Their going did, however, enable Grey to move Stanley to the Colonial Office and replace him by the more tolerant Littleton, afterwards Lord Hatherton. The Bill was, however, passed, and caused a crisis when it came up for renewal the following year. "It combined all or nearly all the different methods of dealing with Irish riots and conspiracies which the Tory Governments of the last thirty years had elaborated." [1]

The Cabinet were no better agreed on the right policy of conciliation. Clearly something had to be done about the Irish Church, with its large revenue and insignificant congregation. Russell and Brougham wished to divert some of the surplus income to education, but Grey and Stanley objected firmly. The position was complicated by a strong feeling amongst English Dissenters against allocating any funds to Roman Catholicism. The Radicals would support a Tithe Bill with appropriation clauses, but the appropriation must be for secular purposes. Stanley's Irish Church Bill of 1833 abolished the Church cess but did not divert any of the Church revenues to other purposes. Brougham suggested the

[1] H. W. C. Davis : *The Age of Grey and Peel*, p. 252.

appointment of a Commission as a middle course; this was not accepted. The dispute within the Cabinet came to a head in May 1834, when Russell "upset the coach" by declaring in the House of Commons that "the revenues of the Church of Ireland were larger than necessary for the religious and moral instruction of the persons belonging to that Church, and for the stability of the Church itself." Shortly afterwards Stanley resigned, and was followed by Graham, Richmond and Ripon.

The coach rocked ominously, and would certainly have been over if Brougham had not taken charge. For the next six months his chief efforts were directed to saving the Ministry, though most of its members were quite willing to accept defeat. Grey, having made England safe for aristocracy, was longing to be back at Howick. Many others were chiefly anxious to be free from the vulgar persistence of Radicals and Irishmen. Brougham could see no reason for undoing the work of the Reform Bill by handing over the Government to a Tory minority in the Commons and a Tory majority in the Lords. He bitterly resented Russell's calculated indiscretion, which must have been made without any previous consultations. "Every effort," wrote Littleton to Wellesley in May, "and some sacrifice must be made to keep the Government together. I mean to talk the whole matter over with Brougham before the time of settlement arrives. On Lord Russell's outburst the other day, he wrote him a letter beginning 'Henceforth the name of Whig and sniveller are synonymous.'"[1] Brougham himself wrote to the Irish Viceroy about the same date.

"I went to the King yesterday morning, and was near an hour with him, and found H.M. in a state of vigour and spirit and confidence and cordial affection towards us all such as I cannot describe, and

[1] Add. MSS. 37307, f. 46.

have never been equalled since we came in. He regrets the resignations but speaks with ease of our filling up the blanks, and it *is* easy, tho' Stanley is an irreparable loss in debate. Our favour with H.M. leaves no chance of failing—and my view of all things and all men were laid before him both verbally and in writing very fully. He says he will stand fast by the Cabinet as long as it stands by itself. *I for one will never abandon* the public service and leave all in remediless confusion as long as I can find any six men to stand with me—that is certain. The confidence and delight of the House of Commons and the publick are unequalled." [1]

Within two months the Whig coach was again nearly upset, another Irish crisis coinciding with the introduction of the contentious and unpopular Poor Law Amendment Act. Some modifications of Stanley's Irish Coercion Act had been accepted by the Cabinet, but Althorp, Littleton and Brougham wished to go further, partly to help the Renewal Bill through Parliament, and partly in hopes of reaching a settlement with the Irish over the tithe question. Littleton, following Grey's precedent of three years before, got into touch with O'Connell, and found that " what he dislikes and fears is the power to prohibit meetings, etc." [2] After consulting with Brougham, Littleton wrote to Wellesley suggesting the dropping of the clauses relating to public meetings, and Brougham wrote informally at the same time. Wellesley felt the risk was worth taking, and sent letters to Grey, Melbourne and Brougham, explaining that he had changed his mind on this point.

Then followed a very confused fortnight. Wellesley had written on June 21st, explaining his willingness to do without the " public meetings clause." Althorp told

[1] Add. MSS. 37311, f. 143.
[2] E. J. Littleton (Lord Hatherton) : *Political Occurrences in 1834,* p. 29.

THE UPSETTING OF THE REFORM COACH

From a sketch by H. B. Doyle.

June 4, 1834.

British Museum.

Littleton that he " might rely on it that the clauses in question should form no part of a new Bill, as he himself was resolved to resign sooner than allow them to be renewed; and Lord Grey would not risk that result." [1] Upon this assurance Littleton let O'Connell know confidentially that the clause would not be re-introduced. Grey, however, proved adamant, relying on a former letter from Wellesley in which he had asked for the clause to be retained. The Cabinet very weakly acquiesced. Althorp did not resign, and the Bill, with the public meetings clause, was introduced into the Lords by Melbourne, whose own omission to answer letters was one minor cause of the misunderstanding. O'Connell in the House of Commons accused Littleton of bad faith, disclosing the general substance of the conversations. This was, of course, a glorious opportunity for the Opposition, who pressed for the full correspondence. On July 8th Grey and Althorp both resigned. The King sent for Melbourne to form a new Ministry, and suggested a coalition with the Tories. It was William IV's solution for all difficulties; his statecraft hardly went further than organizing a Government of " right-minded " men to keep out the Radicals.

Brougham was placed in a very delicate position. He had undoubtedly been one of the prime movers for a more conciliatory Irish policy, and for omitting the public meetings clause, but Althorp was equally involved, was the leader of the Whigs in the Commons, and had given Littleton the assurances on which he had acted. It was not the time for a post-mortem on a badly managed affair, which had not, however, lost the Whigs their support in the Commons. Brougham's main difficulty was the maddening tendency of the Whig patricians to commit political *hari-kari* at the slightest excuse. The gods, we are told, in their wisdom hide from mortal man the calm delight of natural death, but Althorp knew only too well that his political suicide would transport him

---

[1] *Id.*, p. 13.

U

to a heaven where each heifer calf brought a new
interest in life, and his duck decoy an endless pleasure.
Brougham had to apply the scourge before the rot set in.
Accordingly he wrote to Althorp :

> " Your step of resigning has, I fear, sealed the
> fate of this country. Rather than be plagued by
> two or three speeches addressed to a House of
> Commons which has more confidence in you than
> ever, you have done your best to dissolve the only
> Government the country will bear, and I hear that
> Abercromby and Rice are afraid to remain. I
> regard them, next to you, as the cause of all the
> mischief which may ensue ; they, too, are resolved
> to fly from their posts and deliver us over to the
> Tories and the mob in succession, because they
> don't like being badgered. I shall do all I can to
> ward off that calamity ; but how can I if everyone
> in the House of Commons is afraid to keep his
> ground ? " [1]

Brougham managed to persuade both the King and
Melbourne that the Commons would not allow Wellington and Peel to return to office, and Althorp grumblingly
returned to his old position. Grey was hopeless, and
had to be allowed to go back to Howick, where his
woman-folk and intimate friends did their best to persuade him that he had been very badly treated. The
Whig coach started off again. Littleton, with " more
punctilio than was at all wanted, desired to resign in
order, said he, to give the Government a facility," but
Brougham " sent for him, and had him privately *whipped*,
and convinced him that by *facility* he would be giving us
difficulty." [2]   The Government was re-formed with Melbourne at the Treasury and Hobhouse given a minor
post. The affair of the Coercion Act soon blew over,
and before the end of July Brougham could tell Wellesley:

[1] Lansdowne MS.   Le Marchant : *Althorp*, p. 510.
[2] Add. MSS. 37297, f. 399.

" I have much satisfaction in assuring you that nothing could go off better than all did in the Lords last night, and I had a real gratification in both speaking from my heart as to your Excellency, as well as a pride in stating how ridiculous all idea is of any of Lord Grey's colleagues having plotted to get him out, especially Althorp and myself, who had five times in one year kept him in by main force." [1]

The last sentence is in no way exaggerated. During the crises which had occurred every two or three months, the whole of Brougham's energies had been expended in keeping the Ministry in existence, and his original communication to Wellesley about the Coercion Act was clearly intended to help the Government over a difficult period. All this Grey recognized. As he wrote to Brougham in November, " I have at all times disdained all suspicion and belief, though these things had made my immediate retirement unavoidable, that they were intended to produce that result. Of such an intention, whatever share you might have had in the previous transactions, I entirely acquitted you, having in my possession what I consider as the strongest proof of your wish for my continuance in office." [2]

While this Irish business was occupying everyone's attention, the new Poor Law Bill, which had passed the Commons, was waiting to be introduced into the Lords. This would have been undertaken by Lord Grey, but the work was now transferred to Brougham, who had taken a considerable part in its preparation, and thus became doubly identified with a measure which was to arouse the deepest hostility amongst working men and women, whilst it exposed the Whigs to very effective criticism from the Tories. Nearly everyone was agreed that some change was necessary in the system, first formulated

[1] *Papers of Marquis of Wellesley,* ii. 243.
[2] Letter of November 4, 1834. Quoted in Prof. Trevelyan's *Lord Grey of the Reform Bill,* p. 392.

by the Speenhamland Justices, whereby wages were supplemented by family allowances paid from the poor rates. As farmers could pay what wages they liked, and labourers who organized were liable to the fate of the " Tolpuddle Martyrs," this method of poor relief acted as a very unscientific and unsatisfactory form of subsidy for agriculture, while it left the workers with the miserable standard of living which had caused the disturbances of 1830 and 1831. Its tendency was to reduce the worker to one dead level of underfed thriftlessness. " It charged not only the weak upon the strong, but the stupid on the skilful, the lazy upon the industrious, the drunken upon the sober, the dissolute upon the chaste, the honest upon the dishonest." [1]

Unfortunately the task of revising the Poor Law was undertaken at a time when educated opinion was dominated by a number of ill-digested economic ideas about wages-funds and the tendency of population to outstrip production. McCulloch and Malthus were the prophets of this mechanized world. Nassau Senior reduced their theories to practice, and was the most active member of the Commission, appointed in 1832, to inquire into the administration of the Poor Laws. The Report issued in 1834 was a curiously inhuman document, breathing the active hatred of the poor which was so characteristic of this period. Bulwer Lytton's *England and the English* was written while the Commission was sitting. " Let us now look at our Poor. Where is their common sense ? Alas, what imprudence.—Early marriages ; many children ; poor rates, and the workhouse—see the history of the agricultural labourers. . . . In no foreign country, even of far less civilization than England, is there the same improvidence ; in France, where there is a much greater inclination to pleasure, there is yet a much more vigorous disposition to save. The French peasants never incur the wicked, because voluntary, calamity of bringing children into the world whom they cannot

[1] Montague : *The Old Poor Law and the New Socialism*, p. 11.

feed. . . ." This was the point of view of a young and enlightened Whig who preferred to call himself a Liberal, yet he fully accepts the current philosophy.

Nassau Senior and his school went a step further. They looked upon the problem as one of breeding the right number of workers in the right places. To them the old system was vicious because it encouraged population to grow where it was not needed, as in the agricultural South. The Commission tackled the question in a spirit which justified the worst that Cobbett ever said about " feelosofers." Outdoor relief paid to able-bodied workers led to more children, so it must be stopped. The workhouse test which the humane Gilbert had abolished in 1796 was revived. The Commission even suggested that any relief granted should be in the nature of a loan. The Whigs, in accepting the Report, seem to have assumed that wages would immediately adjust themselves; at any rate, there is no provision for an intermediate period. The Commission proposed certain amendments in the law of settlement, and also of bastardy. Finally, the greatest change was the establishment of a central authority for the whole country.

Althorp and Brougham drew up the Bill, and it is to their credit that they did not accept the evil system of paying relief as a loan. Apart from that the Bill followed the lines of the Report. Brougham in his thirties, the Brougham of 1817, with his unconventional economics, might have taken a broader view. As he grew older Brougham's mathematical mind seems to have relished the mechanical theory of human relationships which was being taught by the predecessors of the free trade *laissez faire* movement. He was reaching that stage in a reformer's life when old prejudices are apt to return, and a consciousness of failure is appeased by accepting some generalizations unfavourable to mankind. In fairness it must be remembered that it was very difficult to avoid the excessive centralization which made the new Poor Law so inhuman. There were no trained and reputable

officials working in the counties. The ancient body of
overseers consisted of badly educated men steeped in
petty tyrannies and corruption. The Justices were
honest, but had themselves evolved the Speenhamland
system which was now being abolished. The clergy
were deservedly unpopular with the Whigs. The
office-holders in the ancient municipalities were to be
swept away in the reforms which were to be introduced
the following year. Some central control was essential,
but the three Commissioners and their Secretary were
not happily chosen and were given too free a
hand.[1]

The Bill provoked considerable discussion, but little
serious opposition in Parliament. Grote and the Radicals
supported it in the Commons; the Tories admitted the
need for a change and had no alternative scheme.
Brougham piloted the Bill through the Lords, introducing it with a speech in which he seems to have
amused himself by taking the theories of the economists
to their logical conclusion, and claiming the right of the
Government to lay down the policy on which local
bodies were to work. It was perhaps fitting that this
should have been his last important official action. The
middle-class radicalism, to which he really belonged,
reached its apogee in this doctrinaire Poor Law, drafted
without any consultation with or consideration for the
poor themselves. The Reform Bill had been a middle-
class measure, but was popular because it seemed to be
an attack on the " Old Corruption." Just as people
began to see that Reform had merely substituted a new
corruption, that of Eatanswill, there came this Act which
handed them over to a new kind of official—the " bashaws
of Somerset House." There has been some controversy
over the responsibility of the Commissioners, and their
very efficient Secretary Chadwick, for the too drastic
enforcement of the Act, and for the horrors of the Poor

[1] For Brougham's share in the reform of the Poor Law, see
T. Mackay's *History of the English Poor Law*, passim.

Law institutions which Dickens helped to reform. The Commissioners had scarcely begun operations before Brougham left office, but they helped to bring about the eclipse of Radicalism which marked the last half of the 'thirties, and thus weakened his support in the country.

The new Law was also partly responsible for a sudden change in the policy of *The Times*. The proprietor, John Walter, launched an attack upon the Bill in April, and this developed during the summer into a vendetta against Brougham himself.

Brougham's personal relations with the editor, Thomas Barnes, still continued after the passing of the Reform Bill, but his brother William was no longer in the office, and the rest of the Whig Party were rebelling against this newspaper's growing domination. Palmerston supported for its rival, the *Globe*, and early in 1834 a group of Whigs, of whom Sir John Easthope was the most prominent, purchased control over the *Morning Chronicle*. *The Times* was soon involved in a wordy warfare against "the shuffling *Chronicle* and the slavish *Globe*," which became more bitter when the Whigs proposed to lower the Stamp duty, a change which it was generally agreed would destroy the "virtual monopoly" of *The Times*.

The reasons for the personal animosity with which Barnes began to attack Brougham in July are obscure. There are hints of a quarrel, of a remark overheard at Brooks's, but the change seems to date from an incident, now fully explained in the new History of *The Times*. It appears that Althorp, much disturbed by criticism of the Poor Law, wrote a note to Brougham, who was then in Court. The Lord Chancellor read it, tore it up and threw it into the waste-paper basket, from which the pieces were rescued, and sent to *The Times*. The note was preserved, and has now been reproduced. On the margin is pencilled—" Picked up by a Friend and sent thinking it may be of service as a private principle of action." The note ran as follows—

My dear Brougham,
            The subject I want to talk to you about is the
State of the Press, and whether we should declare
open war with *Times* or attempt to make peace.
                                Yours most truly
                                        Althorp

Downing Street
    June 11.

Barnes immediately wrote to Brougham's secretary,
Le Marchant.

    Show this to the Lord Chancellor.

                                        June 11th, 1834.
My dear Sir,
            I told you I would always treat you frankly :
and in that spirit I think it right to say that I am
aware of Lord Althorp's application to the Chancellor for his opinion whether " the Govt. should
declare open war with the *Times* or attempt to make
peace." What does the Gaby mean ?
                                Yours ever,
                                        T. Barnes.

    Some correspondence followed, of which only a portion
is preserved.[1]   It was probably towards the end of June
that a personal quarrel began with Barnes, but the
Chancellor can be excused a certain degree of bad temper
at discovering that his waste-paper basket was being
rifled, and private letters were being bought by a man
whom he had considered his friend.   Of this we have no
certain knowledge, but the personal venom of *The Times*
against Brougham continued until Barnes died in 1841.
It had little relation to Brougham's political career after
1835, though *The Times* became a supporter of Sir Robert
Peel and the Tories in 1835.

    1 " *The Thunderer* " *in the Making*, pp. 299 ff.

Brougham's own views about this change of front are given in a letter to Wellesley, written in July.

"You'll see the London Press furious at me, especially *The Times*, which must puzzle Lord Londonderry, whose faith is that I am the editor of that journal.   The key to it is that they all wanted dissolution and revolution, and some want government at the mercy of the gentlemen of the Press, and they accuse me most justly, I am glad to say, of having defeated their prospect by standing firm. But my attack in the Libel Committee on their slanders and their monopoly are also a cause of spite. I succeeded, I believe, in putting an end to the newspaper stamps, which the great papers hold to be one of their great securities against competition. I also have fulfilled a threat I then held out of ending the violent and slanderous Press by an association. For, joined by the most respectable merchants and bankers in London (Smith, Lloyd, Grote and Goldsmith) and by lawyers I have launched a Society for Diffusing Political Knowledge, and this *The Times* perceives will emancipate the ' courteous readers ' and put them in the hands of gentlemen." [1]

The antagonism of *The Times*, which caused some of the smaller papers to swing over against him, placed a great strain upon Brougham at the end of an extremely trying year.   Late in 1833 he had lost his favourite brother James, whom he had always consulted in difficult times.   Creevey, with his usual maliciousness, wrote that " there is much speculation abroad whether the event will drive the Chancellor mad.   It is quite true that his brother's influence over him was as unbounded as it was miraculous, for no one ever discovered the slightest particle of talent in James of any kind." [2]   Then in

[1] *Papers of Marquis of Wellesley*, ii. 243-4.
[2] *Creevey Papers*, ii. 271.

March there was a muddle over the appointment of Horne, the Attorney-General, to a Judgeship. The Chancellor's efforts to keep the Government alive through the Irish crisis reacted on his judicial work, and the lawyers regretted " the extreme gravity and patient attention of old Eldon." Greville, who had strong professional as well as personal reasons for disliking Brougham, describes him as " a bad presiding judge, for he will talk so much to counsel" and notices, in March, that " his friends think him much altered in spirits and appearance; he has never shaken off his unhappiness at the death of his brother, to whom he seems to have been genuinely attached." [1] On the top of all this came the " Thunderer." Campbell recounts a remark, possibly imaginary, made by Lord Melbourne. " Have you not seen this morning's *Times* ? Another *Broughamic*, hinting that he is out of his mind, exaggerating his pecularities, vilipending his rhetoric, and, above all, asserting that there are heavy and increasing arrears in the Court of Chancery." [2] It is a sufficiently accurate description of the newspaper abuse to which Brougham was subjected, from July onwards. It was very like a conspiracy to hound him out of public life, and was the more bitter because Brougham had relied upon newspapers as the visible sign of his following in the country when he was opposed to the Whig oligarchy.

Brougham's courage did not fail, but these attacks from an unexpected quarter upset his judgment. With the idea of consolidating the Whig position in the North, he decided to make a vacation tour in Scotland. It was a foolhardy thing to do with the whole pack at his heels, the newspapers, the Tories, the old " Malignants " amongst the Whigs, his enemies amongst the lawyers and in the King's household. There was, at the time, an absurd convention against the Lord Chancellor leaving England, and a still stronger feeling against his becoming

[1] Greville : *Journals*, iii. 78, 84.
[2] Campbell : *Lives of the Chancellors*, viii. 443.

an " itinerant " politician. Brougham's five weeks' journey gave the Press and the King's advisers the opportunity they wanted. Disraeli has referred to the business in a famous passage describing the disruption of the Whigs. It is worth recalling, as it records the views of a keen and hostile observer on the relative shortcomings of the Cabinet.

" The startling rapidity, however, of the strange incidents of 1834; the indignant, soon to become vituperative, secession of a considerable section of the Cabinet, some of them esteemed too at that time among its most efficient members; the piteous deprecation of ' pressure from without,' from lips hitherto deemed too stately for entreaty followed by the Trades Union, thirty thousand strong, parading in procession to Downing-street; the Irish negotiations of Lord Hatherton, strange blending of complex intrigue and almost infantile ingenuousness; the still inexplicable resignation of Lord Althorp, hurriedly followed by his still more mysterious resumption of power, the only result of his precipitate movements being the fall of Lord Grey himself, attended by circumstances which even a friendly historian could scarcely describe as honourable to his party or dignified to himself; latterly, the extemporaneous address of King William to the Bishops; the vagrant and grotesque apocalypse of the Lord Chancellor; and the fierce recrimination and defiance of the Edinburgh banquet, all these impressive instances of public affairs and public conduct had combined to create a predominant opinion that, whatever might be the consequences, the prolonged continuance of the present party in power was a clear impossibility." [1]

What was this " vagrant and grotesque apocalypse " which helped to upset the Government, and later was

[1] *Coningsby*, Book II, Chap. i.

one of the reasons for Lord Melbourne excluding Brougham from office? Some Edinburgh reformers wished to give a congratulatory dinner to Lord Grey in the middle of September. There is evidence that Brougham helped to initiate the idea. As Chancellor, as " adopted son of Scotland," and as a leading parliamentary reformer, he was, of course, invited to attend. Going North to fulfil this engagement, he also agreed to accept the Freedom of Inverness. People in Scotland were hungry for politics, and he found his five weeks fully occupied in travelling round to see friends, and making some half-dozen speeches at Perth, Glasgow, Aberdeen and Dundee. As he wrote to Wellesley, his Scotch visit " was very unexpectedly, and not very agreeably, turned into business instead of relaxation, by the great kindness of the people wherever I went. Had I foreseen it, I should certainly have not stirred from my fireside, but being once in for it, I resolved to go through with it so as to do good to the Government and the stability of the country's institutions. I really think *I preached the word* with some good fruits." [1]

Probably neither Grey nor Brougham anticipated the excitement which their visit would cause in a country which had been so long denied any real voice in public affairs. Hobhouse met Brougham on his arrival at Stirling, where he " was received with salutes of cannon from the fort on the hill and pipers on the lawn." [2] The dinner at Edinburgh, which Brougham attended with his stepdaughter, Miss Spalding, was a great success, in spite of the chilliness of Lady Grey, who always considered her husband had been badly treated. Here, and in his other speeches, Brougham was at pains to meet the charge of failure to fulfil their pledges, which Lord Durham had begun to make against the Government. There is nothing unusual in a Cabinet Minister entering into a controversy along these lines with a former

---

[1] *Papers of Marquis of Wellesley*, ii. 247.
[2] Broughton : *Recollections*, v. 5.

colleague who has resigned. Brougham had a very strong case. The post-reform Ministry, for all its internal disputes, had produced a mass of legislation— the abolition of slavery, the India and Bank Charter Acts, the Factory Act, Brougham's legal reforms, the Poor Law Reform. Durham continued his attack at a speech in Gateshead. Brougham, with considerable justification, took the line that the Government, which had the important Municipalities Bill on the stocks, was working quite fast enough, and possibly too fast. " My own opinion is that we have done too much rather than too little." The dispute with Durham seems to have followed quite normal lines, except that both contestants adopted rather " slogging " tactics, and brought up the question of the part which each had played in the preparation of the Reform Bill. Brougham finally replied to the Gateshead speech when at Salisbury after his return to England early in October, and also in the pages of the *Edinburgh Review*.

The special charges against Brougham's behaviour really may be reduced to the nature of his speeches, and to a " rag " which took place at Rothiemurchus where Brougham was stopping with the Dowager Duchess of Bedford. Some young ladies hid the Great Seal, and made the Chancellor play the game of " hot and cold " to find it. Anyone who reads memoirs and letters written in the first half of the nineteenth century will know the extent to which statesmen unbent in those happy days before the emissaries of the Press had found their way into patrician houses. The affair was only important because it somehow got to the ears of the King, who was already offended by the Chancellor going so far afield, and was surrounded by friends anxious to blacken his character. As for the speeches, it is notable that his opponents, keenly watching for mistakes, all picked upon one unfortunate sentence, in which Brougham, at Inverness, dragged in the fact that, as was then customary, he was in constant communication with the King.

" To find that he lives in the hearts of his loyal
subjects inhabiting this ancient and important
capital of the Highlands, as it has afforded me pure
and unmixed satisfaction, will, I am confident, be so
received by His Majesty, when I tell him (as I will
do by this night's post) of such a gratifying manifestation."

It was not a wise remark, but few politicians making a
series of extempore speeches in the intervals of what was
then a long journey, would avoid occasional bathos or
false emphasis. It seems, however, to have confirmed
William IV's senile mind that " his " Lord Chancellor
was going about to outlandish places making " demo-
cratical " speeches. The King unburdened himself in
this strain to Lord Melbourne. Brougham returned to
England to face the very awkward question of appointing a Master of the Rolls to succeed Sir John Leach. His
choice of Pepys instead of the Attorney-General, Sir John
Campbell, seems to have been fully justified on legal
grounds, but the future biographer of the Chancellors
never forgave anyone who interfered in his career, and
thirty years later took his revenge, as he also did upon
Lyndhurst and others who had somehow offended him.

On November 10th, Earl Spencer died, and his son
Lord Althorp succeeded him. It had long been known
that this event might cause a crisis. The Government
had a weak set of representatives in the Lower House,
largely owing to Grey's refusal to bring middle-class
Radicals into the minor offices. Four days later the King
took a very remarkable step, he simply dismissed Lord
Melbourne's Ministry, though there was no question of
it having lost the confidence of the House of Commons.
It had never, of course, had a majority in the Lords.
Like the " Bedchamber Question " of five years later, it
was an attempt on the part of the Crown to claim its old
prerogative of choosing the Ministry without regard to
the wishes of the majority of the Commons. On each

occasion Melbourne, a Whig but a patrician, accepted this claim, which twenty years later would have been considered an anachronism. Melbourne returned to London from Brighton, and informed Brougham and one or two other Ministers that the King had decided to place the Government in the hands of the Duke of Wellington. There is no evidence that the King had consulted any leading Tories before taking this rash and precipitate action. Peel had gone to Rome for a holiday.

On the morning after Melbourne's return *The Times* alone published the news. " The King has taken the opportunity of Lord Spencer's death to turn out the Ministry. There is every reason to believe that the Duke of Wellington has been sent for. The Queen has done it all." An absurd rumour was spread about that Brougham had informed *The Times* and was responsible for the sentence about the Queen, which caused very great offence. It was Brougham's rule never to deny silly rumours, which is sound policy for a cautious man with a strong political backing, but a dangerous habit for anyone in Brougham's vulnerable condition. There was no reason for Brougham to present a bitterly hostile newspaper with a valuable "scoop." *The Times* had taken Lord Durham's side in the controversy, had unscrupulously travestied every detail of Brougham's Scotch tour, and immediately after publishing this statement, asserted that Brougham's " unbecoming conduct " was responsible for the downfall of the Government. Three days later *The Times* contains the following typical " Broughamic." " There could not, indeed, be a more revolting spectacle than for the highest law officer of the empire to be travelling about like a quack doctor through the provinces, puffing himself and his little nostrums, and committing and degrading the Government of which he has the honour to be a member." [1]

It is almost incredible that Brougham in the middle of this bitter campaign against him should have gone out of

[1] November 18, 1834.

his way to help *The Times*.   Campbell makes no mention
of this story in his life of Brougham, though there is a
reference in his own autobiography.   When writing to
his brother on November 18th, Campbell talks about
the quarrel between Brougham and *The Times*, suggesting
that " spite against Brougham " is probably the motive
for the latter's support of the Duke of Wellington.   If any
Whig sent the message to *The Times*, it may have been
Ellice.   Croker asserts this definitely.[1]   It is equally
probable that the leakage was due to Melbourne himself.
He was very casual in such affairs, and was then intimate
with at least one astute lady, Mrs. Norton, who was
connected with the Press, and some years later was
supposed, probably unfairly, to have given away a
Cabinet secret.   The King, muddle-headed and seldom
up to date, connected Brougham with any machinations
of the Press, and jumped to the conclusion that Brougham
was responsible for the insult to his wife.[2]   When
Melbourne, four months later, was anxious not to have
his former Lord Chancellor back in the Cabinet, he would
certainly not have troubled to defend his old colleague
or helped to dissipate the King's suspicions.

The pack continued to worry round Brougham's
heels, eager to seize any opportunity of discrediting him.
He was accused of disrespect to the Crown because, as
Campbell says, " he sent the *clavis regni* to the King in a
bag, as a fishmonger might have sent a salmon for the
King's dinner." [3]   Actually the Duke of Wellington
asked Brougham to deliver the Great Seal to him
personally on the Friday morning.   Brougham, with
some cases to complete, retained it till the afternoon,
after suggesting to Lyndhurst that as the Duke was

---

[1] J. W. Croker : *Correspondence and Diaries*, ii. 240.   Croker's
view is accepted in " *The Thunderer* " *in the Making*.   " It is astonish-
ing to think that history for long accepted as a fact that the
informant of *The Times* was Brougham," p. 334.

[2] In spite of the alleged insult Queen Adelaide made Brougham
an executor of her will.

[3] Campbell : *Lives of Chancellors*, viii. 460.

holding all the principal offices until Peel's return, he
would also presumably give judgments and hear appeals.
Lyndhurst thought it necessary to reply that the Duke
had no intention of doing so. Brougham took leave of
the Bar with dignity, paying a high compliment to
the ability of Pepys, Master of the Rolls, and pointing
out that the Chancery Court, " represented by its enemies
as the temple of discord, delay and expense, has been
twice closed within the space of six months."

Unfortunately, shortly after leaving office, he once
more exposed himself to attack by making one of those
queerly ingenuous offers which suggest that he was never
able to appreciate the strength and bitterness of those
opposed to him. It will be remembered that Grey had
given Lord Lyndhurst the post of Chief Baron of the
Exchequer, though he was a leading Tory. It was not
considered a strictly political appointment; Canning
had offered it to Brougham in 1827, and also possibly at
an earlier date.[1] When Lyndhurst became Chancellor
for the second time, after Peel returned, the position was
again vacant. Brougham now suggested that he should
take the post without salary, merely retaining his £5000
pension as Chancellor. From a national point of view
there was something to be said for this suggestion, but
it was a lamentable proposal to make in a world of
hungry politicians and lawyers, eager to push the former
Whig, Sir James Scarlett, into the job, and benefit from
the " general post " which would follow. Dr. Aspinall
has printed the letter in which Brougham made his offer.
It is reminiscent of his proposal made over twenty
years before to Castlereagh, but much more open to
misconstruction.

" Having resigned the Great Seal, I am by law
entitled to my pension which was granted to me under
the Act of Parliament as a compensation for the large
professional income which I sacrificed, as well as

1 See above, p. 201.

x

for the expense I incurred by the burden of the peerage. Upon your Lordship resolving to keep the office of Chancellor, that of Chief Baron of the Exchequer will become vacant, and I beg leave to state that I am willing to take upon me the duties of that office, whereby the country will be saved the charge of my pension.

"Although this would throw upon me great labour and effect a considerable saving—with a very small addition to my income not exceeding £1000 a year—yet as I well know all men's motives are liable to be misrepresented, and as I am resolved that no man shall have the possibility of misrepresenting mine—I shall positively refuse to take the salary belonging to the office, beyond the expense, whatever it may amount to, of the circuits and any expense of the Chambers and court—the whole of which cannot exceed £800 or £1000. . . ." [1]

The Press and the Bar naturally seized upon this offer as soon as it was made public. Brougham saw that there was no chance of it being considered on its merits, and withdrew it a week later. Melbourne took the conventional politician's view. "I think it a step which proves a greater want of judgement, a grosser ignorance of his own situation, than any which he has yet taken. The original error is, in fact, only made more glaring by the subsequent retraction; but I am not sure that this will be the general impression. I very much doubt whether the King would have been persuaded to have made him a Common Law judge, and I am quite sure that he would have been right in resisting it." [2] Brougham was really playing the political game with a different set of rules. He could not see why the King should be taken seriously. At the time of the Government's dismissal he had written a letter to William IV, the general

[1] *Lord Brougham and the Whig Party*, p. 204.
[2] W. M. Torrens: *Melbourne*, ii. 51.

purport of which he correctly described to Wellesley.
" The thing is strong, for it tells His Majesty : ' You
choose to ruin the country. I wash my hands of your
proceeding, and hold you answerable for the consequences.' " [1]   But to take such a line Brougham needed
a stronger backing. Revolutions are not won by
arguments but by organization. Brougham went out of
office never to return.

Two great statesmen, Morley and Asquith, have
remarked upon the similarity between Brougham and
Sir William Harcourt. On the day when Gladstone
introduced the Home Rule Bill of 1893, Harcourt, who
objected to the financial clauses, wrote him a strong
remonstrance. This roused a protest from Morley :
" That you should have, on such a morning, written as
you have done to Mr. G. is the kind of thing that
Brougham would have done, and nobody else that I have
read of in modern life."   Mr. Asquith, writing thirty
years later, accepts this verdict.   " The comparison, in
this angry outburst, of Harcourt to Brougham is unhappily only too apposite.   Both were men of the highest
gifts, head and shoulders above almost all their contemporaries ; but in both cases the gifts of nature were
rendered dangerous and even ruinous to their possessors
from inherent defects of temperament, which neither of
them had the power, or perhaps the will, to overcome.
There was something essentially lovable about Harcourt's
nature : the nature of a great breezy, elemental, ungovern-
able child who had never grown up." [2]

Before we accept as just the politicians' sentence of
banishment, we may perhaps allow ourselves, in these
days when democracy only survives fitfully and half
apologetically, a moment's doubt as to whether these
conventions of public life are so valuable and so essential.
Harcourt and Brougham were men who fixed their own

[1] *Wellesley Papers*, ii. 250 *et seq*.   The letter to the King is given
in full.
[2] H. H. Asquith : *Fifty Years in Parliament*, ii. 221.

standards, who were laws unto themselves, and both suffered disappointment—Brougham the greater, because he did not even belong to the governing class. The Whiggism of Melbourne, the Liberalism of the octogenarian Gladstone were but survivals cumbering the ground, and owing their strength to the men who would not have done " the kind of thing that Brougham would have done." Brougham's defeat was inevitable, but England was not necessarily the gainer.

CHAPTER XVII

A FREE-LANCE IN THE LORDS

Itaque veræ amicitiæ difficillime reperiuntur in iis qui in honoribus
reque publica versantur.   CICERO.

BROUGHAM, when writing his memoirs in his old age,
stopped at the year 1834, undoubtedly looking upon this
date as the end of his greatness.   He was only fifty-six
when he handed over the Great Seal.   He had another
thirty-four years to live, a period as long as from 1800,
when as a youth of twenty-two he had been called to the
Scottish Bar, and had not yet made up his mind to come
to England.   Yet his verdict on his own career was
almost certainly right.   A glance at the early numbers of
Punch is sufficient to show the place which he still held in
the public eye during the 'forties, and certainly twenty
of his last thirty-four years were spent very actively,
but his last year of office was a definite turning-point.
It would be no exaggeration to say that, at any time up
to 1834, Brougham's death would have profoundly
affected English history, but after that date it would have
made very little difference.   One of Brougham's last
actions as a Cabinet Minister, one to which he would
have attached little importance, was to help defeat the
East India Company's proposal to have Sir John Metcalfe made Governor-General.   Only those interested
in Indian history will appreciate the full tragedy of the
transaction which Brougham describes so light-heartedly
to Wellesley.   " John Company (your old friend) wants
a Governor-General of John's own shop—*a second-chop
statesman* called Metcalfe—and John is intriguing busily
for this, but we have to-day given his honour a most

positive *no* to this or anything of this sort." [1]   Within
a few months Brougham himself was to become a
"second-chop statesman," active, virile, and independent,
but never again in the front rank.

There is a formlessness about Brougham's later life
which also justifies a rather cursory treatment.   Till
1834 a biographer can find a definite purpose in nearly
every decision, a philosophy behind his expressed views,
and, in spite of his critics, a remarkable freedom from the
politician's besetting sin of allowing personal quarrels
to influence his opinions and actions.   From 1835
began his long quarrel with Melbourne and the Whigs.
This warped his judgment, and later his " Scotch
crotchets" and old half-forgotten prejudices operated
too easily on a mind not disciplined by any Party attachment.   It is not only that he accomplished little in the
last thirty years, but much that he attempted was confused
and illogical,

> " A scribe's work writ awry and blurred,
>   Scrawled after the blind evensong."

Immediately upon the dismissal of the Whig Ministry
Brougham went to France, as he told Wellesley, " to
recreate my health, ruined after thirty-four years of
slavery."   He decided to stay abroad for some weeks.
" I heard that the good people, not of England, but of
Brooks's, had laid me under an *ostracism*. . . . I resolved
to come and see some old and dear friends in the north
of Italy, and to examine minutely the state of affairs of
France, well knowing that the said ostracism would be
soon over, and that it would then be in my power to
make them eat the shells of their own oysters." [2]   Lady
Granville met him in Paris " in roaring spirits, not the
least ashamed of his last extraordinary step, his law
request." [3]   His stay was further lengthened because
" the beast-ridden and priest-ridden Government of

---

[1] *Wellesley Papers*, ii. 247.
[2] Letter to Wellesley of January 1, 1835.   *Wellesley Papers*, ii. 260.
[3] *Letters of Harriet, Countess Granville*, ii. 177.

Sardinia . . . has chosen to place all France and Italy under an interdict," and Brougham was kept in quarantine. It was a fatal mistake. As always, he underestimated the jealous hostility of the Whigs, and Melbourne's cool determined enmity. Brougham's quarrel with Melbourne was not exactly personal. Though they continued to bicker for many years, it was found on Melbourne's death that, much to his family's annoyance, he had made Brougham his executor. Their differences were, however, of a kind which made political co-operation impossible. Melbourne's philosophy of life, *quieta non movere*, was directly opposed to Brougham's, and they had entirely opposite ideas about the rules of the game of politics, the function of the King, the rights of the people, the objects of Government. Yet Melbourne was now the undisputed leader of the Whigs, and Brougham, by supporting the Whig Government and attacking Durham, had ruined himself with the Radicals. It was no time for a man so weakly placed to go abroad and let his enemies consolidate their position.

Melbourne could now see a chance of some years' placid old-fashioned Whig rule, of the kind which he may have honestly believed was best for his country, and which he certainly thought was best for his own class. The King's Tory venture could not last long, and Melbourne began to prepare for a new Whig Government, free from many disturbing or progressive influences. Russell he would be bound to include, but he was quite ready to bring in Sir Robert Peel, and according to Disraeli, opened negotiations with him through the ubiquitous Mrs. Norton, with whom he was to be so entangled the following year.[1] In January he was already writing to Grey about a new point of departure, when he will consider himself entirely free to recast the Ministry.

"I will have nothing to do with Brougham. I need not state to you the reasons of this determina-

[1] Buckle and Moneypenny : *Life of Disraeli*, i. 282.

tion. They reduce themselves readily under two heads—viz. his whole character and his whole conduct. I will have nothing to do with Durham. For obvious reasons I forbear to state to you my reasons for this decision; nor need I account for my third peremptory exclusion, which is O'Connell."[1]

Melbourne then goes on to mention other "difficulties"—Wellesley, Littleton, Ellice and Thomson—he wants the next Whig coach to have a very quiet team. Grey had enough loyalty to the old pre-reform days, when Melbourne was an obscure Canningite and Brougham kept the Whigs together, to protest mildly.

"In concerting the measures to be taken, how can you reject, from merely personal reasons which it is difficult to assign, the co-operation of a person like Brougham, who was intimately connected with you in office, who professes the same principles, and who, whatever may be the justice of the censure which he has so generally incurred, will, immediately after the meeting of Parliament, by his extraordinary activity and talents, again attract the attention, and not improbably conciliate the favour of a great portion of the Public?"[2]

Lord John Russell, one of the few men inside the Whig family circle with any genuine democratic and progressive ideas, gave a less equivocal verdict in favour of Brougham when approached by Melbourne. "I am very glad," he wrote on February 9th, "that Lord Grey recommends, with respect to Brougham, so cautious and conciliatory a course. His merits are great and conspicuous; his demerits vexatious, but not vital."[3] But Melbourne had made up his mind, and he had the Holland House group behind him. Immediately after receiving Russell's letter, he proceeded to write to Brougham a letter which has behind it the whole patrician

[1] Lloyd C. Sanders : *Melbourne Papers*, p. 237.
[2] *Early Correspondence of Lord John Russell*, ii. 86.
[3] *Id.*, ii. 89.

feeling of the eighteenth century. The " professional " had been a nuisance, and was now dismissed. When reading this remarkable letter it should be remembered that Melbourne was slightly younger than Brougham, had not a quarter of his political experience, or done a tithe of his work for the Whigs, that he had been an inefficient Home Secretary, and so casual in his private habits that a year later he had to get his Attorney-General to defend him against a charge of criminal adultery, of which he may not have been guilty, but to which he exposed himself by his manner of life. Yet he writes as follows :

" You must be perfectly aware that your character and conduct have since November last formed the principal and general topic of debate and discussion. I believe myself to have said little or nothing upon the subject. I have written little or nothing, except to one or two persons, and that in the strictest confidence. At Lord Holland's, where politics are talked every day and all day long, it is, of course, to be expected that more observations have been made; but if you believe that any hostility or malignity towards you has prevailed there, so far as I have been witness to what has passed, I can assure you that you are misinformed.

" It is a very disagreeable task to have to say to a statesman that his character is injured in the public estimation; it is still more unpleasant to have to add that you consider this is his own fault; and it is idle to expect to be able to convince almost any man, and more particularly a man of very superior abilities and of unbounded confidence in those abilities, that this is the truth. I must, however, state plainly that your conduct was one of the principal causes of the dismissal of the late Ministry, and that it forms the most popular justification of that step." [1]

[1] *Melbourne Papers*, 257 *et seq.*

This was followed, three days later, by another letter in reply to Brougham's request that Melbourne should be more specific in his accusations. It was written in the same strain, but carefully avoids a final breach. " You seem to consider my letter as putting an end to the political connection which has subsisted between us. You will observe, however, that it does not express such a determination. . . ." Brougham accepted this, and took his full share in turning out the Tory Government. In spite of a slight " swing to the right," Peel did not sufficiently strengthen its position at the General Election, and resigned. Melbourne then showed definitely that he intended to exclude both Wellesley and Brougham. Thus was formed the " Jury-mast " Cabinet, which held office for six years, chiefly because neither Tories nor Radicals had enough enterprise to displace it. It was merely a weakened version of the Government which William IV had dismissed so cavalierly. The new Lord Spencer, having escaped from his purgatory, firmly refused to come anywhere near Westminster.

The dropping of Wellesley was done straightforwardly, leaving the ex-Viceroy an implacable foe. But Melbourne was guilty of some duplicity with regard to Brougham, of whose opposition he was more afraid. The new Prime Minister certainly gave Brougham the impression that the King was the chief obstacle to a return to the Woolsack, and he encouraged this idea by placing the Chancellorship in commission, an unsatisfactory arrangement which was continued for nine months. Brougham again accepted an anomalous position. He was well used to exclusion from office owing to Royal caprice, and during the summer he worked hard for the Whigs. " H. B. " was only expressing the common sentiment when he portrayed Brougham and O'Connell as carrying the Melbourne Ministry between them. Brougham forced the highly contentious Municipal Reform Bill through the Lords. His temper had not improved, but his methods were effective.

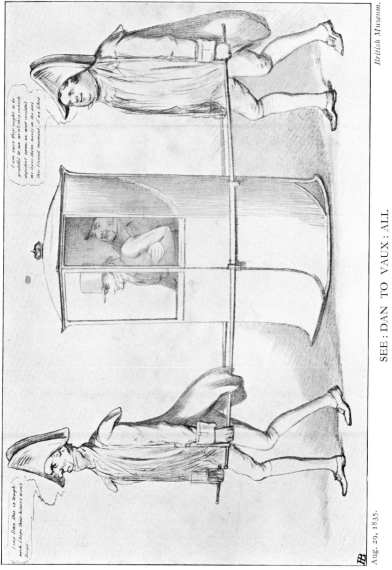

Brougham.　　　Melbourne.　　　O'Connell.

SEE : DAN TO VAUX : ALL
and back again
From a sketch by H. B. Doyle.

Aug. 29, 1835.

British Museum.

"Brougham," wrote Parkes to Durham, "has been like a tiger in a jungle dealing out death wherever he fixed his prodigious claws. Last night he not only knocked Lyndhurst head over heels but jumped on his carcase and stamped the life out of him." [1] In the autumn he accepted, after some hesitation, the chairmanship of the Commission on Educational Endowments, a return to his old interests of sixteen years earlier. It would seem that even this minor appointment was opposed by the King. Russell wrote to Melbourne in September 1835 :

> "You will know before that the King strongly objects to Brougham, but I hope that you will be able to overcome his objections. He considers it as a commission to direct education instead of an inquiry. What is it Brougham did ? I have written to Taylor another long letter, which you ought to see. It must be considered that if Brougham is rejected after having consulted his friends, we shall have ' war to the knife ' from him and, according to an old joke of Dudley's, Mr. B.'s Monarchy Abolition Bill read the first time." [2]

By the beginning of 1836 Melbourne felt strong enough to end the arrangement about the Chancellorship, which was causing congestion in the Chancery Court. In December Brougham had written to him desiring "to be understood as having renounced any claim he may have to the Great Seal." [3] It would have been easy to accept this, and eased Brougham's path. Instead, Melbourne, with calculated bad manners, appointed Sir Charles Pepys without any intimation to Brougham, who first learnt about the elevation of Lord Cottenham from a newspaper. It was a final blow. "I must be a stock or a stone," he wrote to Lord Spencer, who sympathized with him, "not to be sensible that my treatment affords

---

[1] Letter of Aug. 14, 1835. Stuart Reid : *Life of Lord Durham,* ii. 73. [2] *Early Correspondence of Lord John Russell,* ii. 126. [3] *Id.,* ii. 164.

an instance, almost unparalleled, of gross injustice. Whether the Ministers have acted from fear of one or two newspapers, or a set of jobbing members of Brooks's calling themselves the Whig Party, or from all these fears combined, is quite immaterial. They have done or submitted to such an act as never yet, I verily believe, was known among men bound together, even by the tie of party, but still more of Cabinet connection." [1]

Brougham did not immediately cross the floor of the House, as most modern politicians would have done. With more dignity he retired from politics for a year, and spent 1836 between Brougham Hall and Cannes, where he had built a villa in what was still a small fishing village. His disappointments and struggles seem to have reacted on his health, and he underwent one of his periodic fits of depression, but he was also busy writing, his chief solace during the latter years of his life. In 1835 he had published the first volumes of his edition of Paley's *Natural Theology*. He began upon a collection of his own speeches with introductions, and later upon his better-known *Historical Sketches*. Bulwer Lytton wrote to Lord Durham in the summer—" Brougham still moralizes, but I believe is less ill than they give out—writing books for posterity, and ruminating on vanished woolsacks, to express it tersely, in a political soliloquy, which he may be supposed to utter when inspired :

> " New books, I'm blotting 'em ;
> Whigs, I've forgotten 'em ;
> Damn that Lord Cottenham." [2]

The Government suffered severely from Brougham's withdrawal. Melbourne, unnerved by the Norton trial, was totally ineffective. The Lords, knowing the Whigs had little support in the country, treated their Bills with contempt. " The Lords, having no fear before their eyes at present of Brougham, Spencer or Durham, seem determined that if the Whigs continue in office and take their salaries

[1] Althorp MS. Quoted in *Lord Brougham and the Whig Party*, p. 221. [2] Stuart Reid: *Life of Lord Durham*, ii. 96.

they shall not govern."[1] In the following year Brougham returned to London, attended the Lords, where he sat on the ministerial benches, "talked familiarly, if not cordially, with Melbourne," but took little part in the debates. He introduced three Bills, dealing with National Education, the establishment of local Courts, and the abolition of Pluralities in the Church, but seems to have made little effort to press them. He preferred to wait for the approaching end to see what changes might follow the accession of Queen Victoria.

The results of the change were disappointing. Melbourne soon established a complete ascendancy over the young Queen, and the Cabinet under its jury rig continued to drift slowly, without anyone on board, except possibly Lord John Russell, having much idea where they were going. Brougham at first took his own independent line. He was certainly not continually opposing the Government, as Campbell would suggest. On some questions, such as education, the Cabinet was notoriously divided. Hobhouse has left an account of a discussion in 1838. "We discussed Russell's Education scheme. Lord Melbourne confessed that he was against the thing altogether; on which Howick said, ' Thank God there are some things which even you cannot stop, and that is one of them.' Melbourne only smiled."[2] Brougham did his best to fight for Russell's Bill, which was a direct descendant of the one he had introduced in 1820, and had to face much the same opposition from the Lords and the Bishops. Similarly, Brougham would defend those earlier Whig measures which he had helped to advance. In March 1838 Melbourne acknowledged his help in a letter to the Queen.

"Lord Stanhope made a long declamatory speech, very violent, but having in it nothing defined or specific, and was answered by Lord Brougham in a most able and triumphant defence and maintenance

---

[1] Id., ii. 86.   [2] Broughton : Recollections, v. 168.

of the late Act for Amending the Laws for the Relief of the Poor." [1]

To a considerable extent Brougham kept to his attitude of complete independence as the depositary of the true Whig faith, but such a rôle is difficult to maintain, and Brougham was "human, all too human." He could not avoid personal quarrels with Melbourne, or personal friendships with certain Tories, notably Lord Lyndhurst, with whom, apart from politics, he had much in common. By December 1837 there had been what Greville calls " a grand breeze in the House of Lords between Melbourne and Brougham " over a proposal to increase the allowance of the Duchess of Kent. Brougham accused Melbourne of " courtly airs " and Melbourne replied with a rather obvious *tu quoque*. On this occasion Brougham was *Athanasius contra mundum*, but inevitably there were occasions when a portion of the Tory Party would be glad to support him. Peel, Stanley and Wellington strictly avoided all contact with Radicals. Peel wrote to Arbuthnot at the end of 1838 :

> " I am very glad that Hardinge acted so wisely in not meeting Lord Brougham. Nothing could be more injurious than any sort of connection with that man. I know that more than once last Session the Duke of Wellington would not vote for him though he thought him right." [2]

Other Tories were not so conscientious, or from another point of view so small-minded. Many went further than Brougham in exploiting the growing force of Chartism throughout the provinces; others, like Lord Lyndhurst, were willing to find some common ground to co-operate with Radicals in harassing the Government. Brougham did his best to make the slavery question such a subject. Melbourne, it may be remembered, had

[1] *Letters of Queen Victoria*, i. 138.
[2] C. S. Parker : *Sir Robert Peel*, ii. 369.

always been an opponent of emancipation. In 1824 he had resisted Brougham's demand for an inquiry into the case of the missionary, John Smith. In 1833 he had passively discouraged the Cabinet policy of emancipation. The period of apprenticeship was now drawing to a close, and various difficulties arose on which the Radicals disapproved of the Colonial Office policy. There was also the question of the indenture system, in those days very akin to slavery, under which Indian coolies were being shipped to Antigua. In March 1838 Brougham made a great speech on slavery, and Greville noted, " he continues to be the great meteor of the day . . . the Conservatives . . . are not sorry to pat him on the back as a fragellifer of the Ministers."

Brougham sounded Stanley on the subject of Antigua in a letter which suggests a close relationship with some of the latter's party.

> " I am going to bring on slavery and slave trading on Monday. Only think of the Government having, without intending or knowing it, made a new branch of slave trading. Minto and Co. will be beaten on Monday unless the Tories disgrace themselves again." [1]

But neither Stanley nor Peel, nor for that matter the Duke of Wellington, were ready to take up the subject, and they feared that the Radicals would demand a *quid pro quo* on the question of parliamentary reform. The Whigs, as Brougham had foreseen, were now taking the line that the 1832 settlement was " final," though its deficiencies were every day becoming more obvious. Brougham returned to open support of the ballot as the only method of preventing the bribery, which flourished unashamed until well into the Victorian era. While, therefore, Brougham was on very friendly terms with men like Croker and Lyndhurst, the patrician Tories kept studiously aloof. " When I was at Belvoir," wrote

[1] *Id.*, ii. 360.

Peel to Arbuthnot, early in 1839, "Croker received a letter from Brougham which nothing but very intimate terms could have indited. Yesterday's post brought one to Lord Ellenborough from the same pen. I had no wish even to get into the very slightest contact with Brougham which the mere reading of his letter (as I take it for granted it was on Canadian affairs) might bring me into. I expressed, therefore, no wish to see or hear it." [1]

The " Canadian affair " and the famous " Bedchamber question " were two cases in which Brougham came out strongest against the Whigs, and were the usual instances taken by Government men, like Campbell, to prove that Brougham allowed his personal feelings to overcome his political principles. In each Brougham showed that he was still strong enough, merely as an individual, to endanger a Government.

After Papineau's rebellion of 1837, the Whigs suspended the Canadian constitution and sent Lord Durham out as High Commissioner. The first step was probably justified, but the choice of the Commissioner was undoubtedly influenced by Melbourne's desire for a quiet life. Durham, it will be remembered, was the second of Melbourne's "peremptory exclusions" in 1835. Durham, on his return from his mission to Russia, was likely to be a thorn in the Government's flesh. He had decided claims to a seat in the Cabinet, and otherwise would be a focussing point for Radical discontent. Like Mr. Belloc's lachrymose hero, who was sent " to govern New South Wales," Durham was despatched to Canada to get him out of the way. It was an unhappy choice, for " King Jog " was as self-centred, as domineering, and as neurotic as ever. His new mission was a fiasco, though redeemed by an admirable Report which laid the foundations of modern Canada. The paradox was typical of the man. His general ideas were magnificent. He was ahead of his time on social questions, as

[1] *Id.*, ii. 374.

well as in his imperial conceptions, but he had no
political sense. He insisted on taking out to Canada
two men of doubtful antecedents. He formed an
Executive Council of four, none of whom had any
experience of Canadian administration, and three of
whom were his private secretaries. Shortly afterwards
he issued an Ordinance granting an amnesty for all
except twenty-three of the late rebels. Eight of these
exceptions were deported to Bermuda, and the remainder
forbidden to return to Canada on pain of death. Considering the extraordinary powers given him as High
Commissioner, it was something of an achievement to
produce such a doubly illegal order.

Brougham undoubtedly watched these proceedings
with a very unfriendly eye. The quarrel of 1834 had
ended on a note of personal bitterness. Subsequently
each was inclined to blame the other for their exclusion
from office, an illusion which the more orthodox Whigs
did their best to foster. Brougham, as the self-appointed
censor of Whig constitutional orthodoxy, had his chance.
He had objected to the original suspension of the
Canadian constitution, and could now point to the rake's
progress which followed such illegal action. Melbourne
put up no sort of defence in the House of Lords. He
undoubtedly thought that Durham was in the wrong.
" His conduct," he wrote to the Queen, " has been most
unaccountable." [1] Brougham was not a sportsman, but
he must have felt all the joy of the skilled shot in bringing
down his two birds so neatly. Introducing a " Canada
Government Act Declaratory Bill," with the object of
elucidating the original measure suspending the constitution, Brougham was able to say exactly what he
thought of Durham's illegalities, while conferring an
indemnity upon him for his past " evil acts." Melbourne capitulated, the Ordinance was disallowed by the
Home Government, and Durham returned in a huff.
There is some evidence that Brougham originated the

[1] *Letters of Queen Victoria*, p. 163.

Y

famous description of the Report—" Wakefield thought
it, Buller wrote it, Durham signed it." If so he was
unfair to an old comrade in arms, but his attack on the
Ordinance was perfectly justifiable, and Melbourne, if
he found himself in an impossible position, had only
himself to blame. Durham also put himself in the
wrong by his sudden return, and there were some
grounds for the accusations of " desertion " embodied
in " H. B.'s " cartoon.

Some Tories, like Lord Ellenborough, and certain
Radicals, took a prominent part in this attack, but the
Government, though badly shaken, survived their surrender. Many Tories would hardly condemn a pro-
consul for being high-handed, and most Radicals retained their affection for Durham. Even Roebuck, who
was usually Brougham's faithful ally in the Commons,
thought he was " all astray as to Lord Durham in
Canada, and misled by a desire to find him in the wrong."
The next year saw a new constitutional crisis, but with a
different party alignment. It began, as in the case of
Canada, with a Whig Bill to suspend the constitution of
Jamaica, which was carried by such a small majority
that the Government resigned. Then followed Peel's
insistence on certain changes in the Household, including
some of the Queen's "Ladies." The details of this
question are hardly germane to our subject, but Victoria's
refusal to dismiss her Whig " Ladies," and Melbourne's
consequent return to office, must have seemed to many
Whigs a complete travesty of their traditional attitude
towards the Crown. Brougham apparently wrote round
to some of his old Whig friends not to embark on this
perilous course, and worked with certain Radicals to
arrive at a compromise. It was only when these failed
that " the boiling torrent of rage, disdain and hatred,
which had been dammed up upon a former occasion
when he was so unaccountably muzzled, broke forth
with restless and overwhelming force. He spoke for
three hours and delivered such an oration as no other

Durham.

Brougham.

Jan. 29, 1839.

British Museum.

A DESERTER

From a sketch by H. B. Doyle.

man in existence is capable of; devilish in spirit and design, but of superhuman eloquence and masterly in execution. He assailed the Ministers with a storm of invective and ridicule; while he enveloped his periods in a studied phraseology of pretended loyalty and devotion, he attacked the Queen with unsparing severity." [1] This passage from Greville seems worth quoting at length as it suggests the curious mesmeric effect of Brougham's eloquence upon his listeners, even those who strongly disapproved of him.   Here is the actual wording of the reference to the Queen.

"The Government have resumed office only because the Queen has refused to dismiss two ladies of her bedchamber. They stand by the Queen without the confidence of Parliament. Will this standing by the Queen get back publick confidence? I do not believe a word of it. The attempt to pass a falsehood on the nation has signally failed. Considering what an inexperienced person the Queen is, it should be imputed to no fault of her own. She has barely reigned two years. But those who are about her are bound to inform her of the solemn responsibility thrown upon her by the ancient and established principles of the Constitution."

About this time Lord Spencer wrote to Melbourne suggesting that a reconciliation with Brougham would be possible. "I feel confident, without any communication with him to make me so, that he would be conciliated if you offered to him to join the Administration, whether he would do so or not. I think he would." [2] It is unlikely that Melbourne made any advances, and Brougham continued to worry the Government until it fell in 1841. He then remained on the Opposition side, and played the candid friend to the new Administration. A full description of his activities, political and judicial,

[1] *Journal*, iv. 218.   [2] *Melbourne Papers*, p. 401.

education would enable working men to appreciate the rigidly controlled world in which they lived. The franchise would give them a chance of correcting abuses, but no serious interference was possible with the mechanism of production, distribution and exchange. Brougham would not have extended his economic " laws " to the relations between different countries, but at home he accepted the dismal science, and may be considered a founder of the *laissez-faire* school.   In his younger days, when he was more in touch with working men and women, his humanity would keep breaking through, but when Sir Robert Peel took office in 1841, Brougham was sixty-three, and had no popular following in the country.   He still took his own line, but he was far more of a doctrinaire.   This did not necessarily lead him astray on the fiscal question, but he fell lamentably when it came to social legislation.

In an earlier chapter Brougham was described as an empirical free trader.   He retained that attitude when free trade had become a religious dogma, from which any deviation was apostasy.   In politics it is not easy to be *tertius gaudens*, and Brougham found himself hailed as a renegade.   He was in favour of Repeal, but disliked the violence of the Anti-Corn Law agitation.   He was even involved in an acrimonious controversy with John Bright, whom he accused of inciting people to murder Sir Robert Peel.   Brougham would have been prepared to retain for a period the very low sliding scale on wheat. Worse was to follow, for in 1849 Hobhouse recounts how " the renegade Brougham moved the amendment, protesting that the Repeal of the Navigation Laws had nothing to do with free trade.   Russell told me he expected this move as Brougham hopes to be Stanley's Chancellor. . . . Sir James Graham told me a joke of Russell's, viz. that Brougham ought to be well acquainted with the Navigation Laws, having so long engaged in the *seal* fisheries." [1]   Russell may be allowed his little

[1] Broughton : *Recollections*, vi. 237.

ferocity, nevertheless addressed the following " open letter " to the President of the United States, when Brougham made his American visit in 1850:

> " I have much pleasure in making yourself and my friend Brougham—the Brougham whose fame is not European but world-wide—better acquainted. With all his drolleries, he is an excellent fellow; and with all his oddities, he has worked like a stable boy at our Augean Courts of Law. He has cheapened costs; he has well-nigh destroyed the race of sharp attorneys. Indeed, if you seek Brougham's monument, look round every attorney's office, and you will *not* find Brougham's picture."

So far would Brougham go, but, like so many later Liberals, he could not see that there can be no equality of contract between a rich man and a poor man. His sojourn in the Lords, and a life spent between London, Cannes and Brougham Hall, only made him more dogmatic when it came to dealing with Factory Bills. Lord Shaftesbury, looking back on his early struggles over the Ten-Hours Bill, said of the Liberals, " O'Connell was a sneering and bitter opponent, Gladstone ever voted in resistance to my efforts, and Brougham played the doctrinaire in the House of Lords. Bright was ever a most malicious opponent. Cobden, though bitterly hostile, was better than Bright." [1] Brougham's logic would enable him to agree to the exclusion of children from mines in 1842, but not to anything approaching interference with the " right " to sell one's labour. " If we leave the question open," he said two years later on the Ten-Hours Bill, " every man had a Ten-Hours Bill already : he might work ten hours if he pleased, and no power on earth could make him work more unless he liked—no man need work longer than he pleased." Later he seems to have dropped something of the

---

[1] E. Hodder : *Life of Lord Shaftesbury*, II. 378.

doctrinaire, opposed the miserable business of the
" compromise " over the Ten-Hours Bill, and in 1860,
as an octogenarian, came down to the Lords to support
Shaftesbury on the question of special legislation for
Bleach Works.   It is, perhaps, evidence that Brougham's
economic bark was worse than his bite that, in 1858,
Shaftesbury refused to move a vote of thanks to Lord
John Russell at the Social Science Congress " because I
could not honestly praise him (a social intriguer and the
unfeeling adversary of the wretched chimney-sweepers),
but agreed to move one to Lord Brougham." [1]

[1] *Id.*, III. 75.   See also J. L. and B. Hammond, *Lord Shaftesbury*,
passim.

CHAPTER XVIII

ALL PASSION SPENT

The Seas are quiet, when the Winds give o're;
So calm are we, when Passions are no more;
For then we know how vain it was to boast
Of fleetings Things, so certain to be lost.
Clouds of Affection from our younger Eyes
Conceal that emptiness, which Age descries.

The Soul's dark Cottage, batter'd and decay'd,
Lets in new Light, thro' chinks that time has made
Stronger by weakness, wiser Men become
As they draw near to their Eternal home.

EDMUND WALLER.

In the first chapter of this book it was suggested that
Brougham had two difficult horses in the team which
was to drag him through life—a restless inquiring mind,
and very high animal spirits.   Looking back upon his
career, he had certainly accomplished a remarkable
journey, even if his mettlesome team sometimes took
him through unnecessarily dangerous places.   Up to
the age of about fifty-seven he had driven with great
firmness and determination, though he had taken an
unconventional line of country.   After that there was
a period when his hand seemed to lose control.   But he
gradually pulled back on to the high-road, and entered
upon a very peaceful, mellow old age.

"A full busy youth," wrote Stevenson, "is your
only prelude to a self-contained and independent
age."   As middle age turned to old age Brougham
could certainly look back upon a life which had been
full and busy.   There had been the first period when he
drove straight through all that maze of legal and con-

stitutional barriers which had hemmed in his generation, making a trail through which others were to follow, and forget the pioneer. A contemporary, William Hazlitt, has left a good description of Brougham as an iconoclast.

" The Opposition, it seems, with Mr. Brougham at their head, ' attack all that is valuable in our institutions.' So says Lord Castlereagh; and, to make the thing more incredible, so says the *Courier*. They attack Sir Judkin Fitzgerald and the use of torture; and *therefore* they attack all that is valuable in our institutions. They attack the system of spies and informers; and therefore they attack all that is valuable in our institutions. They object to the moral characters of such men as Castles and Oliver; and therefore they attack all that is most respectable in the country. They consider Lord Sidmouth, who is ' to acquaint us with the perfect spy o' th' time,' as no conjurer, treat his circular letters and itinerant incendiaries with as little ceremony as respect; and therefore they are hostile to all that is venerable in our constituted authorities. They do not approve of the Suspension of the Habeas Corpus, of Standing Armies, and Rotten Boroughs; and therefore they would overturn all that is most valuable in the Constitution." [1]

This was written in 1817. There followed the strange drama of the " Queen's Trial," and let no one imagine that it required scant courage to stand up against a ruling monarch in the years which followed the Napoleonic wars. Then came those ten busy years which saw the gradual liberalizing of English politics, the defeat of the Old Tories, the struggles over legal reform, the founding of London University. Finally, as the great climax, were the four years of Brougham's Chancellorship, with the Reform coach rattling along at a speed

[1] W. Hazlitt: *Collected Works*, iii. 240.

which terrified nine out of ten educated Englishmen. It had been a wonderful journey, but when the next stage had to be undertaken Brougham was a disillusioned man, wearied and without any clear objective. The guiding hand relaxed. Bagehot, who wrote a very wise and sympathetic sketch of Brougham's career, understood the strain which this later phase placed upon his character. " To a man so active, to be out of action is a pain which few can appreciate; that other men should enter into your labours is not pleasant, that they should be Canningites does not make it any better. We have witnessed many escapades of Lord Brougham; we perhaps hardly know his temptations and vexations." [1]

Brougham had a strong Puritan trend, due to his birth and upbringing, but those two troublesome steeds, his restless mind and his exuberant vitality, began to take charge when they felt the reins slack upon their backs. There is a curious interval in Brougham's life when he was the intimate friend of Count D'Orsay, was Palmerston's rival in the affections of Mrs. Petre, supped with Lady Jersey, and gambled with what Creevey called " the usual list of dandies and swindlers (D'Orsay included)." Greville, strongly disapproving, describes Brougham as having " frittered down his really great powers to the level of his new friends and companions, but he has no notion how to converse or live with ease, and nothing can be more awkward or ungraceful than this exhibition he makes of himself as a man of fashion." [2] He drifted into foolish scrapes. In 1839 a report of his death reached London from Brougham Hall, and produced a crop of obituary notices. It seems to have originated in a joke on the part of D'Orsay and a Mr. Shafto. Brougham's own responsibility is doubtful, but most people imputed the hoax to his usual love of notoriety, and many would not take it so good-naturedly as the Duke of Cambridge, who " hunted

[1] H. W. Bagehot : *Collected Works*, iii. 77.
[2] Greville : *Journals*, vi. 240.

Brougham round the room, saying, ' Oh, by God, you wrote that letter; by God, you did it yourself.' "[1] Brougham would never quite grow up, there was always a suspicion of the " card " treating life in general, and London Society in particular, as a kind of harlequinade. Hobhouse, in 1844, describes how he

> " went to an assembly at Lady Brougham and Vaux's. The invitation, of course, came from the lady, and I thought there was no objection to accepting it, although the freaks of my former friend and colleague made it a doubtful case. Brougham came in a little tipsy, as Lady Malmesbury observed to me, fully dressed, having dined with the French Ambassador, and made grimaces and bows to his wife on the sofa, and then to Lady Jersey and others. He told me that the dress suit was one that he had when he went to the Bar. He called me ' My dear Hobhouse.' The Duke of Wellington was there in regimentals. Miss Fanny Eden showed me a piece of tapestry given to Brougham by Louis Philippe of which B. is very proud."[2]

This phase lasted about ten years, into the later 'forties, after which Brougham gradually relapsed into a very decent and dignified old age. He was never wholly absorbed either into the " world " of Miss Fanny Eden and the Duke of Wellington, or the " half world " of Lady Jersey and the Count D'Orsay. These ten years were occupied with political and legal activities which would have been sufficient for many men of his age. He continued to sit on the Judicial Committee of the Privy Council until 1850, and took an active part until still later in the judicial business of the House of Lords. He presided over the Law Amendment Society, and helped with its quarterly journal, the *Law Review*. Above all he found in literature a solace during the last thirty years of his life.

[1] *Id.*, iv. 256.   [2] Broughton : *Recollections*, vi. 100.

Brougham just failed to earn his niche in the temple of literature. He was a very able journalist, or rather a writer for periodicals, but so were most contemporary authors. Coleridge was, for a time, a daily journalist; Southey supported himself by writing for periodicals. As Professor Saintsbury said of William Cobbett, Francis Jeffrey, Sydney Smith, John Wilson, Charles Lamb, William Hazlitt, Thomas De Quincey and John Gibson Lockhart, " they were such frequent contributors to periodical literature of one kind or another that in some cases nothing, in most cases little, would be left of their work if contributions to newspapers, reviews and magazines were to be excluded from it."[1] Brougham, in spite of the eleven volumes of his collected works, never quite reached the literary standards even of the more pedestrian amongst these authors. One reason for this comparative failure was that Brougham, until nearly sixty, almost always wrote to further some political end, while after 1836 he chose his subjects, and wrote chiefly to distract himself. He was not content, like Robert Browning, to read Greek prose in his old age, but he had to translate and annotate it, a specialist's job for which he had not the knowledge. As Grote wrote to G. C. Lewis : " Your criticism upon that kopis, hedulogos, democraristos Brougham is quite just; and I daresay you will find material for ample annotation in his inaccuracies. Speakers are privileged to be inaccurate, and Brougham seems to have abnegated his peculiar and appropriate weapon when he exchanged the tongue for the pen."[2]

Unfortunately Brougham had an itch to publish as well as to write. Most of his eleven volumes should never have left his study drawer. This weakness was most conspicuous during the five years which followed his break with Melbourne. He smothered his admirable *Historical Sketches of Statesmen and Philosophers*

[1] G. Saintsbury : *Nineteenth Century Literature*, p. 168.
[2] Letter of Sept. 1840. *Life of George Grote*, p. 133.

between a four-volume collection of his speeches and a lamentable translation of Demosthenes, which simply invited the most scarifying criticisms from all those old classical scholars, who had never forgiven him for his " Patent Omnibus," or his efforts to popularize education. *The Times*, with a curious lack of proportion, allowed Joseph Blakesley, a Fellow of Trinity College, Cambridge, to castigate this work in the longest review which the paper has ever published—a serial running into several pages of small type. The future Dean of Lincoln obviously enjoyed the " vapulation which we intend to inflict upon Lord Brougham's literary hide" for his "foul, wallowing, boisterous and unEnglish" translation, but it is doubtful whether many readers of *The Times* can have appreciated this outpouring of academic venom. Barnes, the editor, who died a year later in 1841, might have shown a little more mercy to a man who had been his friend for years, and a little more understanding of the urge which was driving Brougham into authorship.[1]   Only the urgent need for distraction can explain why, just after his sixty-first birthday, he should have "been writing sixteen hours a day, and about to bring out two more volumes of Paley." [2]

Great literature may be produced for a thousand different causes, but hardly as a relief from an attack of ergomania, or as a sedative for frayed nerves. Yet Brougham's *Historical Sketches* and his *Lives of Men of Letters and Science* are very readable, and crammed with a queer unstressed erudition.   It is, perhaps, characteristic that his collected speeches are dedicated to Wellesley, his fellow-sufferer, but the *Sketches* to his wife.   He was beginning to free himself from the thraldom of Party politics, and from the rancour of his dispute with the patrician Whigs and the Canningites.   Although he was violent in controversy, he was not a good hater, and he gradually returned to his old friendships with

[1] " *The Thunderer* " *in the Making, 1785–1841*, pp. 443–5.
[2] Greville : *Journals*, iv. 154–5.

Grey, Durham, and even with Melbourne. In his last letter to Princess Lieven, written in 1841, Grey describes his own aloofness from politics. "Correspondents I have none, except Brougham, who is very good in writing to me frequently the *on dits* of the day."[1] Abraham Hayward noted early in 1839 that "Lord Durham dines with Brougham—so much for the quarrels of statesmen."

Brougham Hall and Cannes steadily absorbed a greater part of his life, between these two he could keep in touch with every side of life. At some time or other everyone of importance seems to have drifted down to see him in the south of France, or struggled up to Westmorland. Towards the end of the 'forties Brougham's political passion seems to have spent itself, but his enthusiasm for life was not abated, and he remained a " card " till the end of his days. A letter from Campbell to his brother describes a visit to Brougham, and suggests that, like so many old men, he was absorbed in establishing an obviously spurious ancestry.

> " In the church of Brougham there was the grave of an Edwardus de Broham, who accompanied Richard I to the Holy Land, and fought many stout battles against the Saracens. My noble and learned friend lately opened his coffin, brought away the skull, framed it and placed it in his baronial hall, under the purse which contained the Great Seal of England. Being called upon to admire the grinning Crusader, I could only say that ' I was much struck by the family likeness between him and his illustrious descendant—particularly in the *lengthiness* of the *jaw* ! . . .' We had a grand ball to celebrate the birthday of William Brougham's eldest son, who, in derogation of the right of blood which is in John's eldest son, is to be called to the throne."[2]

[1] *Correspondence with Princess Lieven.* Letter of August 19th.
[2] Hardcastle : *Life of Lord Campbell,* ii. 244.
Brougham Hall, in 1934, finally passed out of the Brougham

Brougham might here be pictured as the complete but somewhat senile Victorian patriarch; but this was in 1848; the same year in which he had spent some time studying the latest French Revolution on the spot, and had got involved in the last of his scrapes by applying to M. Crémieux, the Minister of Justice, to become a naturalized Frenchman. The last was a gesture in the grand manner of Henry James, and from the same motive of friendship to a country passing through a difficult period, but Brougham had not understood that it meant renouncing English citizenship, and the incident closed in a good deal of laughter. It also inspired an admirable cartoon in *Punch*.

Brougham, as always, remained completely unperturbed by criticism. Two years later he was back in Paris. Abraham Hayward describes how " he took me to the *Institut* on Monday, where he introduced me to the leading men of science. On Tuesday I dined with him, D'Orsay, Alexandre Dumas (the celebrated writer), Lord Dufferin and Stuart of the Embassy." Hayward had previously found him " in a squabble with a Frenchman whom he had engaged to translate a scientific paper to be read that day at the Institut, and whom he ended in calling *bête comme une oie*." Brougham read his paper, " which (barring accent) was not a bad or unsuccessful performance. No less a person than Arago remarked, in answer to a timid inquiry (from Hayward), ' *C'est bien ; mais il n'y a rien d'original là dedans*.' " [1] The paper was presumably on the " optical discovery " which he discussed with Campbell while they were both sitting on the Judicial Committee of the Privy Council, and of which he said " Newton had very nearly hit upon it." [2]

The Association for the Promotion of Social Science

---

and Vaux family. It is at least pleasant to learn that the Crusader's skull, having been the cause of wit in John Campbell, has at last been reinterred.

[1] H. E. Carlisle : *Correspondence of Abraham Hayward*, pp. 146–8.
[2] *Life of Lord Campbell*, ii. 250.

THE CITIZEN OF THE WORLD;
Or, Lord Brougham Naturalized Everywhere.

From the cartoon which appeared in *Punch*, April 19, 1848.
Reproduced by permission of the Proprietors of *Punch*.

was almost a revival of the old " Steam Intellect Society,"
and helped to keep Brougham in touch with reformers
of different schools.   It held its first Congress in 1857,
and was the chief interest of Brougham's later days.
Robert Owen attended the following year.

> " It is now a matter of public history how
> kindly Lord Brougham, as soon as he saw his old
> friend, took him by the arm, led him forward,
> and obtained a hearing for him.   Then Mr. Owen
> in his grand manner, proclaimed his ancient message
> of science, competence and good-will to the world.
> When he came to the conclusion of his first period,
> Lord Brougham, out of regard to his failing strength,
> terminated it.   He clasped his arm, applauded his
> words, then said, ' Capital, very good, can't be
> better.   There, that will do.'   Then in an under-
> tone, ' Mr. Rigby, convey the old gentleman to
> his bed.' " [1]

The scene is very typical of Brougham, especially the
last remark.   Robert Owen was eighty-seven, but
Brougham himself was eighty.   He refused to be beaten
by time, any more than he had been beaten by life.
Two years later, he received honorary degrees at both the
older Universities, which had at last forgiven his old
activities.   At Oxford he had a tumultuous reception;
" many of the young men in the gallery probably had
never heard of his anti-Oxford movements, and the
elder ones willingly forgot them for the sake of his
recent good services.   The noble veteran was in good
health, full of energy and spirits, actually *knocking up*
more than one Oxonian, considerably his juniors, in
lionizing Oxford during two successive days." [2]
Cambridge seems to have been more of a strain, for
Delane noticed that he " was uncommon shaky, but—
what nobody expected—quite concise."   He was a

[1] F. Podmore : *Life of Robert Owen*, p. 626.
[2] G. V. Cox : *Recollections of Oxford*, p. 450.

Z

lion-hearted old man, who liked the younger generation, and did his best for them. He helped to launch his numerous nephews on to the world, and when his old rival Lord Campbell was appointed Chancellor in 1859, he wrote warmly congratulating him, and, as Campbell writes, " condescended to ask me to appoint his nephew a Registrar in Bankruptcy, which I very readily promised to do, reminding him that he, when Chancellor, had given a similar appointment to a nephew of mine." [1] So the two octogenarians, who had sparred so often in the past, united amicably to " do a job."

Brougham Hall became a great resort for a younger generation of writers. Whitwell Elwin, of the *Quarterly Review*, was a frequent visitor, helping to entertain the Countess of Westmorland, for whose coming " a statue of Lord Erskine was dragged out from some lumber room and placed in a conspicuous position in the hall, and we all scrubbed the statue for an entire morning with soap and soda to try and get off the stains and dirt of a quarter of a century." Elwin used to supply, and even at times invent, suitable quotations for Brougham's addresses to the Social Science Congress, and the old man did his best to help him in his career. " It is very touching," wrote Elwin in 1855, " to see him after a public career, which would have seared the hearts of most people, as tender in his feelings as persons who have all their lives been cultivating the domestic affections. He has never recovered the death of his own daughter, though it is more than fifteen years since she died. In company he is very silent, often not opening his mouth during an entire meal, but when you are alone with him he talks in an uninterrupted flow, and then nothing can be more animated and entertaining." [2] Another guest, whose coming marked the passing of an old feud, was John Delane of *The Times*. He found " the people here all mad for coursing, and the court-

[1] *Life of Lord Campbell*, ii. 370.
[2] W. Elwin: *Some Eighteenth-Century Men of Letters*, i. 151.

yard full of squires and greyhounds." [1]   There was certainly an infinite variety about Brougham, even after he had passed his threescore years and ten.

In the early days of the Society for the Diffusion of Useful Knowledge, which expired in 1844 in the effort of bringing out the Penny Cyclopædia, Brougham invented what would now be called a slogan.   A man, he said, should know something of everything, and everything of something.   Another later saying was— Man is not responsible to man for his belief, over which he has no control.   There is much of Brougham's philosophy of life in these two ideas, both of which had a considerable influence on Victorian thought.   He belonged to an age which believed that salvation lay in the acquisition of " facts "   Man was sent into the world to experiment and to acquire knowledge.

Mention has been made of Brougham's almost pathetic faith in the value of education to cure social discontent. It is equally characteristic of him that we know little about his religious beliefs, except his interest in spiritualism.

Frank Podmore, himself a trained observer of psychical phenomena, has given, in his biography of Robert Owen, an account of the rather childish experiments in table rapping which the old philanthropist carried on during the 'fifties.   Brougham became intensely interested in these, and attended engagements at Mr. Seaton's who " boasts a good medium for superior spirits."   The spirits were certainly " superior," for it was usually the Duke of Kent who announced his presence, and on one occasion at least insisted that Brougham should attend for the next meeting.[2]   We do not know how seriously Brougham took these phenomena, or whether they affected his beliefs at a time of life when men have usually given up their search for new doctrines.

[1] A. Dasent : *John Thaddeus Delane*, i. 301.
[2] *Life of Robert Owen*, passim.   A. Aspinall : *Lord Brougham and the Whig Party*, p. 223.

z 2

Probably Brougham would have been content to describe his religion as that of all sensible men. He certainly was not a fervent son of the Scottish Church in which he had been reared, but a reformer of his period had little cause to love any established religion. Catholics and Dissenters, as well as the Church of England, had at one time or other helped to thwart his educational schemes, and a rather cynical agnosticism was common amongst those with whom he worked. Zachary Macaulay, towards the end of his life, took it upon himself to defend Brougham from attacks made upon him in the *Christian Observer*, and the editor, making some amends, describes a meeting with Brougham at the funeral of Henry Thornton, a leading " Saint." Brougham then remarked that " he had been accustomed to hearing Christianity spoken of in a sceptical manner . . . but that when he saw such dispassionate men as Thornton and Macaulay all in the same story, it did strike him there must surely be more in it than the Edinburgh wits dreamed of." [1] This frigid acknowledgment of Christianity was followed by some twenty years during which Brougham was looked upon as the hammer of the Anglican Church, yet he fought the Bishops and the older Universities as a Dissenter rather than as an agnostic, and later he defended Christianity against the infidel in his *Introduction to Paley's Natural Theology*. But at no period of Brougham's life was religion the spur which drove him to action. Morley, contrasting Gladstone and Brougham, said that all the latter's projects were secular, " dealing with man from the outside, none touching imagination or the heart." [2] It is true that so far as Brougham was a prophet, he was a secular prophet. In the first part of the nineteenth century there was little hope of leading men to a better world. Brougham saw men in bondage, and in helping to free them he paved the way for the Victorian Liberals.

[1] Viscountess Knutsford : *Life and Letters of Zachary Macaulay*, pp. 481–2.   [2] John Morley : *Life of Gladstone*, i. 156.

It may not be irrelevant to remember Gladstone's own record in 1833, at the climax of Brougham's long and dangerous struggle. Gladstone " voted for the worst clauses of the Irish Coercion Bill, including the court-martial clause. He fought steadily against the admission of Jews to Parliament. He fought against the admission of Dissenters without a test to the universities, which he described as seminaries for the Established Church. He supported the existing Corn Law. He said ' No ' to the property tax, and ' Aye ' for retaining the house and window taxes. He resisted a motion of Hume's for the abolition of military and naval sinecures, and another motion of the same excellent man's for the abolition of all flogging in the army save for mutiny and drunkenness." [1] He had previously spoken against the abolition of slavery. When later Gladstone " saw the light " as a Liberal it was in an England which had forgotten the trammels of the eighteenth century, and the reaction Brougham fought so successfully.

Amongst Brougham's *Men of Letters* the author with whom he has most sympathy is Voltaire, and he sums up his work in words which consciously or unconsciously apply to his own career. After describing the debt under which Voltaire had placed mankind by his writings, Brougham continues :

> " Great as these services are . . . they are really of far inferior value to the benefits which have resulted from his long and arduous struggle against oppression, especially against tyranny in the worst form which it can assume, the persecution of opinion, the infraction of the sacred right to exercise the reason upon all subjects, unfettered by prejudice, uncontrolled by authority, whether of great names or of temporal power. That he combated many important truths which he found enveloped in a cloud of errors, and could not

[1] *Id.*, i. 106.

patiently sift, so as to separate the right from the wrong, is undeniably true; that he carried on his conflict, whether with error or with truth, in an offensive manner has been freely admitted. But we owe to him the habit of scrutinizing, both in sacred matters and in profane, the merits of whatever is presented for our belief, of examining boldly the foundations of received opinions, of making probability a part of the consideration in all that is related, of calling in plain reason and common-sense to assist in our councils when grave matters are under discussion; nor can anyone since the days of Luther be named to whom the spirit of free inquiry, nay, the emancipation of the human mind from spiritual tyranny, owes a more lasting debt of gratitude."

Unconsciously Brougham has here written his own *apologia pro vita sua*. He saw mankind not only in the slough of despond, but shackled as well. He may have had no vision of the Delectable Mountains, but we, in England, still struggling to reach firmer land, should be thankful to the man who more than anyone of his generation saw to it that we should at least be free to find our own way out.

INDEX

PRINTED IN GREAT BRITAIN BY RICHARD CLAY & SONS, LIMITED, BUNGAY, SUFFOLK.